About Island Press

Since 1984, the nonprofit organization Island Press has been stimulating, shaping, and communicating ideas that are essential for solving environmental problems worldwide. With more than 1,000 titles in print and some 30 new releases each year, we are the nation's leading publisher on environmental issues. We identify innovative thinkers and emerging trends in the environmental field. We work with world-renowned experts and authors to develop cross-disciplinary solutions to environmental challenges.

Island Press designs and executes educational campaigns, in conjunction with our authors, to communicate their critical messages in print, in person, and online using the latest technologies, innovative programs, and the media. Our goal is to reach targeted audiences—scientists, policy makers, environmental advocates, urban planners, the media, and concerned citizens—with information that can be used to create the framework for long-term ecological health and human well-being.

Island Press gratefully acknowledges major support from The Bobolink Foundation, Caldera Foundation, The Curtis and Edith Munson Foundation, The Forrest C. and Frances H. Lattner Foundation, The JPB Foundation, The Kresge Foundation, The Summit Charitable Foundation, Inc., and many other generous organizations and individuals.

The opinions expressed in this book are those of the author(s) and do not necessarily reflect the views of our supporters.

Vaquita

Vaquita

Science, Politics, and Crime in the Sea of Cortez

Brooke Bessesen

ISLANDPRESS

Washington | Covelo | London

Keywords: acoustic monitoring, alternative fishing gear, Alto Golfo, American border patrol, animals in captivity, aquatic cocaine, baiji, Baja California, Baja peninsula, *buche,* bycatch, c-pod, captive cetaceans, Chelonia Limited, Chinese mafia, CITES, cochita, collateral damage, Colorado River Delta Biosphere Reserve, corruption, corvina, critically endangered, disappearing biodiversity, drum fish, El Golfo de Santa Clara, endangered species, Endangered Species List, endemic to Mexico, fish maw, fish soup, ghost nets, gillnet ban, gillnets, Gulf of California fishing, Gulf of California harbor porpoise, Hong Kong, illegal fishing, jinqian min, la vaquita marina, Mexican cartels, Mexican fishermen, Mexican species, Mexican Standard NOM-059-ECOL, Mexico's sea life, money fish, organized crime, panda of the sea, passive monitoring device, *Phocoena sinus*, Phocoenidae, poaching, porpoise, Puerto Peñasco, Rocky Point, San Felipe, sciaenid, Sciaenidae, Sea of Cortez, shifting baselines, smallest cetacean, smuggling operations, Sonora, swim bladder, totoaba, *Tototaba macdonaldi*, US crime, Upper Gulf of California, vaquita, Vaquita Refuge, Vermilion Sea, wildlife conservation, wildlife trafficking, Yangtze River dolphin

For Mom, who in my darkest hour wrote,
"I love you and want your heart to be calmed.
Hang on and know you will be given the strength
to carry on and give the vaquitas a voice—
for the world to know their story."

Contents

Foreword

In 1991, I was invited to visit the Upper Gulf of California, in Mexico, with US federal employees of the National Oceanic and Atmospheric Administration. We were there to see and discuss the issue of gillnets, the illegal capture of an endangered fish called the totoaba, and—the real reason for our visit—the predicament of the vaquita.

The vaquita is a little porpoise, the world's smallest cetacean. It is a fragile species, specialized to living in a unique place, inhabiting a tiny range. Its looks are unique: light-colored face highlighted by dark eye patches. A little panda of the sea.

At the time of my trip, vaquitas were drowning as collateral damage in several fisheries. There were, we were told, only about six hundred left where once thousands had thrived. But nothing much has been done in the intervening decades to remove the source of their decline, and now only a remnant of even that small population remains.

The vaquita is an emblem. A mirror that reflects back at us. If the vaquita disappears, we will be left to reckon with who we are. And those species we have not yet driven to extinction will be left to navigate a different world than the one they evolved to succeed in, as they are trying to do now.

Partly, this is a global story of human limitations, of empathy, of greed, of need, of simply not caring. It's not that fishermen are bad. It's that there are simply too many of us for the living world to bear. But the vaquita story is equally about how a group of brave souls refuses to accept extinction on our watch, at the hands of our own species. Against all odds, they are determined to keep the smallest porpoise in our realm.

Brooke Bessesen is the ideal author to tell this story—because she has lived it, immersed herself in its nuances and complexities. Giving voice to those at the core of this remarkable drama, she leads us on a journey not soon forgotten. We need to know what has happened to the vaquita so we can prevent it from happening again and again, so we can protect other species from suffering a similar fate. We need to know this story because we need, the world needs, a happy ending. And the story is not over. Not yet.

Carl Safina

Goodbye Baiji

Gone.
Done.
No more to do, not do.
We stood along the banks and watched you go under,
popping up, desperate gulps of air.
Again. Again.
Time ticked between sightings.
Too much time.
We bored of your life, your struggle—
turned away, turned the channel.
We tired of your incessant need,
your slow demise.
Your death.
Yet when at last the obituary was written,
we cried out,
shock and grief wetting our voices,
What?
You are *gone?*
Done?
Now what will we do, not do?

Prologue

"Just don't stop," I told myself as my Prius skidded sideways through a maze of ragged shrubs. Sliding in the sand like a stunt driver, I pressed on the gas pedal and held fast to the steering wheel. If my car bogged in the sediment, if it got stuck, I would be sitting lost in a remote patch of Mexican desert, alone and miles from help.

I had been traveling a paved thoroughfare that promised a highway connection above the northern tip of the Gulf of California when my cell phone's navigation system failed me. The self-assured Siri had indicated a left turn some miles back, but I found no such road to take. Soon my path had petered to dirt and then narrowed to trail before dead-ending in a lonely thicket of brush.

When navigating into remote terrain and forging into the unknown, there are always uncertainties—dangers even. I was on my first trip into Mexico to learn about vaquitas, and my plans were already off course. Perhaps I should have turned back. Instead, I crossed a rickety irrigation bridge and jolted along a washboard canal road in search of a way forward.

Now I was snaking wildly across the dry riverbed of the Rio Colorado, fishtailing through several inches of silt, dodging thorny shrubs, pushing the gas, and praying that luck would prevail.

∼

When China's Yangtze river dolphin, the baiji, was pronounced extinct in 2006—the first cetacean species to be driven to extinction from the effects of human activity—the dooming title of "world's most endangered marine mammal" was handed down to Mexico's tiny endemic porpoise.

La vaquita marina. An animal as adorable as a plush toy.

Vaquita (pronounced *vuh-KEY-tuh*) is a somewhat recently discovered species. Found only in the Upper Gulf of California, it was first described by science in 1958 and given the name *Phocoena sinus.* Unlike many other critically endangered species, vaquitas are not hunted. Neither is their habitat disappearing nor degraded. The species is even protected by law. Still, it is now on the verge of extinction.

What circumstances could be driving down the vaquita population so rapidly? Why was a timid little porpoise being wiped out before the world could even care? Most important, what was being done to stop it? In seeking the answers to these questions, I found myself caught up in a story line worthy of a crime novel, complete with cartels and corruption, an international black market, and angry fishermen willing to risk their lives for profit or drugs.

When I began researching this book in March 2016, vaquita expert Barbara Taylor told me, "If you walked the streets of San Diego today and asked a thousand people, you would probably not find a single person who knows what a vaquita is—despite the fact that we've been trying to get the word out for twenty years."

Indeed, until 2017, most Americans had never even heard of vaquita.

Now locked in a bizarre and dangerous international crisis, *Phocoena sinus* is at last being introduced to the world—and not a moment too soon. As news of its annihilation surges in the media, more and more people are taken by the dramatic circumstances of its plight. Charging to the cliff's edge, it suddenly feels as though there is a global breath-hold. Can vaquita be saved?

It has been a demanding endeavor to stitch together the deeper history and troubling politics that brought us to this current crisis. I made numerous trips to Mexico to meet people involved in the drama. I tagged along with scientists to see their research firsthand. I talked with local residents to get a pulse on the cultural perceptions shaping their communities. I interviewed fishermen, American expats, and even artists. And I met with or phoned several nongovernmental organization leaders on both sides of the border.

I must admit that I was unprepared for the twists and turns of the journey, the obscurities and contradictions that at times made the experience of researching vaquita as out of control, nerve wracking, and thorny as skidding across the barren sand bed of the Colorado River.

Above all, I learned that conservation is messy business.

Dozens of individuals come and go throughout this book. They represent the plethora of generously shared stories and opinions that contributed to my overall understanding. Some characters stay with me from beginning to end: Gustavo Cárdenas, Paco and Javier Valverde, Lorenzo Rojas, Armando Jaramillo, Barb Taylor, and Oona Layolle. These trusted scientists and conservationists became my touchstones and sounding boards. They are the voices of change, the defenders of hope. They are lights on the path.

The intense and haunting story that unfolds on the following pages tracks my experiences and discoveries over a twenty-month time frame between spring 2016 and fall 2017, a hinge-pin period marked by nail-biting shifts in both vaquita population estimates and legislative policy. It explores the intricacies creating confrontational opposition to the protection of vaquita as well as the acoustic science, social media, and international collaborations being applied to its recovery.

The baiji is gone, and the vaquita is quickly disappearing, conceivably destined for the same fate.

What will we do, not do?

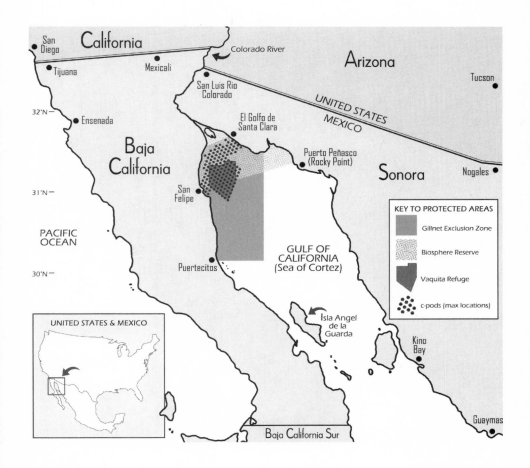

California

San Diego
Tijuana
Mexicali
San Luis Rio Colorado
Colorado River
Arizona
Tucson
Ensenada
32°N
Baja California
El Golfo de Santa Clara
UNITED STATES
MEXICO
Puerto Peñasco (Rocky Point)
Sonora
Nogales
31°N
San Felipe
PACIFIC OCEAN
30°N
Puertecitos
GULF OF CALIFORNIA (Sea of Cortez)
Isla Angel de la Guarda
Kino Bay
UNITED STATES & MEXICO
Baja California Sur
Guaymas

KEY TO PROTECTED AREAS

Gillnet Exclusion Zone

Biosphere Reserve

Vaquita Refuge

c-pods (max locations)

CHAPTER 1

The Dead Girl

Don't be nervous. It's safe," Gustavo offered preemptively as we pulled into a dirt lot facing the dark entrance of a brown concrete building. The structure had the angular foreboding of an abandoned prison, with open, rusty-barred windows jutting evenly along the front. Not one to worry, I hadn't been a bit nervous until Gustavo made this statement, which now had me attentive to deep shadows cast by the cool evening light. Still, I followed him inside.

Eyes adjusting, I scanned a panorama of dilapidated brick and tile stalls. *Se renta o vende* read sloppy strokes of graffiti. For rent or sale. As Gustavo's stocky silhouette sidestepped piles of rubble, his flip-flops echoed down spoked halls, which stretched into the building's blackest recesses.

I had met Gustavo Cárdenas Hinojosa, a thirty-something scientist with INECC (pronounced *EE-nek*), Mexico's National Institute of Ecology and Climate Change, just twenty minutes earlier, at five o'clock at the Hotel Los Angeles as planned. We had fumbled through our initial greeting, each trying on a language we hadn't worn in a while—my Spanish, his English. His English fit better, so we stuck with that.

I'd made my first ever trip from Arizona to San Felipe, Mexico—a six-hour drive—to ask a single question: why was the world's most critically endangered marine mammal still dying in gillnets when gillnets were supposedly outlawed? Gustavo, field coordinator for INECC's vaquita acoustics study, had generously driven over from Ensenada to introduce me to some people who might offer insight, starting with a well-known fisherman named Javier Valverde.

Gustavo and I quickly checked into the hotel, a new kelly-green monolith at the edge of town. After dumping our bags in two convenient first-floor rooms, we hopped into his red truck, a Ford Ranger that looked to be a multitour veteran of fieldwork. Five minutes later, I was being ushered down this dusty corridor.

A right. A left. Twenty paces forward.

Like the warm glow of a farmhouse on a dark night, we came upon a single, brightly lit window. In such a gloomy edifice it was strange to find a satellite office for CONANP, Mexico's National Commission of Natural Protected Areas. It was a respite of pale yellow walls and encouraging environmental posters. As Gustavo directed me through the door, a middle-aged man wearing a *viva la vaquita* T-shirt stepped forward to say hello. Paco Valverde is a biologist and administrator for CONANP and is Javier's son.

Paco offered me a friendly smile, but his features were lined with stress, and after shaking my hand, he turned to Gustavo and delivered some piece of terrible news in such rapid-fire Spanish that I was left struggling to interpret their anxious expressions. Several minutes passed before I could even begin to grasp the situation, and it wasn't until Paco clicked through gruesome images on his computer screen that the issue became clear.

A vaquita had washed up on the beach—dead—just that morning. It was March 15, 2016. Gustavo's arms folded across his body as if holding something fragile together. It was the second vaquita corpse in eleven days; a male had been found floating offshore on March 4.

The vaquita, scientifically named *Phocoena sinus*, is the world's tiniest cetacean, a stout, glossy-skinned porpoise whose entire frame, rostrum to fluke, spans a mere five feet and tips the scale at just ninety-five pounds. On the whole planet, there is but one population of vaquitas, and that population, living in the Upper Gulf of California, has endured continual decline since the early 1940s. A prestigious group of scientists conducted a population survey in the fall of 2015. Six months later, they would announce their unfavorable findings: fewer than sixty vaquitas were left on the planet.

Chris Snyder, a Flagstaff, Arizona, transplant, had discovered the dead vaquita during her morning walk. Chris lives in an expat community called El Dorado Ranch, seven miles north of San Felipe. The porpoise was on the beach "in front of EDR golf course," she wrote in a 10:37 a.m. Facebook post along with a photo of the body—bruised and bloated skin beginning to tear, empty eye sockets fixed and vacant. Her husband, Tom Gorman, deciding that more images were needed, had hurried back down to the body and loaded several more shots to Facebook. One showed a hungry turkey vulture lurching like a Western movie character over purple flesh.

It was the Snyder-Gorman Facebook photos that first alerted authorities to the dead cetacean and set off the firestorm of official calls, texts, photos, and reports. Paco showed Gustavo video he had taken of the corpse being loaded onto the bed of a truck for transport to Mexicali. I fretfully snatched at any Spanish words I could recognize and pieced together the basics. Despite significant decomposition, they identified the victim as a female, 1.3 meters long (about fifty-one inches). Every loss bodes poorly for the survival of the species. But with so few vaquitas remaining, I knew the forfeiture of a female's breeding potential was a sharp twist of the knife.

As Paco spoke, Gustavo texted wildly on his cell phone, and I stood by, trying to follow the narrative. I asked a few questions, but it was obvious that these men had no attention for my inquiries. Neither seemed to possess the mind power for a second language at such an upsetting time, and I felt foolish that my crash course in refresher Spanish had failed to take. The stress was palpable, so I slipped into an adjoining room to give them some space. My heart ached for Gustavo and Paco, but I could not console them. It was like I'd accidentally stumbled into the private funeral of someone famous but whom I did not personally know. I was an interloper, an observer, a distraction.

It wouldn't be until a couple weeks later, in a moment of deep personal contemplation, that the image of that dead vaquita would flood back to my mind. With my heart wide open, I saw her, really saw her, not as one of a disappearing population but as a single, distinct individual—a daughter, a sister perhaps—who lived freely and died tragically. I imagined her final moments: the terrified thrashing, the tangle of rope, holding her breath against the murky midnight water for countless frantic seconds until at last her burning lungs insisted on one final inhale.

In my mind, her little frame cast out on that isolated beach transformed into the body of a young girl dumped by the side of the road outside a rural town.

She'd been murdered. And everybody knew who'd done it.

There are always clues at a crime scene. In this case, there were eight totoaba carcasses strewn about on the sand.

~

Totoaba is a fish. It also is endemic to the Gulf of California and is also listed as critically endangered. *Totoaba macdonaldi* is the largest member of the Sciaenidae family. Sciaenids are commonly called drum fish, or croakers, because they can produce a thrumming sound by vibrating special muscles against an internal gas-filled organ—the swim bladder—which regulates buoyancy and helps the fish go up and down in the water column.

Totoaba (pronounced *toe-TWA-buh*) are now being heavily poached for their swim bladders, called *buches* in Spanish.

And what are those *buches* used for? For soup.

The swim bladder, called fish maw in Asia, is boiled into a Chinese soup that is coveted for purported curative powers, including improved skin complexion and circulation. Although such remedial properties remain unsubstantiated, the feeding frenzy continues. Since 2012, hundreds upon hundreds of *buches* have been smuggled and sold in what has become a multi-billion-dollar international black market for wildlife products.

China's main source of fish maw—the Chinese bahaba, another drum fish—has all but disappeared. *Bahaba taipingensis* once resided in great numbers along the coast of the China Sea, from Shanghai south to Hong Kong. With the bahaba completely fished out and nearing extinction, however, the cost of a bahaba swim bladder rocketed to astronomical heights, so Chinese marketeers redirected their interests to extract Mexican totoaba from the northern half of the Gulf of California. Both are large and long-lived sciaenids, and their life cycles and bladders are very similar.

It is not the first time China has promoted poaching. The country is notorious for trafficking wildlife parts, and its unrelenting appetite for endangered species poses a catastrophic threat to many beloved animals on the threshold of extinction.

Rhino horn, tiger bone, pangolin scales, totoaba bladder. Each attracts its own cast of assassins.

For the right price, local poachers are always willing to take a risk, especially in countries like Mexico where penalties are rare. (Totoaba poaching has not been a felony, and arrested parties are typically freed within a couple of days.) Of course, fishermen who poach *buches*, known as *bucheros*, are not selling directly to China. Chinese and Mexican mafias are said to have joined forces to traffic the "aquatic cocaine"; with similar pound-for-pound profits, bladders really are as lucrative as drugs.

Unlike powdery and flowery drugs that are measured only by weight, *buches* are also valued by size. Size matters, a lot. The larger, thinner-walled bladder of the male totoaba is particularly valued. And the older the fish, the bigger the *buche*. The more perceived strength and vitality, the higher the price.

As the black market booms, fishermen rush to the water like gold miners, tossing gillnets to collect their claim. Some *bucheros* even "clone" their pangas, or skiffs, painting the same number on both hulls to secretly run two boats under one permit. In the dark of night—or worse, under the guise of catching legal species—local fishermen capture football-player-sized totoaba and quickly carve out their *buches*. Those *buches* are then dried for transport.

A well-connected cartel syndicate is said to smuggle the contraband across international borders and distribute it in China or to Chinese restaurants in the United States. As China's economy grows stronger, there are more wealthy people who can afford gastronomic luxuries, and dried swim bladders are said to be standard fare at Hong Kong markets and openly auctioned in China. The illegal commodity is even sold through online sources like Alibaba.

Mexico blames China for not coming down hard enough on the sale of totoaba parts. China blames Mexico for allowing fishermen to poach the animals in the first place. They're both right. It's a bit like drugs. Countries that produce the merchandise must be held accountable, but countries that consume the imports are also culpable. Government leaders, fishermen, smugglers, bosses, buyers, restaurateurs, diners, and, of

A dried totoaba swim bladder, buche *in Spanish; with long tubes of attached tissue, it looks something like a Mesoamerican drawstring sack. (US Fish and Wildlife Service)*

course, corrupt law enforcement officers are all part of the organized criminal chain.

To date, China doesn't seem fully committed to destroying a profitable business model, and Mexico doesn't seem fully committed to abolishing loopholes for poaching. Meanwhile, the illegal industry gains traction.

Unfortunately, totoaba is not the only critically endangered animal to be caught up in this international scandal. In death, vaquita is totoaba's mammalian twin. Both large, lovely, silvery imperiled species fall victim to the same *bucheros*. The gillnets deployed to capture totoaba, left adrift in the water column, are either indistinguishable or confusing to vaquitas' sensitive sonar. When the tiny porpoises accidentally hit the nets and catch a fin or fluke, they panic and roll themselves into inescapable knots. As air-breathing mammals like us, they cannot survive indefinitely beneath the sea surface and soon succumb to asphyxiation.

Gillnets—locally called *chinchorros* or *redes de enmalle*—have been the mainstay of fishing in the Upper Gulf since the 1940s. The contraption is simple: two ropes with netting strung between. Buoys tethered to the upper rope act as floats and markers, and lead weights attached to the bottom rope stretch and shape the net. Once deployed, the apparatus may remain unattended for many hours, sometimes days, anchored to the bottom or adrift in the current. Although gillnets are designed to snag the gills of particular species—the mesh size is selected to fit the target fish's head—they inevitably capture nontarget species as well.

It's called bycatch.

Bycatch is the incidental capture of nontarget species, and some researchers estimate that bycatch of nets, longlines, and trawls accounts for up to 40 percent of total global catch. In other words, for every one hundred pounds of targeted fish hauled in and sold at market worldwide, forty pounds of nontarget animals—rays, sharks, seahorses, marine birds, corals, crabs, octopus, sea turtles, seals, and cetaceans—may be dumped, dead or dying, back into the sea. That adds up to sixty-three billion pounds per year.

Collateral damage is a pitiful part of the food industry that most of us don't want to look at. Bycatch is a sobering problem in every ocean around the world. Vaquitas, however, fall victim in just a single location, the only place the species has ever existed: a pinpoint spot on the map of Mexico.

Baja California is Earth's second-longest peninsula behind the Malay Peninsula of Southeast Asia. This skinny strip of land, like an old man's finger pointing toward Argentina, hugs a bio-rich aquatic environment against the continental mainland. Many geographically challenged people are confused by the different names given to the seven-hundred-mile-long embayment. Americans typically call it the Gulf of California;

Spaniards call it the Sea of Cortés. Its original moniker—the Vermilion Sea—dates to 1539. Some historic references dub it the Red Sea. Perhaps Jacques Cousteau was the most insightful when he branded it "the aquarium of the world" because some six thousand animal species have already been recorded in its boundaries.

In the highest reaches of the northern Gulf of California exists one of the most productive coastal marine habitats in the world. Characterized by brackish bays and marshes, the Colorado River delta region supports an array of endemic species and migratory birds. It is there in the Upper Gulf—locally called Alto Golfo—that the rarest member of the whale clade resides.

La vaquita marina is uniquely adapted to eat small bottom-feeding fish and squid in the shallow, silt-laden waters of Alto Golfo. Of the sixty-eight thousand square miles of aquatic habitat provided by the lengthy Gulf of California, this pint-sized porpoise with enigmatic dark-ringed eyes and black-lined lips that seem curved into a perpetual smile inhabits only about fourteen hundred square miles. Indeed, this dusky gray cetacean has the most limited range of any marine mammal.

More than fifteen hundred fishermen earn their living in and around vaquita habitat. Most hail from one of three fishing villages: San Felipe in the Mexican state of Baja California, El Golfo de Santa Clara just east of the Colorado River delta in the state of Sonora, or, ninety-three miles south from there, Puerto Peñasco, better known to Americans as Rocky Point. Nearly every fisherman in the Upper Gulf owns a gillnet, and many are directly or indirectly involved with the totoaba trade. A satellite image taken in December 2014 shows almost one hundred pangas engaged in illegal fishing activities.

In 2015, responding to rampant poaching and alarming vaquita-mortality statistics, the Mexican government took unprecedented action. President Enrique Peña Nieto traveled twelve hundred miles from his capitol building in Mexico City to the sandy pueblo of San Felipe; it was the first presidential visit there in history. On April 16, he declared a two-year emergency gillnet ban across vaquita habitat. Permits for all gillnet fisheries, Peña Nieto announced, were to be placed on hold until the spring of 2017, while a multiple-million-dollar compensation program would pay fishermen for lost income.

The president's presence in San Felipe implied real and urgent concern. Both vaquita and totoaba are endemic species, unique to Mexican waters and recognized as part of Mexico's rich biological heritage. Furthermore, the vaquita is actually the country's national marine mammal. No respectable leader wants to be accountable for losing a national treasure. It's bad for business.

Indeed, a 2015 press release from the Center for Biological Diversity stated, "The [president's gillnet] ban announcement came in response to growing international attention and outrage over the plight of the vaquita, including calls for trade sanctions against Mexico and a possible boycott of Mexican shrimp."

But if protecting endangered species is all about business, so is killing them. A single *buche* can put $1,500 to $1,800 into the pocket of the fisherman who poached it (and dozens of *buches* may be harvested in one catch). Smuggled into the United States, a *buche* is worth about $5,000. Once in China, its price shoots up to around $10,000 and can go as high as $50,000 for a large specimen.

Not all these illegal products are consumed. Many are bought as gifts and collectibles. The most impressively sized bladders are traded by high-end investors and secured in company safes like gold bricks. One Chinese trader in Qingping Market reported investing more than ten million RMB (that's about $1.5 million) in totoaba. He and his countrymen call it *jinqian min*, or money fish.

It makes no matter that the totoaba fishery was closed by the Mexican government in 1975, that the fish was marked by the International

Union for Conservation of Nature, or IUCN, as endangered in 1986 and was upped to critically endangered in 1996, or that the vaquita, the most endangered marine mammal on Earth, declined a shocking 80 percent in just four years as totoaba bycatch. None of that dissuades criminals in China or Mexico from embracing the profits of illicit trade. Scarcity only serves to drive up prices and make prospects more lucrative.

As Paul Fleischman wrote, "Science explains what nature is doing; money often explains what we're doing."

In March 2016, a twenty-eight-year-old San Felipe man was arrested after the Mexican Federal Police detained his pickup truck on the road to Tijuana. Hidden behind the spare tire were 121 *buches* wrapped in plastic wrap. With a dry weight of eighty-six pounds, the booty was estimated to have a black-market value of more than $750,000.

Dr. Jorge Figueroa, former mayor of San Luis Rio Colorado, pointed out that even as the fish were poached (translated), "nobody noticed— not the Navy with its Coast Guard anchored in San Felipe, equipped with radar, a helicopter and more than twenty speed boats; nor the Army with its roadblock, nor the police, federal or state, who have been extorting the totoaba poachers."

That was neither the first nor the biggest bust in recent history. More than two dozen seizures have been cited in the United States and Mexico, accounting for thousands of bladders. In one confiscation, a seventy-three-year-old California resident named Song Shen Zhen was caught transporting twenty-seven *buches* from Mexico into the United States. He arrived at the border station after midnight, declaring nothing in his possession, but officers noticed that the floor mats of his vehicle bulged. When they lifted the mats and discovered the *buches*, they played it cool. Instead of making an arrest, they let Zhen go. The subject then unwittingly led federal agents to his Calexico home, which, when subsequently raided after some period of surveillance, proved to be a *buche*-drying factory. Inside, agents found an additional 214 swim bladders. There was almost no furniture—just stinking fish parts, pink with blood, drying under a whirl of fans.

The plunder was valued at $3.6 million.

~

"The problem is the fishermen down here, and the big money that they get with this totoaba thing," Chris Snyder later told me. She confirmed seeing the dead totoaba at the tide line near the vaquita's body. The fish had washed up the day before. "They were pretty much intact except for the middle being cut out," said Chris. "'Cause you know they do that and then they throw them overboard. There are lots of illegal boats during totoaba season. Campers on the beach say they hear them coming and going all night long. Without lights, of course."

The *buche* trade is threatening to wipe out vaquitas. Would it be unreasonable for an investigator, seeing the two species side by side, to make a mental correlation or at least propose a possible link? Don't one dead vaquita and eight gutted totoaba equal circumstantial evidence?

How did the Mexican government respond? In the first article covering this vaquita's death, published by Mexico's national outlet *Excelsior*, an on-scene agent reported (translated) "no apparent evidence on its body, no nets or other fishing gear or foreign objects attached to it; no traces, cuts, amputations, lacerations or obvious marks indicating it suffered entanglement." The totoaba were not even mentioned. The article then stated that water samples were going to be analyzed for phytotoxins (the culprit of red tide) or other contaminants that might be causing the mortalities.

Red tide concentrations do sometimes occur in the Gulf of California, and blooms of toxic algae can cause death in marine birds, sea turtles, fish, even mammals. But not a single vaquita corpse has ever been found in connection with red tide. Besides, those events are usually identified by a mass die-off of a wide range of species. Because there were no dead birds, dolphins, or other kinds of fish associated with the incident, red tide would have been an implausible conclusion.

Why would a government spending $32 million a year to save vaquita avoid suggesting the possibility of gillnet entanglement when it seemed the most likely cause of death? Why allow misleading information to be published?

I felt like I was stumbling into a pit of quicksand.

Not surprisingly, the agent who said there was no evidence of entanglement was wrong. Whether by oversight or inexperience, he missed an array of cuts and bruises around the animal's head, neck, and pectoral flippers that were "very characteristic of entanglement."

On March 24, 2016, the little female vaquita was lifted onto a stainless steel table at the Alexander veterinary clinic in Tijuana and prepared for necropsy. For identification, she was labeled Ps2. She was joined by two dead males: the one found before her (Ps1) and another (Ps3) discovered floating out in the Gulf on March 24, nine days after her.

Three dead vaquitas in three weeks.

Five percent of the remaining population—an unspeakable loss.

The grim, gloved work, which required careful and thorough inspection of all bodily organs under intense medical lamps, was conducted over two days by veterinarian Frances Gulland, a member of the US Marine Mammal Commission, and Kerri Danil from the Southwest Fisheries Science Center. Although submitting samples for pathology is standard protocol for necropsies and lab results later confirmed gross examination, the veterinarians didn't need help to figure out what had killed the animals. Based on distinctive tissue damage, they concluded that the official cause of death for all three was "trauma, entanglement."

Lorenzo Rojas Bracho, Mexico's most renowned vaquita expert (and Gustavo's big boss at INECC), was in attendance for the necropsy proceedings. He knew the vaquitas were bycatch as soon as he saw them but believes the agents who recovered the body just had no idea what to look for.

Ps2 turned out to be a subadult female, an otherwise healthy sixty-four-pound teenager. Among the necropsy remarks about her reproductive tract (immature), stomach (full of fish), and fitness (no signs of parasites) were grisly signs of struggle: "Notch in right mandible typical of monofilament. Linear cuts in leading edge right pectoral flipper. Bruising of blubber right thorax and neck area."

A precious young life snuffed out. Another flicker of hope gone cold.

Surprisingly, Ps1, Ps2, and Ps3 were the first vaquita necropsies conducted in quite some time. The death count may be rising, but the reclamation of corpses has flagged. Back when Lorenzo was doing his thesis work, he was able to recover thirty-five to forty bodies for analysis. That's because fishermen used to openly report mortalities. Those days are gone.

Once vaquita deaths became scandalous, the fishermen started keeping them secret. Even fishermen working legally don't want trouble, so if a porpoise is accidentally caught in their nets, they usually toss it overboard without an utterance. Totoaba poachers most certainly don't want them found; they are rumored to hide them or sometimes to weigh down the bodies mafia-style before dumping them in deep water. How many vaquita deaths have gone uncounted in the vast waters of Alto Golfo?

Another homeowner from the El Dorado community says she saw a fourth dead vaquita washed up on the beach on March 23, but the species could never be verified. The body was reportedly "disposed of" by a maintenance man before anyone could track it.

~

Back in Paco's office, reeling from the spin of bad news and fast Spanish, I stared at a drawing of vaquitas—a mother and calf—taped to the CONANP office window and considered turning tail for home. I was unprepared for such a ghastly introduction to the story of vaquita. Could I really bear to dive deeper into this heartbreaking topic?

Suddenly, as if he'd forgotten something important, Gustavo popped out and told me to follow him. He briskly escorted me back into the darkness, and, cutting right, we tottered past more (or the same) decaying stalls. Several flip-flop echoes later, we approached another glowing room in the dusty building.

As we entered the space, decorated like an employee lounge, Paco's father, Javier, stood up from his cushioned chair.

"You're late."

CHAPTER 2

Resource Extraction

Despite the hint of blame in his words, Javier's face wore a gentle expression, and his manner bore the patience of a man who can sit for hours, bobbing in a small boat. His calm energy settled mine. With a deep breath I eased into a padded chair and expressed my sincere thanks for his time.

"I don't mind to help," he responded kindly in English and returned to his seat.

His mahogany hands found a quiet place in his lap, like two napping kittens. Beneath his easy smile, an oval saint charm hung from his neck on a humble filament of twine.

Señor Valverde is one of the good guys. Somewhat famous in vaquita-conservation circles, he openly risks career and reputation to stop porpoises like Ps2 from dying in gillnets. As an active member of a civil association called Islas del Golfo Co-op, Javier works with the World Wildlife Fund, Pronatura (Mexico's oldest and largest environmental organization), and other organizations that promote *alternativa*—Spanish for alternative fishing gear. He is also a trusted contractor for

INECC, hired to deploy underwater acoustic devices that monitor vaquita activity.

Sadly, the man is practically alone among peers.

Nearly all regional fishermen oppose the president's gillnet ban, and most have acted in direct defiance. Of course, the surging black market is blamed for their audacity. News outlets are riveted to the criminal trade of totoaba with its sensational million-dollar cartel busts and bloated corpses. It's natural to assume that if this current scandal can be cleaned up in time, vaquita will be saved. But thinking the situation is that simple is simple thinking.

Although *bucheros* may be today's biggest and most pressing problem, they are not the whole problem. There is a poignant chronological discrepancy: the *buche* market boomed in 2012, but efforts to save vaquita have been foiled for decades. So my first question to Javier was simple.

"What do fishermen think about vaquita?" I asked.

He answered that most fishermen see vaquita not as a biological treasure, but as an obstacle to their professional goals. He believes that it is because measures taken through the years to protect the species have had a negative impact on the local economy, whereas the animals themselves have no fiscal value whatsoever. He paused and replied, "I feel sad about that."

Antivaquita sentiments, strongly held throughout the Baja-Sonoran region, are a real impediment to conservation. An intense dependency on fishing-derived income, whether legal or illegal, makes the trials of defending the species from extinction even more challenging.

Any hope of grasping the intricate cultural and political interplay shaping today's struggles requires a brief trip into the past. By establishing a concise time line of fishing in the Upper Gulf, I was quickly able to comprehend the relevance of gillnets to both provincial and commercial development and make better sense of the industry conflicts that continue to overshadow vaquita conservation.

At sixty-nine years old, Javier has witnessed much of the region's history firsthand. During our conversation, he filled in the formal record with some insightful, personal memories.

The most startling discovery? It all began with totoaba.

~

1920–1950

If one were to presume, as I did, that Mexicans have lived and fished from the waters of the Colorado River delta for hundreds, perhaps thousands, of years, they would be wrong. Indigenous tribes have, though. For example, the Cocopah, whose name means River People, and their ancestors have engaged in sustenance fishing for more than three thousand years. Nowadays, those native cultures have all but disappeared, and tribal members struggle to retain their heritage.

Permanent Mexican settlements actually didn't develop around the delta until almost a hundred years ago, when muscled laborers arrived in pursuit of their most-prized aquatic quarry: totoaba.

It was the early 1920s, and the Chinese market was growing hungry for fish maw soup, supplementing the supply of bahaba swim bladders with those of totoaba. (Is it coincidence that the names sound so similar?) At that time, the torpedo-shaped totoaba grew upward of seven feet long and more than three hundred pounds and ran in schools so massive they were said to roil the seas. During their counterclockwise coastal migrations up Sonoran shores and back down the Baja, hordes of shimmering backs could be seen for miles—a skilled fisherman could step right into the surf and stab one with a spear.

Some strategic fishermen followed the totoaba's migratory path. Pushing north from Guaymas, they paddled over whitecaps in dugout canoes or rowboats powered by small gasoline motors. They slumbered in ramshackle fishing camps along parched and barren shores. It was not an easy journey. But in Alto Golfo they discovered the totoaba's annual reproductive grounds, where the fishes predictably arrive in late winter and spawn from March to May. They had hit the jackpot.

The men tossed in their commercial hooks. Shelters were built from adobe or desert wood. Families relocated.

Here, perhaps, we find one of the fundamental hindrances to environmental conservation in Alto Golfo: the people who colonized the region came specifically to extract resources. They had no birthright, no time-honored love of land. The water was not their ancient backyard to be celebrated and protected as a matter of aboriginal inheritance. Instead, it was their workplace, valued primarily for its productivity.

During the earliest totoaba hunts, *buches* were carved out, dried by the desert sun, baled like hay, and paddled back to Guaymas. Uneaten carcasses totaling thousands of tons of meat were left strewn about in various stages of rot. If this take-what-you-can attitude was passed down through the mere four to five generations that have since called the upper shores home, it is no surprise that many of today's fishermen still see everything in the water as a commodity. And that mind-set seems to play into their present-day conflict with vaquita.

The totoaba's tender flesh eventually found its way to commercial export. No longer wasted in stinking heaps, the value of the fish, and thus the fishery, rose exponentially. Lives improved, villages grew, and cultural roots took hold.

Remote communities enjoyed few comforts but were bonded in the sense that they had each other—and fishing, of course, although that was surely a tedious affair. Totoaba were caught one at a time using the simplest tackle. Each run of quarter-inch rope terminated in a seven-inch hook that had to be dropped and attended until some unwitting giant took the bait.

By the late 1940s when Javier was born, totoaba fishermen had abandoned those hook-and-line techniques for handy contraptions called gillnets, which could harvest fish by the hundreds. Jumbo totoaba were scooped from the sea with gillnets cast and hauled as quickly as sinewy muscles could withstand. Catches often exceeded two thousand tons.

It was at this point that fishermen first started finding dead vaquitas in their gear. However, little thought or concern was spent on dewy-eyed mammals, or any other marine animal, limp or living, heaved up as bycatch; totoaba was all that mattered. What percentage of the original vaquita population was lost in those early years when gillnets and porpoises first met discord remains a mystery.

1950–1970

Javier remembers the days when totoaba were legal to hunt. "When I was a kid, we overfish the totoaba because it was easy to see the big schools," he said. "They used the same net as now, the gillnet. And I remember my father, he used to invite me to go fishing for totoaba. I was young. There was maybe twenty-five, thirty, forty boats. Little boats. And they'd load them up in March and April."

Where did all those totoaba end up? Mostly on American tables. The flesh, cheaply imported and commonly found in the fish aisle, was praised for its delicate texture and flavor. "Cutting the heads and the tails, we bring them to the trucks, and they take them to the United States. I remember that the totoaba use to go to San Pedro. Los Angeles somewhere," said Javier.

"I'm talking about"—he smoothed his white mustache as he calculated the year—"about 1958." The meat was sold in regular grocery stores, while swim bladders went to California's Chinese neighborhoods for fish maw soup.

By and by, the totoabas' natural reproduction could no longer keep pace with the hunt. Numbers dwindled. Paychecks dropped. Clever fishermen, though, simply shifted their attention, pushing shrimp to the top of their hit list. It was a brilliant business move. Shellfish became the new economic mainstay, especially in Puerto Peñasco, where the harbor

Fishermen hoist totoaba onto a beach in Alto Golfo. Photo by Tony Reyes Baca circa 1954, published in The Unforgettable Sea of Cortez. *(Permission to reprint by Cortez Publications)*

was deep enough to dock and off-load large trawlers. Sometime after the middle of the twentieth century, tourism also took root, but shrimp continued to dominate as the primary source of revenue throughout the Upper Gulf.

It is essential to understand that although the totoaba fishery weakened, it did not disappear. Alto Golfo fisheries are highly dynamic and seasonally variable; there is never just one in action. For example, a gillnet shark fishery emerged in the 1940s. Shark fins were sold to the Asian market to make another kind of soup—shark-fin soup—and shark liver oil was processed for vitamin A and industrial lubrications. (Unlike the totoaba, which has a swim bladder for buoyancy regulation, a shark has an oil-filled liver that does a similar job; once vitamin A was synthesized and readily available, the demand for shark livers declined. Conversely, the demand for shark-fin soup grew more intense and, to this day, continues to decimate shark populations around the globe, with a frightening number of species now endangered.)

Dozens of fisheries, including corvina, sierra, dorado, flounder, sole, guitarfish, octopus, and various shellfishes, developed in Alto Golfo through the years. Certain species may have arrived at market in higher or lower percentages, but there was always a mix. Be that as it may, San Felipe, El Golfo de Santa Clara, and Puerto Peñasco really grew up on a diet of shrimp. Puerto Peñasco's seaside plaza even hosts a bronze sculpture of a fisherman riding a bull-sized shrimp.

Industrial trawlers—huge, rugged vessels with overhead beams that extend out like the arms of a colossal scale—joined small-type commercial gillnetters among the colliding waves, and together they hoisted a tremendous amount of shellfish for export. Fishermen formed cooperatives, which sought and secured political power.

Somewhat quietly, in 1958—the same year Javier was hauling in totoaba with his father—a new species of porpoise was introduced to science by Ken Norris and William McFarland. They called it *Phocoena sinus*.

Although fishermen had been netting the mammals as bycatch for nearly two decades, Norris and McFarland lacked a complete specimen and had to write a limited species description based on three bleached skulls found along the beach. Even so, discovering a marine mammal endemic to Mexican waters was truly exciting.

The biologists bestowed their new cetacean with the common name cochito, but it didn't stick; instead, the moniker *vaquita*, used by the locals, took residence in scientific literature by 1961. When I asked Javier why people called it vaquita, meaning little cow, he gave a reasonable, if somewhat disconcerting, answer. Early fishermen ate a lot of bycatch, he said. "Maybe that's why they called it a vaquita," he speculated, "because the back, the filets in the back is red like a cow."

It's disturbing to speculate how many porpoises might have been dispatched to the kitchen, given the frequency with which they were captured in large-mesh gillnets strung out for sharks, totoaba, and other large prey as well as in medium-mesh gillnets set for rays, snapper, and groupers. I would later hear secondhand about a man who tried to barbeque a vaquita and said the smell was so vile that he had to throw the whole stinking bundle away.

Javier is primarily a shrimp fisherman. He says even shrimp *chinchorros*, which are made with light monofilament in a mesh size of just two and three-fourth inches, are known to entangle vaquitas. Traditional shrimp gillnets may be small-meshed, but with extended lengths and strong water currents, they still pose serious danger to unsuspecting porpoises.

He sat forward in his chair and gestured with his leathery hands. "The vaquita is here, and the net's coming fast. . . . *Whoosh!* They can't escape."

I cringed.

What about large-scale trawls, which are known to wreak havoc on the seafloor, reaping up to 90 percent bycatch? They do not appear to be a major concern for vaquitas. Presumably, the little cetaceans hear the grumbling motors and steer clear.

Just five years after the discovery of *Phocoena sinus*, a pivotal event took place that would later spur debate regarding the decline of the species. The Glen Canyon Dam in the southwestern United States finally halted the flow of the Colorado River into the Gulf of California.

The loss of fresh water indelibly altered the appearance of the delta. The once-lush riparian habitat became windswept desert. Before 1963, Javier recalled, "There was a lot of water in the river. And there were a lot of shrimp 'cause the salt water and the fresh water was mixing. The fresh water means a lot for the shrimp. They are like mosquitoes."

1970–1990

Despite any change to the ecosystem, shrimpers continued to carve a living from the sea. In fact, when shrimp reached peak dollar in the 1970s, workers from Mexico's interior flooded to the Gulf of California to ply the waters. "Pink gold" filled ship holds by the tonnage, and development for tourism was left on the back burner as all hands were called on deck.

The Sea of Cortez became a minimetropolis of commercial pangas and industrial shrimp trawls. In this watery realm, the groans of men and the creaks of winches gave way to sputtering sea life spilled over wooden decks, where fishermen shuffled around their hulls, knee-deep in wriggling fish and crustaceans.

Although the totoaba population was severely depleted by now, gill-nets were still set for that giant drum fish. And access to fresh filets persisted in US markets.

Here, another point must be made. Many countries, including the United States, depend on their national fisheries departments to conduct stock surveys for major fisheries. Such studies guide governmental permit allowances and ensure that baseline populations of economically valued fish are not razed. In Mexico, the National Fisheries Institute, INAPESCA (pronounced *EE-nuh-pes-kuh*), is responsible for that kind of work, but no stock survey of totoaba was ever conducted. Thus, the inevitable happened, and the totoaba fishery collapsed.

The year was 1975. By then, totoaba schools were no longer massive or common. Indeed, catches landed at less than sixty tons, just 3 percent of their 1940s landing weights. Acting decisively, Mexico officially closed the fishery and made illegal the capture and sale of its largest endemic sciaenid.

That same year, an international treaty, the Convention on International Trade in Endangered Species, or CITES (pronounced *SY-tees*), was signed. It united governments in the effort "to ensure that international trade in specimens of wild animals and plants does not threaten their survival." It is an interesting bit of conservation history that totoaba was the first marine fish ever considered endangered. It made the CITES list in 1976 and was pulled from American dinner plates under the Endangered Species Act in 1979.

Scientists who later scrutinized the totoaba situation cited three causes for the collapse. Of course, the primary trigger was overexploitation—plain, old overfishing—especially during the reproductive season when aggregating adults are snagged by gillnets before they spawn. Species that mature late and live long are particularly vulnerable to overfishing; totoaba live up to fifty years in the wild and don't reproduce until age six or seven.

Loss of juvenile totoaba as bycatch was considered a secondary contributor to the species' decline. Juvenile totoaba do not immediately attend the adult migration but remain in the river delta for two to three years. There, they face their own brand of peril: industrial shrimp trawlers. Vaquitas may not get caught by large-scale trawls, but young totoaba most certainly do.

The Glen Canyon Dam was also suspected to have played a third, albeit minor, role by altering the species' spawning grounds.

The closure of the totoaba fishery in 1975 was the first major restriction in the Sea of Cortez. It was also the first (but not last) time a government proclamation proved insufficient. Commercial export ceased, but gillnets did not. Totoaba simply became a private treat for local fishermen lucky enough to catch them. The meat was eaten at home, shared with neighbors, or sometimes sold under the vague order of bass. Nobody took notice of infractions that could be viewed as sustenance poaching, and so the practice continued. A study review by Miguel Cisneros-Mata and colleagues estimated that each year in the decade following the fishery closure, sixty-two hundred adult totoaba were poached and 120,300 juvenile totoaba fell victim to the shrimp industry.

As the plight of totoaba took 1970s headlines, the vaquita gained some attention too—at least in certain scientific circles. Conservation was becoming mainstream, and given the porpoises' limited range, losses as bycatch raised legitimate concern for the future of the species.

In 1978, based on mortality figures ascertained from fishermen interviews, vaquita was placed on IUCN's Red List as vulnerable with this statement: "The Mexican Government has declared a total closure of both sport and commercial fishing for [totoaba]. These measures, if enforced, should halt or greatly reduce the number of *P. sinus* killed in the course of fishing operations."

A few years later, in 1982, biologist Robert Brownell published a scientific paper that focused heavily on vaquita exploitation. He wrote that "during totoaba gillnet fishing operations around San Felipe . . . [an observer] reports a catch of 10 porpoises in one day in the early seventies."

Ten dead porpoises in one day. Just in San Felipe.

Although Brownell also described more diagnostic characteristics for *Phocoena sinus*, including physical measurements such as total length, flipper length, and vertebral count, it's remarkable that twenty-four years after Norris and McFarland first presented the species to the world, Brownell still could not describe the animal's color pattern. Indeed, the vaquita's unique markings—its dark fins, silvery face, and attractively tinted eyes and lips—would remain unknown to science until 1987. That's a full two years after it was listed as endangered under the US Endangered Species Act.

The 1980s also saw Mexico's peso stumble and fall. Currency devaluation, which toppled businesses throughout the country like an economic earthquake, provided unexpected opportunities for waterfront communities in the Gulf of California. The cost of travel within Mexico was inexpensive, especially for foreigners with money to exchange, and tourism blossomed. Lured by the promise of sandy beaches, lovely sunsets, cheap *cervezas*, and freshly caught shrimp, Americans scuttled across the border to enjoy new shoreside amenities. The influx of US dollars rapidly transformed certain fishing villages into holiday hot spots. Many beach towns soon earned a dichotomic reputation for relaxation and chaos.

An overabundance of alcohol and no age limits on drinking incited some rowdy escapades, which in turn attracted an imprudent crowd. Every year during spring break in the United States, a wave of California high schoolers and college kids rolled five hours south from San Diego to stagger along the San Felipe *malécon*, while Arizona's party-hungry youth poured into Rocky Point (Puerto Peñasco) for a foolhardy week of beer bongs. Tourism not only added income to the Upper Gulf economy, it diversified it.

It is unfortunate for vaquita that most Americans have never heard of El Golfo de Santa Clara. Despite its close proximity to the US-Mexico border—less than seventy miles south of San Luis, Arizona—that pueblo never managed to hook a lot of visitors. Entrepreneurs opened restaurants and hotels, prepared fresh *ceviche*, and smoothed crisp linens in ocean-view rooms. Still, the village went relatively unnoticed, passed by for the bustling streets and neon nightlife of Rocky Point. So, during the tourism boom, residents of El Golfo de Santa Clara were forced to survive as they always had—by fishing.

The situation hasn't changed much there. That community is still heavily dependent on gillnets for income. In some ways, El Golfo de Santa Clara is the lost triplet, the one rarely seen or spoken of, the one left behind, entrenched in the needs and habits of the past.

In San Felipe and Puerto Peñasco, vacationers indulged their appetites for all things Mexico. They drank a lot of tequila and Corona beer. And they ate a lot of shrimp. Every day, dusk or dawn, restaurateurs and street vendors were obliged to wait near the docks, circled by frigate birds and vultures as trawlers and gillnetters motored to shore to replenish their soon-to-be-gobbled supplies.

Local demand, as high as it was, only accounted for a small portion of annual landings, however; the vast majority of shrimp was being exported to the United States. Such rampant consumerism was predictably unsustainable, and soon catches had dropped by as much as 50 percent.

Repeating a shortsighted pattern of unrestrained resource extraction, the shrimp fishery was headed toward collapse—following totoaba as the second to do so in only two decades.

1990–2005

Workers ran out of work. Banks repossessed boats. In Puerto Peñasco alone, the fishing fleet was slashed from two hundred twenty boats to fewer than one hundred, and residents began to shuffle away in search of other work. Alto Golfo communities might have been deserted if not for the resilience of the fishermen, who cleverly switched gear—again.

Some headed into deeper waters to focus on sportfishing fare like marlin and dorado that tourists would enthusiastically pay to reel in themselves. Others cast nets for previously underappreciated fish like milkfish. Gillnets of various sizes were sent out to work like autonomous employees. Gauzy mesh drapes zigzagged the turbid, current-swirled waters of the Upper Gulf, seeking anything that could still be snared.

Alas, something spine-chilling now warrants mention: ghost nets.

By the 1990s, gillnets were celebrating their fiftieth anniversary in Alto Golfo, having been deployed by the thousands, decade after decade. As translucent and dangerous as spiderwebs, they were set adrift at every depth, in every quadrant, to take advantage of every possible line of attack. Many of those nets were never recovered by their owners. Abandoned or lost, they continue to tremble about like phantoms in the darkness, towing the remains of vaquitas, totoaba, dolphins, stingrays, sharks, crabs, sea lions, shrimp, and other casualties.

Some creep along the bottom, weighted by the bones they carry, gathering healthy passersby into their makeshift cemeteries. Others waft through the midwaters, committed to their ghoulish task of collection, unaware that they've been freed from duty. To this day, the Upper Gulf remains haunted by ghost nets that secretly hunt the territory.

All those nets, old and new, took a terrible toll on vaquita. Whereas pregillnet populations were likely upward of five thousand individuals, the first reliable population estimates for *Phocoena sinus* showed fewer than six hundred remaining.

Moreover, mortality studies at that time indicated that gillnets from El Golfo de Santa Clara alone were drowning vaquitas at a mind-blowing rate of up to eighty-four per year. Many of the victims were youngsters—a 1991 photo shows five calves lined up on a bench awaiting necropsy with gillnet indentations crisscrossing their soft, gray skin. One of the earliest vaquita scientists, marine biologist Omar Vidal, documented 128 porpoises killed in gillnets set for sharks, mackerel, shrimp, and (already outlawed) totoaba. His body count included twelve young babies and one near-term fetus. Vidal wrote in 1995, "These 128 captures certainly represent only a fraction of the total mortality from fishing operations."

Such devastating statistics pushed *Phocoena sinus* to endangered status on the IUCN Red List in 1990 and to critically endangered in 1996. In 1994, the species was added as a Mexican Standard NOM-059-ECOL for species *en peligro de extinción*. As Mexico's tiny endemic porpoise took center stage in conservation, protection strategies were prescribed, and for the first time ever, prohibitions were placed on fishing gear.

In 1992, a commemorative hundred-peso vaquita coin was minted by the Bank of Mexico in association with the United Nations Environment Programme. But more valuable than those silver medallions was Mexico's new law: totoaba-sized gillnets—ten-inch or larger mesh size—were banned in the Gulf of California.

The following year, the Upper Gulf of California and Colorado River Delta Biosphere Reserve was established by SEMARNAT, Mexico's Secretary of Environment and Natural Resources. The goal was (translated) "to preserve and protect natural and cultural richness while integrating conservation." The reserve was thought at that time to cover a good portion of the range of vaquita, so it was designated for special protection measures. But with zero enforcement, fishermen didn't feel much effect.

It is telling that when Richard Cudney Bueno and Peggy Turk Boyer, researchers from CEDO (pronounced *SAY-doe*), the Intercultural Center for the Study of Deserts and Oceans, interviewed fishermen in 1998 regarding their feelings about the Biosphere Reserve, the men reported that it had neither positively nor negatively impacted their livelihoods. They saw it as a conservation concept rather than an area of actual regulation.

Although the Biosphere Reserve did little to curb the rapid decline of vaquitas, it would be erroneous to think it did not have an effect. From a broader perspective, the reserve was the first step toward protective management and—as a sign of the world's budding conservation mindset—was a serious threat to the status quo. Vaquita soon emerged as a controversial mascot and scapegoat for the troubles of Alto Golfo.

The year 1997 marked the establishment of the International Committee for the Recovery of the Vaquita, still known today by its Spanish acronym CIRVA (pronounced *SER-vuh*). Two dozen world-class scientists and fisheries experts were appointed to that advisory committee by the Mexican government and were charged with providing data and recommendations. In its inaugural year, CIRVA proposed a large-vessel survey, which soon provided the first dependable population estimate for *Phocoena sinus*.

Only 567 individuals were said to remain.

Scientists also studied potential causes of the species' decline, including water pollution (barely any), lack of prey due to the low flow of the

Colorado River (no problem; vaquita's diet is diverse, and necropsies of entangled individuals showed them to be plump and healthy), and inbreeding (low genetic diversity appeared natural for the population, so it was not a pressing problem). In the end came the official declaration that "gillnets are the greatest risk to the survival of vaquita."

Those findings caused a rift between scientists (who worried about losing a global treasure) and fishery leaders (who worried about losing their livelihoods). Certain authorities refused to enforce the gillnet ban or regulate fishing grounds just to protect a rarely seen and fiscally irrelevant cetacean.

I have been told that CONAPESCA, Mexico's National Commission of Aquaculture and Fishing, actively transferred gillnet permits to fishermen afield and suggested they come and harvest as much fish as possible from the Upper Gulf. Their intention was to wipe out the last of the vaquitas before those sweet-faced porpoises could garner too much public attention and elicit further restrictions on the habitat. If there ever was such a scheme, it failed, thankfully.

In the early years of the new millennium, distribution data revealed that 80 percent of vaquita sightings occurred in a polygon-shaped area off the coast of San Felipe. This "core habitat" was eventually given protective status by the Mexican Ministry of Environment.

In December 2005, approximately eight hundred square miles of primary porpoise habitat were mapped out and labeled as the new Vaquita Refuge. All gillnets were banned within its boundaries. To repeat: the use of gillnets, any size whatsoever, was banned by law inside the Vaquita Refuge—in 2005.

2005–2015

Shortly after designation of the Vaquita Refuge, two significant events swayed the course of history.

First, in 2006, the baiji, China's Yangtze river dolphin, was declared extinct. That shocking loss effectively thrust vaquita into the position of the world's most endangered marine mammal.

Phocoena sinus, swiftly recognized as an EDGE species—evolution-arily distinct, globally endangered—was attracting international attention. The Zoological Society of London wrote after the baiji extinction, "We need to act fast to ensure that this tragedy is not repeated." Such proclamations implied that there would be profound ramifications for failing to rescue vaquita from the same fate. Mexican leaders could not afford to be seen as negligent. If they did not take action, they would surely end up in the same hot seat as Chinese leaders, trying to defend a preventable extinction as the world clucked disapproval.

The second significant event occurred in 2008. A new large-vessel vaquita survey was recommended by CIRVA. It estimated just 245 survivors—less than half of the 1997 population.

Mexico responded with a comprehensive protection and recovery plan: the Species Conservation Action Plan for Vaquita, abbreviated to PACE-Vaquita. This multi-million-dollar government plan incentivized fishermen to respect gear restrictions within the Vaquita Refuge. There were three options to the program: rent out, switch out, or buyout.

The rent-out option issued a payment of forty-five hundred pesos, about $230, per season to each fisherman who agreed to keep his gillnets outside the boundaries of the refuge. The fishermen were allowed to keep their gear and simply promised to abide the ban imposed inside the polygon. It was a trust deal—no supervision.

Fishermen who chose the switch-out option could continue working in the refuge as long as they exchanged their gillnets for *alternativa*. Shrimp baskets, longlines, and diving hookahs probably didn't seem appealing. But a new prototypal "vaquita-friendly" small-scale shrimp trawl offered promise, so Javier and a few friends took the trade, hinging their careers on the future of sustainable fishing.

"We are the pioneers for PACE-Vaquita, the first people to convert the gillnets," Javier said of his 2008 decision, his voice tinged with pride.

The goal of PACE-Vaquita was to eliminate gillnets entirely by 2012. That should have been a fairly easy task given that regional fishermen had successfully transitioned equipment several times as depleted fisheries demanded. Yet only about fifty of fifteen hundred fishermen opted into the switch-out program. Most of Javier's peers simply ignored the restrictions—there was no enforcement anyway—and plied their traditional practices unabated.

As for the buyout option, fishermen could retire their permits and pangas and start a new career. About eighty fishermen submitted small business proposals and received up to $50,000 per permit. They used the money to start renting motorcycles or bungalows or to open a barbershop, launch a restaurant, or provide some other kind of service. Some buyout participants fared well for a while. But when the drug war ramped up in 2009 and 2010, a situation compounded by the economic recession in the United States, Americans quit going to Mexico.

Businesses faltered. Many failed. PACE-Vaquita crumbled. Men returned to fishing, but no longer owning permits of their own, they had to work as hired hands in conglomerates. These alliances place several fishers as employees under one owner's permit. With no other substantial revenue streams in San Felipe and El Golfo de Santa Clara, men held to their conglomerates with unbreakable solidarity.

It is vital to note that Puerto Peñasco fishermen were excluded from the 2008 incentive program (as well as the 2015 gillnet-ban compensation program). They vehemently argued for government imbursements, but the vaquita's range—once thought to be at least thirty-one hundred square miles—has narrowed, and the porpoises no longer frequent the waters near Rocky Point. Requests were refused on the grounds that those fishermen could stay close to home or motor south into unrestricted regions.

Of the three Alto Golfo communities, Puerto Peñasco enjoys the most diverse economic composition. As little as 10 percent of its populace still works in fisheries. So, not only is there geographic distance from the Vaquita Refuge, but people also have occupational alternatives. By contrast, it is said that there is no such thing as a nonfishing family in San Felipe or El Golfo de Santa Clara.

By July 2012, Mexico's highest government was in flux. President Felipe de Jesus Calderón was exiting office. Enrique Peña Nieto, governor of the state of Mexico, had just won the seat with 38 percent of the vote, but the legitimacy of the election was being protested under accusations of corruption. Nobody was paying attention to sleepy fishing villages.

During a six- to nine-month period of limited government oversight, cartel leaders evidently slithered into the profitable trade of totoaba. Poaching was nothing new; although never openly acknowledged, it had been going on to a lesser extent for almost forty years. The *Totoaba macdonaldi* population was far from recovered. Left relatively unmolested for decades, however, the species had produced prodigious offspring. Numbers were up, and that gave criminal capitalists an economically viable fishery to exploit.

With big money to make and no precedence of jail time for poaching, the *buche* business flourished, and fishermen in the Gulf of California embraced the benefits of criminal life.

By the time Peña Nieto enacted his emergency gillnet ban in 2015, things were well out of control. An article for the Society for Marine Mammalogy described total disregard for the Gillnet Exclusion Zone: "Within days following the President's announcement and launch of the new program, reports were received of 85 pangas entering the water at San Felipe and of more than twenty pangas fishing within Vaquita Refuge."

∼

Why would anyone have expected anything different? Historical bans and restrictions have rarely been enforced, and poaching has never been punished.

Furthermore, gillnets have been part of the region's culture since before the mid-twentieth century. They have been unfurled for shrimp, corvina, shark, and totoaba as well as rays, mackerel, mullet, sierra, and flounder, among other fish. Even though there are other types of gear used in the Upper Gulf—traps, trawls, and lines—a gillnet is arguably the single most valuable tool a fisherman can own. It's no wonder that declaring a ban on that equipment has created frustration in the community, conflict instead of cooperation.

Families want to preserve their culture, their livelihoods, and who can blame them? As Frances Hesselbein once wrote, "Culture does not change because we desire to change it. Culture changes when the organization is transformed; the culture reflects the realities of people working together every day."

Cudney Bueno and Turk Boyer discovered an interesting psychological component to collapsing fisheries in Alto Golfo. When questioned, fishermen considered booms and busts as normal; they held to the idea that fisheries come in cycles rather than in steady, reliable harvests. Stability is simply not part of their historical knowledge.

To be fair, there are natural years of abundance or scarcity, which can make trends difficult to recognize. But even when common sense suggests that, say, restricting fishing operations during a species' reproductive period is good for long-term business, most fishermen oppose such restrictions—especially because reproductive periods often coincide with spring Lent, a time when committed Catholics abstain from red meat and fish markets are booming.

If communities won't apply conservative measures to protect their legal fisheries—to protect their own economic future—they are unlikely to apply them to sustain overvalued totoaba, let alone undervalued vaquita.

There is no doubt that the recent government crackdown on gillnets is necessary if *Phocoena sinus* is to persist in the wild. Still, trying to regulate the actions of fishermen by giving them money not to fish is only a temporary, resource-draining solution. Until minds are converted and conservation embraced, the future does not look bright.

"All the world has eyes on the Gulf of California," Javier said at the conclusion of our discussion, and his manner gained an edge as though troubled by what might be seen with all that looking.

My own eyes slipped past him to a map of the Baja region centered on the yellow wall. Vibrant icons touted rich marine life. Soaring pelicans. Barking sea lions. Whales and fish leaping from a cobalt sea.

"They are watching to see if Mexico saves the vaquita," said Javier.

I looked back up at the map.

There was no vaquita.

CHAPTER 3

Chasing a Myth

THROUGH THE YEARS, I have conducted marine research in Golfo Dulce, Costa Rica. In that rain-forest-fringed embayment—twenty-five hundred miles southeast of Alto Golfo but still part of the eastern Pacific Ocean—I once undertook a biodiversity study that examined an assortment of charismatic species, including bottlenose dolphins, *Tursiops truncatus*, and pantropical spotted dolphins, *Stenella attenuata*. Those lithe, muscular cetaceans were a pure delight.

Almost daily, one group or another would sprint to our boat to surf the wake and ride our bow, demonstrating exceptional athletic grace. They often leapt flamboyantly, several feet above the water, eliciting spontaneous cheers for their stunning feats. Then, with tail flukes flapping to match our speed, one or two would approach our side rail and roll upside down below the glassy surface a mere arm's-length away—as though begging for an on-the-go belly rub.

With time, I was able to identify and catalogue the residential *Tursiops* based on the shapes and markings of their dorsal fins. Thereafter, a heart-racing enthusiasm filled me every time I saw them. They became cherished friends. There was Notchpox, for example, who always hung around with Dorsal S. There was Playbaby, who, with youthful enthusiasm, zipped around like an overcaffeinated aerobatic pilot. And there was B9, who earned the name Mama after being logged solo one morning only to reappear that afternoon in the protective folds of her family with a wee newborn calf by her side. What a thrill it was, not only to see the dolphins, but also to recognize them, appreciate their unique personalities, and witness tender moments of their lives.

Vaquitas are not like dolphins.

Vaquitas are incredibly timid. They are also remarkably adept at avoiding boats. A brag-worthy sighting is naught more than a charcoal fin breaking the water surface at a distance, a black triangle spotted only by the most perceptive or lucky of eyes. Indeed, few people have ever seen a vaquita alive. This elusiveness impedes the species' path to recovery in the most unexpected way.

People don't believe vaquitas exist.

That's no joke. It has been proclaimed for decades throughout the region that *la vaquita marina* is a purely mythical animal, like Bigfoot or the Loch Ness monster. To say that a species known to science doesn't exist is absurd. Still, the idea persists, and the myth has been told and retold throughout northwestern Mexico for long enough to be held as truth.

So pervasive, so insidious is this myth that Gustavo grudgingly admitted that there was one good thing about finding dead vaquitas. "Their bodies are evidence," he stated in his straightforward manner. "Proof that they exist."

Even in the face of such proof, citizens seem reticent to accept vaquitas as real. When shown photos of dead porpoises tangled in gillnets, naysayers maintain that plastic models were employed to stage the shots—much like conspiracy theorists who claim that the US moon landing was a put-on.

It's the opposite with Bigfoot. One tantalizing hint of perceived presence—a broken tree branch or shabby footprint, a fuzzy shadow in a nightfall photo—and folks become convinced that eight-foot nocturnal simians are stalking America's northwestern forests. Why is a living wonder like vaquita being denied a place in the tangible world?

I queried Gustavo further. Is the myth pure propaganda, or do people really believe it? He said, "Most fishermen, of course, know vaquitas are out there. But the nonfishermen? I don't know. Some probably believe the myth. Others may think that even if they do exist, there are too few to justify protecting them." Anyone who doesn't want to deal with conservation can conveniently duck behind the lore.

For some, the argument is not that vaquita never existed, only that it does not exist today. From the 1940s to the 1990s, perhaps 90 percent of the original population was wiped out. Fewer porpoises naturally meant fewer sightings by fishermen, which led to the belief that the species was extinct. Then, from 1997 to 2008, the remaining population plummeted another 57 percent. Such a rapid decrease in visibility, which continues today, serves to strengthen the notion that *Phocoena sinus* has already gone the way of the dodo.

Unfortunately, whether the animal is believed to be a mythological creature or an extinct species, the end result is the same: preservation is deemed pointless. In certain ways, irrelevance is worse than contention. Battling indifference is like battling a shadow—there is nothing of substance to push against. Just imagine the challenge it poses for educators and conservationists. It's quite impossible to save a species that nobody will even acknowledge.

When I broached the topic of *la vaquita* while traveling around Alto Golfo, some people furtively avoided conversation; as though the subject could prove dangerous, they dodged it altogether. Other people who seemed curious about yet unconvinced by my enthusiastic *Phocoena sinus* facts acted as if I were a magician attempting to dupe them with a well-contrived illusion. Most people, however, simply shrugged indifference, either baffled or bored by my fascination with nonsense.

To understand their responses, one must understand the communities in which they live. There are three pueblos: San Felipe, El Golfo de Santa Clara, and Puerto Peñasco. Together, they form an arch over the top of the Gulf of California, respectively positioned at the left, top and right of the curve.

~

San Felipe

On the western side of the Gulf of California, where rugged mountains tumble into sand dunes, lies the midsized community of San Felipe. Off-road racing fans recognize it as home to the SCORE San Felipe 250, "the toughest and most brutal 250-mile race on the planet." Every spring, drivers carve a dirt course between desert shrubs, sliding sideways along ridges and braving hairpin turns before crossing salt flats that look like freshly fallen snow, where they reach speeds greater than one hundred miles per hour.

During the remainder of the year, vacationers arrive predominantly from San Diego, Ensenada, and Mexicali. They tend to stay in town, strolling the beach boardwalk—the *malecón*—which hosts an array of vividly colored shops, restaurants, and clubs. Despite a scattering of half-built hotels and derelict structures, proof of a struggling economy, San Felipe is developed enough to sustain numerous resorts, rental properties, and dining establishments. In many ways, it's a charming little town.

One sunny morning, while Gustavo was busy with computer work, I found myself wandering the *malecón*. Peeking into each shop, I perused an assortment of merchandise: straw hats, woven blankets, festive curios, open briefcases lined with silver charms, and the expected variety of San Felipe T-shirts and trinkets. Among the fare, I could not locate a single vaquita knickknack.

When I asked shop owners if they had any vaquita-themed items or might consider carrying some, they simply shook their heads. I suggested that cute porpoises might attract foreign buyers. Americans would love vaquitas, I told them. And because the Vaquita Refuge is less than twenty miles offshore, I even threw out my idea of calling San Felipe *El Hogar de la Vaquita*—Home of the Vaquita. It seemed like a slogan that could earn a few bucks on the *malecón*.

No one was interested.

So I went to talk with Jose.

Jose Maria Cuevas is tall and poised, with round glasses and a thick mustache. He owns two markets and a wonderful restaurant where I have eaten many times. Because all three of his establishments are named La Vaquita, I was eager to hear the backstory.

Chatting at a colorful dining table during the quiet hours between lunch and dinner, he freely admitted that he used to believe vaquita was a fabrication of the imagination. But thirteen years ago, someone showed him a photo of a dead porpoise. That's when he realized, "*Sí, existe!*" Yes, they exist.

Jose decided to name his businesses after the tiny porpoises to help bring awareness to their plight. He established his restaurant in 2003 (translated) "as a way to call attention, to make an impact . . . because people, a lot of people, think *la vaquita* does not exist."

Regardless of any controversy the name may have originally provoked, La Vaquita Marina Restaurant is now a gathering ground for local families and events. Serving up live music and good food, it's also frequented by American and Canadian expats, who have no prejudice against, or in many cases knowledge of, the namesake animal.

When I asked Jose how the myth about vaquita stays alive, he said fishermen are to blame. He then added, more as a statement of fact than judgment, "The fishermen have no interest in vaquita. They have more interest in money and politics."

El Golfo de Santa Clara

The Upper Gulf's tiniest and most northern community of El Golfo de Santa Clara feels desolate compared with San Felipe. It was a sweltering 114 degrees Fahrenheit when I arriving in August with my friend Gary Elbert, who was traveling with me along the Sonoran seacoast. Only one restaurant was open for service. Granted, it was low season for tourism, but El Golfo de Santa Clara is clearly *un pequeño pueblo pesquero*, a tiny fishing village.

For those who cherish remote locales, it has lovely beaches with warm water for swimming and a certain quaint appeal. Given that only the main road is paved, however, an adventuresome spirit is also required. The side streets that map a grid of modest to ramshackle houses are coated with such deep sand that my Prius threatened to get stuck if I drove too slowly. And there's something else that's not in brochures: a lot of cartel activity is said to occur here.

Because the majority of El Golfo de Santa Clara residents work in fisheries, I was hoping to talk with Carlos Tirado, president of the Biosphere Reserve Fishermen Association. Rumor has it that he became a vaquita believer after spotting one while a guest aboard a scientific vessel, although he remains a well-spoken opponent of fishing restrictions. My timing was bad, however. Carlos was gone for vacation. The doors to his family's restaurant, El Delfin, were locked and the windows dark.

Looking for some community contact, Gary and I wandered into a local bar, empty but for one customer. Ordering a beer and enjoying some small talk, Gary casually introduced the topic of vaquita. The sympathetic bartender just as casually switched to a different, although perhaps related, topic. He told us his bar had been broken into the night before. "All they took was some shrimp and chicken to eat," he said, adding an explanation. "Crime is up. People aren't working."

Even as visitors, we could see the truth of that. Later, near the town's windswept *malecón*, we peered into the office for CONAPESCA. It was vacant, a bare shell. The sign on the door gave a contact number for questions about the fishermen incentive program, but there was no on-site staff to deal with daily complaints, of which I was sure there were many.

As people sometimes do in small hamlets, Gary and I sat ourselves on the curb and waited for something interesting to happen. Eventually, a young couple ambled by, carrying two crabs and a conch in a Styrofoam cup. They stopped to talk and were very friendly. After some chitchat, I mentioned *la vaquita*. Suddenly they were tentative—not upset exactly, just uncomfortable, wary. They swiftly took exit, shellfish in hand. Another conversational dead end.

Walking back to our hotel, I noticed a twenty-something fisherman raking a dirt yard around a couple of trailer-bound pangas. A faded sign said that the property belonged to the local production fisheries co-op, so I took a moment to stop and comment on the lack of boats in the bay. Stepping forward and leaning on his rake, the young man told me that the government had ended fishing in San Felipe and El Golfo de Santa Clara—no gillnets for two years.

What are fishermen doing for work? I asked in Spanish.

"*Nada*," he answered.

He readily disclosed that he receives eight thousand pesos (about $425) per month in government compensation but said it's not enough with a wife and rent and utilities. He told me the reason for the ban is *la vaquita*, which he incorrectly described as a dolphin with a black head. When I proposed that it must be frustrating to have one animal causing so much trouble for everyone, opening the door for him to express resentment, he instead shrugged indifference.

"*La vaquita está bien*," he said. The vaquita is fine.

The real problem, he explained, is that the government is planning to drill oil for the United States, and the animal is just a way to get the fishermen out of the water. He possessed neither the rancor of a conspiracy theorist nor the savvy of a resistance spokesperson. He just sounded like an average kid telling me the truth as he knew it: the vaquita crisis is nothing but a ruse to reap and sell oil to Americans.

I would eventually come to hear other fishermen around the region make the same assertion. They saw the conservation of vaquita as a contrived distraction from a darker political ploy. It's true that President Peña Nieto has worked toward deregulation of his country's energy industry to allow foreign access to Mexican oil and gas reserves, but drilling in the Upper Gulf has never been publically proposed.

Puerto Peñasco

Compared with San Felipe and El Golfo de Santa Clara, Puerto Peñasco—known to Americans as Rocky Point—is big. Far more a vacation hotspot than fishing hub, it boasts shops and restaurants for almost every taste. On the southeast end of the bustling *malecón*, where residents and visitors gather every Sunday for clowns and ice cream, music and dancing, the coastline is speckled with lovely upscale homes in private communities. On the northwest end, towering hotels and fancy condos bedeck the beaches.

El Edificio Municipal is a two-story cube of white stucco located in town with an impressive brass bell hanging above the portal. I had been told that Puerto Peñasco's City Hall has a vaquita mural in its courtyard, and with a bit of nosing around, Gary and I found it in the main corridor. The paint was flaking from neglect, but there, among other regional marine life, in the lower left-hand corner, was *Phocoena sinus*.

What did this civic exhibit reflect about the community's awareness of the species?

Entering the office, I asked if someone might be able answer a few questions about the mural, about *la vaquita*.

"*La vaquita?*" repeated the woman at the front desk in a tone that made clear I was broaching an unconventional topic.

I smiled with humble hope of assistance. "*Sí, por favor.*"

Raising a chunky phone receiver to her ear, the woman pressed a dial pad and brusquely restated my request and then motioned for us to wait. We did—while the five or six people sitting in the reception area openly stared at us with skeptical curiosity. The reaction was obvious enough to make for an uncomfortable few minutes and caused Gary to remark later as we left the building, "Wow. Did you see their faces? They looked like we were asking about a ghost."

Although we didn't obtain any information, a gentleman named Mario López offered to show us some better vaquita murals around town. He looked to be an educated professional, dressed in a nice shirt and slacks, with short, receding hair and well-carved smile lines. To our pleasure, he proved a friendly and knowledgeable guide—who refused a single peso for his help.

Standing at the popular Playa Blanca, looking at a festive mural by a popular local artist named Memuco, I asked Mario what he knew about vaquita. He responded in earnest (translated), "I know many local fishermen who have worked in the water for twenty, even thirty, years. They have never seen one." When I asked if his neighbors in Rocky Point believe in vaquita, he gave the exact same answer. The fishermen have never seen one.

I told Mario that scientists had recently seen them over by San Felipe. I supplied a few tidbits about the animal's unique biology, its historical decline as bycatch in gillnets, and its plight for survival, adding that Mexico really needed the support of local communities to save the species from extinction.

A twinkle of assent flickered over Mario's face—the idea of vaquita as a living animal was clearly provocative, but could he trust me to be telling the truth? As though stumped by the contradiction, he awkwardly reiterated his mantra. The fishermen have never seen one.

In his defense, it's true that the range of *Phocoena sinus*, perpetually shrinking, no longer overlays the fishing grounds near Puerto Peñasco.

And dead vaquitas, which used to wash onto the shores of Rocky Point, no longer do. The remaining population resides farther to the west and north, apparently at a distance too far for drowned bodies to float. It's quite possible that Mario's fishermen friends might never have seen one.

I gently persisted. Fishermen aside, what does he personally believe? Do vaquitas exist?

He took a moment to weigh what he thought he knew against what I'd told him, looking a bit like a cornered animal. I could tell he didn't want to be rude by insinuating that I was a liar, and settling on diplomacy, he finally answered, "I don't know. Maybe. Maybe not."

It was the kind of answer someone might give regarding the conceivable existence of extraterrestrial life.

~

Lorenzo Rojas Bracho, INECC's lead scientist and long-standing chairman of the International Committee for the Recovery of Vaquita (CIRVA), is convinced that fishermen say the porpoises don't exist for convenience's sake—they don't want to deal with them. He assures me, however, that as recently as the mid-1990s, even top government officials denied the existence of vaquitas.

"I started working on my PhD thesis with a species that 'didn't exist,'" he once told me over a cup of coffee. "Everybody said the vaquita didn't exist. Especially in Mexico, but also some people in the US too. Almost everybody would say, 'Vaquita's a myth, it doesn't exist.'"

Despite public disbelief, Lorenzo forged ahead with his scientific plans. He teamed up with acoustics apprentice Armando Jaramillo Legorreta, who was interested in "looking" for vaquitas by means of the clicks they produce underwater. The pair then connected with another scientist named Barbara Taylor, who works for the US National Oceanic and Atmospheric Administration, stationed at the Southwest

Fisheries Science Center in La Jolla, California. Already a porpoise specialist, Barb had written a paper about the difficulty of monitoring vaquitas through visual surveys alone and was excited to explore additional avenues for establishing population statistics. The burgeoning discipline of acoustics offered promising results.

Uniting with other respected researchers, including Tim Gerrodette, Robert Pitman, and Jay Barlow, an impressive team of marine mammal experts was rallied to collaborate on vaquita studies. Soon—and with the assistance of a then-much-younger Javier, a sympathetic fisherman who had seen porpoises and knew his way around Alto Golfo—the scientists headed into the field.

Lorenzo gives a lot of kudos to Javier. He said that when he and Armando first began their work and didn't know anything, Javier put them on the right track. He added, "There isn't a biologist that Javier has not supported in the last twenty-five years."

The survey team's 1997 data not only confirmed that *Phocoena sinus* was real but also that, as earlier scientists like Robert Brownell had noted, the species was rapidly disappearing. Left unprotected, the world's smallest cetacean would surely become the imaginary creature it was publicly presumed to be.

Gaining traction with officials proved exceedingly difficult, but with substantive evidence, the scientists eventually persuaded a few political leaders to heed their concerns. Lorenzo, Armando, and Barb have toiled ever since then to keep Mexico's porpoise on the political radar—a task complicated by regular administrative turnovers. CIRVA members to this day, they strive tirelessly to foster binational support and influence change at the highest levels.

"Now our team has official status in the Mexican government," said Lorenzo. "The species is getting more and more attention. It's even been in the *New York Times* and some major newspapers in Europe. Most importantly, people recognize the low numbers. Now, it would be hard to find an authority in Mexico that would say the vaquita does not exist. So we went from nonexisting to where we are now."

He took a sip of coffee and added, "I think that's good progress."

Such progress is encouraging and certainly commendable. Gustavo once said, "Without the conservation of the past, the vaquita would already be gone by now. It might even have won the Guinness World Record for shortest time between species description and extinction."

It's thanks to the diligence of pioneering scientists that vaquita is no longer considered mythical among mainstream advisors. With a growing body of comparative data to document the nosedive of the population, better protection strategies have landed squarely on the discussion table. Some of those strategies have been implemented to varying degrees of success, but it's been a long, slow slog, and the hourglass is running dry.

Too many Mexican nationals still believe vaquita is fictitious. Awareness must be raised, fables erased. Only then can local citizens unite in the effort to protect the last surviving porpoises that swim through their watery backyard. Of course, with the species now potentially dipping below 1 percent of its original numbers, there is not enough time for education alone to seed the change. Gillnetting must be stopped—immediately and permanently—with or without the unification of local citizens.

The most obvious, if hard-line, solution is to tell fishermen that they just can't fish anymore. But people who truly understand the complexities of the vaquita problem respect this simple fact: if fishing is unsustainable, so is not fishing. As Lorenzo put it, "You cannot save vaquita and have fishermen go extinct."

Alternative gear, then, seems to be the best solution.

Research biologists Jamie Afflerbach and colleagues agreed that "cessation of fishing [in the Upper Gulf] is not considered a realistic option since it is the principal economic activity for the region." Their 2013 group thesis focused on bioeconomic trade-offs in policies relating to vaquita conservation. Project members modeled theoretical effects of 340 policy scenarios that included spatial closures, fishery closures, gear buyout programs, alternative trawls, and varying levels of compliance. Although "46 policy combinations were identified that will achieve vaquita population growth," they bore associated "economic losses ranging from approximately 21–100% of current total fishery revenue."

The researchers found, however, that artisanal "trawling would lead to a substantial reduction in the economic impact of successful conservation policies" and indicated that "a bioeconomic optimum" would result from "closing a larger area to gillnetting, but allowing use of the zero-vaquita bycatch trawl."

As an advocate for both fishermen and fish, Barb Taylor wholeheartedly promotes a full and effective transition to alternative gear "so workers can continue to work." But alternative equipment has been available since 2008, and it's still not in use. Fisheries managers have not complied with government directives. Even with the 2013 Mexican NOM-002 mandate requiring a three-year switch from gillnets to artisanal shrimp trawls, no progress has been made.

Barb says there is pushback from fishermen, and she understands why. Switching to alternative gear requires something of a professional overhaul. "Gillnetting's very efficient in terms of making fishermen money," she explained. "I mean, you go out there, you stick the gear in the water, you turn off your engine, float around for six or eight hours, and then you pull it out again. You haven't burned any gas, and it doesn't take much skill, if any. When you move to small, light trawls, it's an active gear, so the engine is running to pull the net through the water. It takes gas. And quite a bit of skill."

Still, something needs to happen straightaway. "Mexico can't pay fishermen to sit on their hands indefinitely," Barb told me. "It's really sort of now or never." Otherwise, all those years of hard-earned prog-ress—of collecting and analyzing data, publishing papers, and cam-paigning in government offices and lecture halls—will go to waste. And the story of vaquita will end as the story of baiji did.

Too little. Too late.

CHAPTER 4

Tangled Agendas

One hot spring afternoon in 2016, Gustavo trundled me into a quiet San Felipe neighborhood and dropped me off in front of a modest but respectable house. A twenty-six-foot panga sat in the driveway with its name dancing along its sideboards in lovely blue and yellow cursive lettering. *Islas del Golfo*. A ficus tree drooping with plump green leaves gave the resting beast shade.

A few out-of-work fishermen milled around the dirt yard. Spotting Javier near a mound of turquoise netting, I strode over and was welcomed with a smile. Knowing nothing about fishing equipment, I was grateful for this invitation to his home to get a primer on alternative shrimp trawls.

After introducing me to his co-op buddies, Javier summoned another mustached gentleman, Luis Martínez, who goes by the nickname Taladro, to help him stretch out his lightweight net so that I could see the shape it takes on in the water. At first I couldn't distinguish any shape at all; it looked like a giant wad of twine left too long in the junk drawer.

With a bit of expert pulling and pointing, though, I was able to decipher the basic system.

I could see how shrimp swimming in the water column are scooped into the concaved net and then funneled into a long catch tube. The fifty-foot net has buoys every five feet along the upper rope to keep it suspended, while a chain along the bottom pulls the net down and open. Javier explained how the whole contraption is slowly towed, with the corners of the assembly attached to a metal V right behind the boat, which cuts the water and holds the net open "like the mouth of a whale shark."

Cleverly designed, this type of trawl—fittingly nicknamed *chango* for change—has two essential features to reduce bycatch. First, a special six-inch gap between the bottom of the net and the chain allows bottom-dwelling animals, like rays and crabs and flounder, to pass through without capture. The second feature is seen in the bottleneck of the catch tube: a large metal grate called a TED (turtle excluder device). The barred gate does not impede shrimp, but it blocks the passage of large finfish and slow-moving sea turtles. If a big animal gets caught in the tube and hits the TED, it's bumped out sideways through a floppy opening in the net wall—a secret escape hatch. The sound of the boat motor would presumably keep porpoises at bay, but should one accidentally be taken in, the TED acts as a safeguard.

Predictably, holes and gaps diminish a net's productivity—some of the shrimp undoubtedly slip out—so a *chango* is less profitable than a *chinchorro* or traditional trawl. Javier estimates that his alternative gear can catch 135 pounds of shrimp in three hours, but he says he might get double or triple that with traditional gear. Plus, the new equipment costs about $3,000. That's three times more expensive than a gillnet. So he pays more and catches less.

He stays focused on the fact that *chango* is considerably safer for non-target species. It is so much safer, in fact, that if this kind of gear can become commonplace, there just might be a chance for vaquitas to recover. Of course, fisherman alone cannot save a species.

Blue shrimp, *Litopenaeus stylirostris*, which can grow to more than seven inches in length, accounts for 90 percent of the shrimp catch the Upper Gulf. Roughly 435 miles of gillnets are set each and every day during the shrimping season to secure an annual landing of around seven hundred tons. Because 80 percent of that haul is exported to the United States, American buyers have a powerful role in the future of the region.

Would they, we, be willing to pay a bit more to eat jumbo shrimp caught with vaquita-friendly gear? If the popularity of dolphin-safe tuna is a reliable precedent, the answer is yes. And I would soon come to discover there is a complete production chain—eco-minded importers, processors, restaurants, and consumers—eagerly waiting for vaquita-friendly shrimp to enter the sustainable-seafood market.

By thinking along those lines, the solution may seem perfectly clear. All Mexico needs to do is mass-produce these light trawls and give them to Alto Golfo fisherman in exchange for gillnets. Thereafter, gillnets should become illegal to make or own. With everyone employing the same alternative gear, market prices would naturally adjust for productivity.

Men keep fishing. Vaquitas keep living.

If only it could be that easy.

It turns out that even though Javier has been equipped with *chango* since 2008, he has never been able to use it. "Me, I don't go for illegal," he said. He was facing the sun, his eyes shaded by the brim of his cap. "But I don't know what the government is going to do with us because they don't give us the opportunity to use the *alternativa*." Despite having all their paperwork turned in on time and in order, their permits are being withheld. "The permits they finally give us are out of season, so we go and we don't fish nothing," he explained.

It's Mexico's fisheries agencies that keep delaying approval of the equipment. INAPESCA keeps revising the design and then requiring new tests. Also, whenever the trawls have been taken out for official trials, the test boats were surrounded by sneering gillnetters, who block-aded their movement and then denounced their limited catch as proof that alternative gear doesn't work.

Javier has experimented with several never-approved versions. Near the sidewall of his yard, he showed me an earlier TED, which he said performed much better than the one I previously examined. Whether better or not, that grate is now obsolete, rusting away in the driveway next to his forlorn panga, which sits on blocks like a soccer player cut from the team.

The whole situation is such a mess. Although Mexico's federal ad-ministration is spending tens of millions of dollars to incentivize fisher-men to give up gillnets, its agencies are failing to support those who actually do it. As Javier's friends stood chatting in remnants of shade, I imagined their bright enthusiasm wilting to bitter disappointment. They were living in an endless loop of testing and waiting. Eight years. No progress. How exasperating that must be.

I thought of Javier out fishing with his father so long ago, enjoying the sea breeze in much less complicated world. "You've seen a lot of change," I said as he quietly wrapped up his *chango*. The net had re-sumed its tangled-twine appearance.

He smiled in that sad, ponderous way that older people sometimes do.

"*Sí, mucho cambio.*"

~

One thing that hasn't changed is the aggressive energy directed at alternative-gear fishermen. For surrendering their gillnets, they are treated as traitors—literally and figuratively attacked by their communities. The social rejection they endure ranges from being conspicuously ignored by neighbors to braving cutting remarks across the aisle at the grocery market to suffering direct threats and intimidation.

After one fisherman went out as a paid observer on a test run of alternative equipment, he was bullied in an El Golfo de Santa Clara bar. The ensuing fight ended with a hospital visit and deep-seated fear in the heart of the observer, who swore he would never do the job again. Another proponent of *alternativa* had a gang of unruly adversaries pounding at his door in the middle of the night. Yet another had his truck set on fire.

If social harassment is not enough, the men of Islas del Golfo Co-op are suffering economically too. As part of his initiative, President Enrique Peña Nieto agreed to compensate fishermen for loss of income incurred by the 2015 gillnet ban. However, the exact payment policy and its accounting have lacked transparency. "The money the government give to the other fishermen, it's supposed to be equal," Javier told me. "It was not equal. They don't give us the money they are supposed to give us. We only get 12,500 pesos." That's $700, about one-third of the promised payout.

Alt-gear fishermen have not been rewarded and are still not being allowed to fish as promised, even though they're willing to use vaquita-friendly gear. Rather than being praised as conservation heroes and thanked for helping Mexico move toward ecological sustainability, they appear to be abandoned by their government. They are being penalized for relinquishing their gillnets.

How can that be?

Alex Olivera of the Center for Biological Diversity, who has been investigating the government gillnet-ban-compensation structure, has uncovered some disturbing statistics. There are about 2,770 people in the gillnet compensation program—people considered directly reliant on income from fisheries and their production chain—who are now receiving regular imbursements from the Mexican government. Beneficiaries

Gustavo Cárdenas, who coordinates alternative-gear fishermen from Islas del Golfo Co-Op to assist INECC's acoustic studies, is seen with mooring buoys for underwater vaquita monitoring devices. Front row, left to right: Ramon Arozamena, Javier Valverde, and Gustavo (squatting); Alán Valverde and Gilberto "Giby" Ruiz (holding buoys), and Paco Valverde from CONANP (holding paperwork). (Brooke Bessesen)

on the lower levels receive about four thousand pesos, or $200, per month. Those at the highest level receive more than two million pesos. That's more than $100,000—a month!

To look at this from another angle, 42 percent of the multi-million-dollar dole-out goes to about thirty individuals. More precisely, 20 percent goes to the top thirteen men, who hold numerous permits and receive a payment for each. How did so few people come to hold so many permits? Olivera reports that Mexican fisheries agents have power to manipulate the permit list. And the judicial guidelines for obtaining said permits are *claro como el barro*—clear as mud. It even happens that at least thirty-eight compensation recipients are confirmed totoaba poachers who have run illicit rackets while procuring government subsidies.

Exactly who secures permits is of serious import, especially right now, when, despite what outsiders may believe, gillnet permits are still being issued.

This fact took me a while to figure out because every public report—every commentary, every news article, every broadcast—describes a complete gillnet ban. It's not true. There is an exception: gillnets for a fish called corvina are still allowed. When I learned that corvina lives and spawns in the same waters, during the same months, as totoaba, it was like tripping sideways off a street curb I hadn't known was there.

~

Corvina, *Cyonscion othonopterus*, is another sciaenid endemic to the Sea of Cortez. A totoaba relative, it too has been hunted extensively through the decades, leading to a partial closure of the fishery in 2005. Author Joaquín Humberto Ruelas-Peña and colleagues concluded that "the average biomass [of corvina] from 2006 to 2010 was 52% of the optimum level of the fishery." That explains why the species is still considered vulnerable by IUCN.

Conservation status aside, allowing a corvina exception to the gillnet ban has had a devastating effect on regulation and enforcement for totoaba. The hunting season and spawning grounds for corvina and totoaba (suspiciously) overlap. That is to say, *curvina golfina* are found—and gillnetting for them is permitted—in the Gillnet Exclusion Zone. In fact, the only area where corvina fishing is prohibited is within the boundaries of the Vaquita Refuge, and there are constant violations, especially at night.

Needless to say, legal corvina gillnets have proven an excellent cover-up for poachers. Totoaba nets are easily hidden beneath corvina nets in the hulls of pangas where they can be motored out into unattended waters. As a matter of fact, anyone can carry illegal gear across the water—it's not illegal to transport banned gillnets, only to deploy them. There's slim chance that illegal casting will be recognized in miles of open water.

If the act of fishing corvina is a cover-up for poaching totoaba, the same holds true for the sale of their organs. Corvina is a legal fish; thus, its swim bladder is a legal article of trade. Around 2010 or 2011, Chinese buyers in El Golfo de Santa Clara began purchasing corvina bladders. Chopped and boiled in soup, they served as counterfeit fish maw. Soon fishermen from San Felipe upped the ante, offering "real" *buches* for those willing to pay poaching prices. Anyone still wanting to do business with Chinese buyers was pushed to compete. By 2012, the totoaba black market had grown horns like a devil, leaving many to blame corvina for the resurgence.

It should not come as a surprise that forbidden totoaba *buches* have been shipped to China with authorizing documents stating that they were corvina bladders. *Mexico News Daily* wrote that "the main modus operandi of traffickers is to camouflage the bladder with other swim bladders, for which the proper trading permits have been authorized." It only takes one police officer, one soldier, one customs agent to give the stamp of approval, and contraband becomes commodity.

Although some agents may legitimately lack training to distinguish between the two bladders (which actually look quite different), it would be naive to believe that nobody has accepted under-the-table bills to feign ignorance.

Totoaba and corvina. Smoke and mirrors.

With the two endemic drum fish so intricately interlinked, how could the Mexican president justify his perplexing exemption to the gillnet ban?

His allowance is said to be based on three factors. First, corvina meat serves only the regional market, going to Ensenada and other cities in

Baja and Sonora. Second, corvina fishing is an active rodeo-style process, so the nets, used like purse seines, are attended by pangas, and vaquitas seem to keep their distance. Finally, six-inch mesh is not designed to catch totoaba (designed is the operative word, since fishermen admit that young totoaba can be caught with corvina nets).

Even Lorenzo said, "We told the government many times, if you allow corvina fishing, it will be a perfect cover-up for fishermen to take out totoaba nets under their corvina nets. Or say they will go corvina fishing and instead check totoaba nets already in the water." He said he strongly believes that possessing, selling, or transporting gillnets should be illegal because "as long as you have gillnets in the water, vaquitas are at risk."

Yes, wasn't saving vaquita the whole reason for the gillnet ban in the first place?

～

Everywhere, the C-word is whispered.

Corruption.

From customs agents to police officers, military soldiers to politicians, everyone seems suspect. On the surface, the weather is good. People are collaborating to end the totoaba crisis and to protect a vanishing cetacean. Underneath, however, secret covenants generate an unethical undertow, deep and deadly.

In El Golfo de Santa Clara on Saturday, March 26, 2016, a *buchero* named José Islas Armenta, alias "El Compa Pepe," was killed in a shootout with municipal police. Municipal officer Jaime Arreola Valdez also took fire and died from bullet wounds. It was 6 a.m. on the morning before Easter—*Semana Santa*, the busiest week of the year. With some thirty thousand visitors having clambered into the fishing village to catch a little beach time, the *ra-ta-ta-tat!* of an AK-47 submachine gun did not go unnoticed.

Social media was soon flooded with accusations of municipal and state police corruption. Armenta was known for trafficking totoaba swim bladders obtained under the guise of corvina fishing. In addition to his earnings as a kingpin, he had been receiving more than $5,000 a month through the government compensation program. He was a wealthy and powerful man who was allegedly being extorted by the municipal police—someone even claimed that they had beaten Armenta's wife while demanding a $30,000 kickback.

The night before his death, Armenta was arrested by two Sonoran state police officers who also supposedly extorted him before letting him go. Several hours later, just before sunrise, the municipal police stopped Armenta's Ford truck, and he engaged them in gunfire.

Speculation followed. Were both state and municipal officers extorting the *buchero*? If so, were they acting separately, or was there some higher level of corruption at play?

Two days after the shoot-out, 121 dried bladders were confiscated in a separate news-making event. Those *buches* originated in El Golfo de Santa Clara. Pointing to both incidents and the scale of collusion required to sustain such far-reaching crime, political figure Dr. Jorge Figueroa remarked in an article (translated), "That size implies corruption and pretense in the federal government of Peña Nieto and the state government of [Sonoran Governor] Claudia Pavlovich."

My late father-in-law had a rancorous saying about institutional corruption. "The fish stinks from the head down." It means that trouble in the ranks is always a reflection of trouble with the leader. I have found the adage to be true. As I read the miscellany of reports about the shoot-out, I felt a new level of angst. It was deeper water than I'd intended getting into. Delayed permits and lies about bycatch are one thing; killings potentially linked to state or federal corruption are quite another.

I was further unnerved by the reticence of average citizens to talk about the criminal element. When I spoke with residents around the Upper Gulf about corruption, most refused comment without assurance that their names would not be mentioned. They feared retaliation, even though none had anything particularly damning to disclose.

"It is the exact fishermen who have ignored the laws, who have fished illegally and created the crisis of totoaba and vaquita, that are now getting paid $600,000 a year by the Mexican government."

"It is easy to see who is corrupt. They have big houses, pickups, boats."

"Too many authorities are corrupt."

"Is so easy to be corrupt. It's too easy! It's a part of our culture."

"If gillnets in the water is illegal, it is the Mexican government's obligation to enforce their laws. They have all the resources and equipment to do it. They don't do it because they are paid not to do it. I have no words for that. As a Mexican, I feel ashamed."

"Some authorities stay in San Felipe or El Golfo de Santa Clara one month, three months. Then they change with other people. It's a big problem. They say, 'I receive the money of the illegal fishermen. I know in two months or three months I will go to San Felipe.' It's the same with federal authorities and the state police department. They just take the money and go."

Government and military officials are said to switch posts regularly, which purportedly contributes to corruption, as fraudsters may be restationed before being caught—or even investigated. With ready-made opportunities for financial gain and no real penalties, it's clear to see why authorities would take advantage.

Still, I put forth that some government workers, especially those on the local level, are not necessarily corrupt but afraid. Maybe they don't want to risk going against the system. After all, with organized crime, one regretful decision could bring real harm. Everyone wholeheartedly agreed. They said nobody wants to draw attention that could put them or their families in jeopardy, themselves included.

To be honest, I sometimes worried myself. Vaquita is becoming an increasingly hot topic, not merely because of media attention and rapidly expanding awareness, but also because the situation is emotionally charged with adversaries fully invested and rearing for combat.

So far, nothing drastic has happened to anyone lacking a criminal background, nothing like what occurred in Costa Rica in 2013, when outspoken environmentalist Jairo Mora Sandoval, working to protect the nests of endangered sea turtles along the shores of Limón, was abducted by egg poachers and dragged behind a truck until dead. Mora was murdered for obstruction of business.

Costa Rica is notably different from Mexico in its tolerance for lawlessness. The chief judge for the Mora case announced in court, "This crime is more than just a horrible murder, it has also damaged Costa Rica's reputation as a green country. It has scared away environmentalists." He handed the convicted men fifty years in prison for their crime.

Comparable prosecution is rare in Mexico. Sometimes there isn't even a trial.

On Tuesday, June 11, 2014, another El Golfo de Santa Clara fisherman by the name of Samuel Gullardo Castro was killed in a drive-by shooting. "El Samy," as he was called, was the director of the Alto Golfo Fisheries Cooperative and purportedly an organized crime boss. Although known for trafficking drugs, he is said to have been murdered over a $1 million debt on a totoaba-swim-bladder shipment. Nothing more is known about the case because the investigation lost steam after the man who admitted to the crime was released. Authorities said they doubted the validity of his report.

Such stories haunt me. But whenever concern sneaks in and elbows me, I summon the words of a knowledgeable conservationist who works in Alto Golfo neighborhoods frequented by black Suburbans with tinted windows. When I had asked if she ever feels that her job is too risky, she said, "I'm not scared. The [criminals] know our role in this. They understand our place. We are no threat to them."

Despite the reservation that colored her voice, I believe there is logic to her words.

Besides, change cannot be wrought without courage—the courage to speak up, to stay the course. As I forged into ever deeper and murkier political waters, I thought of all the Mexican nationals who willingly put themselves in the line of attack to save vaquita from gillnets. The conservationists, who openly strive for unpopular policies. The alt-gear fishermen, who endure the backlash of their communities. The scientists, who remain steadfast even when their voices seem lost to the wind. And those stalwart politicians who pledge honesty in an ethos of corruption. Admirably, they all stand fast, even as their fellow citizens are clutched in the talons of fear and frustration.

RUSSELL

Expires: **8/12**

Hold for **MELODY RUSSELL**
Route Item to:

Public Holds Shelf

Title: **Vaquita : science, politics, and crime in the Sea of Cortez**
Barcode: 78551000539654

Request Date: 2019-07-31 11:36
Slip Date: 2019-08-05 14:35
Printed by KRISTI at JCKSN-SEY

CHAPTER 5

Death, Drugs, and Accountability

THERE IS A PURIFIED-WATER STORE in San Felipe with a towering rectangular sign that reads Agua Purificada Mar de Cortez. The blue stucco building accommodates a mural. Amid a static blue sky, gulls dip and swoop, a sea lion peeks above the waves, dolphins leap on the horizon, and a sea turtle and totoaba pass in the depths. On the left side, just behind a lone whale, a pretty little porpoise mama swims near her calf.

Because vaquitas are rarely promoted in San Felipe, the painting caught my attention, and I stopped with Gustavo to meet the shop's owner. Seated in foldout chairs near a display of oversized water bottles, Daniel Gonzales was generous enough to talk with us about his mural—painted by local artist Pedro Camancho—and to tell us about his business.

Daniel used to be a fisherman. He was one of the first buyout participants in the PACE-Vaquita program. He turned in two fishing permits and all related equipment (pangas, *chinchorros*, and so on) for a single payment of one million pesos, about $54,000. That money bought him two rental apartments, which currently fetch a combined rent roll of

$380 per month. Along with the lump cash, Daniel received three weeks of business administration courses to learn how to manage budgets and marketing and other aspects of enterprise.

Taking the government deal banned Daniel from fishing for life, but he's content with his choice. I asked him why he selected the buyout when so few did. He said his gear was old, but even more pressing was the trouble he saw in the fishing industry, namely that it wasn't successful anymore. "Fishermen may work all day and not catch much," he said in Spanish. Plus, the United States was threatening embargoes on shrimp—another layer of trouble.

He knows about twenty-five fishermen in San Felipe who took the buyout. Almost all of them are still in business, running apartment rentals, internet cafes, and tire repair shops—more or less successfully. One person who held several fishing permits only turned in enough to purchase a hotel; with the remainder he still manages a fishing conglomerate.

In 2013, Daniel and six partners entered the water purification business. The venture was sponsored by ENDESU, a nongovernment organization that helps ex-fishermen earn money in provaquita businesses (which explains the beautiful mural). Regrettably, the shop hasn't proved very profitable, so Daniel is glad to have his apartments and his federal aid check.

Federal aid?

It turns out that Daniel gets compensation from the gillnet ban. The government program provides for all parties along the production chain. As a member of his fishermen's association, helping with quality control on fish exports, Daniel qualifies for a monthly imbursement. Although few of Daniel's businessmen friends still fish professionally, many are still connected to the fishing industry and, like him, receive some level of compensation.

Daniel believes that fishermen are privately happy about the ban because they are getting money without having to work, but he conceded a darker side to the story. Fishermen who worked under other owners' permits are not necessarily compensated as intended. The owners of the boats, the ones who hold the permits and receive the money, he told us, systematically misdirect their designated funds to family members instead of paying the fishers who worked for them. Many men who lost their day-to-day labor are now destitute.

～

In March 2016, the *ZETA* article "Crisis en San Felipe" described a hopeless dilemma for a fisherman named David. David had been employed by an unnamed permit holder and had worked right up until the day before the gillnet ban, but when it came to drawing up the list for federal compensation, the article reported (translated), "the permittee knocked him out and stuck in his daughter, his nephew, a grandson," which has left David to "wander the boardwalk on his bicycle with no work, no money."

There are countless such complaints of fishermen being bypassed as beneficiaries.

"The effect [of the ban] has been negative," Roberto Ledón of the Economic Development Council was quoted as saying in the article. "There is less cash flow, fewer people are busy, there is a lack of investment in every way and it shows in closed businesses, people without occupation." The article reported that "arrests skyrocketed from May to September 2015, after the fishing ban resulted in hundreds of people out of work." Aside from the totoaba busts plaguing the region, vagrancy, robberies, and drugs were said to be the root of the arrests.

Drugs, I would come to learn, are toxic threads in the social fabric of San Felipe and El Golfo de Santa Clara—and a grave, if rarely discussed, part of the poaching culture. When I first heard about a drug issue, I presumed it had to do with transporting cocaine or crystal methamphetamine along a northbound corridor to the United States. Naively, the words *drugs* and *Mexico* made me think of meth labs and human mules. That kind of drug trafficking is not much of a concern in the seaside pueblos of the Upper Gulf, however. Addiction is the problem.

Historically, fishermen smoked marijuana and drank beer. Now many are hooked on amphetamines. Because stimulants act on the central nervous system, amphetamines are highly habit-forming and affect impulse control. Side effects of amphetamine use include a false sense of well-being and rare but possible hallucinations. Elevated blood pressure, an irregular heartbeat, insomnia, confusion, and anxiety or agitation can also be added to the list. Addicts are edgy, irresponsible, and worst of all, in need of money.

As drugs take control of their lives, these fishermen frequently turn to poaching for quick cash, which hooks them in with cartels and crime. How far does desperation lead them? Since the black-market surge, up to a dozen fishermen have died while attempting to hunt totoaba in stormy, night-blackened waters. They are said to have been "drowned by ambition." Yet I can't help wondering where the ambition actually lies: with the fishermen or with their bosses?

Did personal greed drive those men into the dark, white-capped mountains of a hostile sea? Did they accept the consequence of death by their own volition? Or did they go because they were told to go? Little is known about how much, if any, cartel pressure is put on poachers to secure *buches* or the role of drugs in the choices those fishermen make. Rehabilitation facilities may help addicts get clean, but by and large, most go back to using.

So, not only are porpoises suffering; humans are too. Their lives—and their deaths—are interlinked in a complicated lattice of social injustice.

One morning I strolled the beach with Chris Snyder, the woman who found Ps2's body. I asked her about drug use in San Felipe. By way of answer, she told me that she and Tom paid more than $200,000 in 2008 for their lovely El Dorado Ranch home, but today would be lucky to get $40,000. Because real estate has lost so much value, the master-planned community has had to cut two-thirds of its staff. "That's added to high unemployment," Chris said. "Now there is petty crime. Nothing too dangerous, just mostly theft. But they cannot hire enough security guards because people have a hard time passing the drug tests."

Chris wishes there could be more education to help fishermen secure new jobs. She'd like to see a push for literacy, too, so that kids have career options. She also wishes her Mexican neighbors could see the value of vaquitas for their community. *Malécon* shops could offer T-shirts, jewelry, and artisan goods for visitors to purchase, she suggested. Charming porpoises could be capitalized as a tourist draw—but only if poaching and drugs can be brought under control.

As we wandered south along the coast, I asked Chris to take me to the spot where she found Ps2. When she showed me the site, I struggled to reconcile the picture-perfect scenery with thoughts of Ps2's young body limp at the tide line. The photos on Paco's computer had turned my stomach queasy. Ps2's lips and tail had been eaten away by salt water and nibbling fish, leaving gaping holes of red flesh and honey-colored bone. Her bloated skin was marbled purple, and her sturdy flippers, which once carried her alongside her mother and once ruddered her in play, had begun to blacken with decay. The memory sent a shudder up my spine.

Now all that remained was a sweep of warm sand beneath idyllic palms and powder-blue sky. I listened to the gentle rush and draw of the surf. It was like I had woken from a bad dream to find everything peacefully in its place.

But Ps2's death wasn't a dream.

~

The only institution with enough power to determine the fate of Mexico's porpoise is Mexico's government. Nongovernmental organizations

Dead vaquita, Ps2, attended by a turkey vulture on the beach at El Dorado Ranch, north of San Felipe, March 15, 2016. (Courtesy of Tom Gorman)

can sponsor, educate, support, and even badger. Scientists can contribute knowledge-enhancing data. People can picket or boycott. In the end, though, it will all come down to what the Mexican government does or does not do. Unfortunately, the country's chain of command is divided along a hierarchical fault line as active and dangerous as the San Andreas.

Of the two federal offices relating to the environment, one deals with conservation (SEMARNAT) and the other with industry (SAGARPA). Beneath them are several national agencies. The trouble appears to be that although certain agencies are leading the effort to keep vaquita from going extinct, other agencies are acting counter to that goal. More specifically, there is an unbridgeable chasm between the conservation and fishing sectors of government, and the persistence of gillnets is but a symptom of that deep-rooted partisanship.

Two critically endangered animals are trapped in a battle of wills. As head of nation, where does the Mexican president's allegiance lie? The answer is impossible to pinpoint because he issues mixed messages. Signing off on a $32-million-a-year gillnet ban while condoning a ban-defying corvina exception. He's giving with one hand and taking with the other.

Admittedly, Enrique Peña Nieto is in a political pickle. He is being asked to stop the eradication of a national biological treasure while simultaneously subsidizing his constituents who rely on the very system causing the eradication. I'm sympathetic. It must be a difficult line to walk. But no matter what action he's taken on behalf of vaquita, the burden of failure will fall squarely on him. Losing a whole species— Mexico's national marine mammal, no less—would be another black mark on his already questionable record.

When Peña Nieto became Mexico's fifty-seventh president in 2012, he returned the Institutional Revolutionary Party, or PRI, to power. The PRI had warmed the executive seat for seventy-one years from 1929 to 2000. It also earned Mexico its enduring reputation as a corrupt nation. A US Library of Congress *Country Studies* book explained that the PRI "used electoral fraud, corruption, bribery, and repression when necessary to maintain control over individuals and groups."

In fairness, the standing president cannot be rebuked for his political party's past indiscretions. After all, Peña Nieto was a student of justice. He received his law degree from PanAmerican University in 1991.

Alas, it has since been discovered that he plagiarized almost a third of his law thesis. *The Guardian* confirmed that "29% of the thesis was material lifted from other works, including 20 paragraphs copied word-for-word from a book written by former president Miguel de la Madrid without citation or mention in the bibliography."

In another scandal, it was alleged that Mexico's first lady accepted the gift of a mansion built by a multi-million-dollar government contractor. Notably, the investigative journalist who broke the story was promptly fired.

Biography.com points to the 2014 capture and subsequent escape of notorious drug lord Joaquín "El Chapo" Guzmán as another example of the "unevenness of Peña Nieto's presidency." Peña Nieto ran on the platform of stopping drug cartels, yet five months after the kingpin of the Sinaloan cartel was captured, he somehow managed to escape—from a maximum-security prison. Peña Nieto's now meager public approval rating (23 percent) purportedly "reflect declining public confidence in the president being able to take on important issues."

What important issues? Like protecting the world's most endangered marine mammal?

The salvation of *la vaquita* is ultimately in Peña Nieto's hands. When the outcome of this saga is revealed, either humiliation or celebration will be his reward. Despite that, he seems to be holding the ineffectual middle ground between conservation and industry. Instead of taking decisive measures that would pull Mexico's national marine mammal out of crisis and allow it to thrive—namely, to make gillnets illegal to own or sell and to lock poachers in prison—he does just enough to appear preservation-minded. But he also betrays his fishery-dependent constituents by refusing to cut the red tape for alternative gear, instead dolling out poorly regulated funds and abandoning the Upper Gulf to turmoil.

If the saying is true—if the fish stinks from the head down—then Mexico's commander in chief is to blame for the current situation. And if his lack of commitment didn't create the gridlock of his cabinet, it surely isn't helping.

~

Make no mistake about it: this is a fight for control, waged by real people with real consequences.

To trace the threads of loyalty and comprehend the destructive rivalries they provoke, it's essential to grasp the organizational structure of those in power, the who's who of government. After grappling with too many unfamiliar agencies, I constructed a sight map with English translations. In Mexico, institutional acronyms serve as common names, phonetically pronounced just as they're written.

On the conservation side is Rafael Pacchiano Alamán—a handsome forty-year-old politician representing the Ecologist Green Party of Mexico. He is Mexico's minister of the environment and head of SEMARNAT (pronounced *SEM-ar-nat*). Minister Pacchiano oversees many environmental agencies, including PROFEPA and CONANP, and is said to be one of Mexico's most dedicated advocates for science and preservation. As vaquita expert Lorenzo has opined, "Pacchiano is the best minister for vaquita we ever had."

Under SEMARNAT is Mexico's Federal Agency of Environmental Protection. PROFEPA, sometimes referred to as the environmental

President Enrique Peña Nieto	
Conservation	**Industry**
SEMARNAT (Secretary of Environment and Natural Resources)	SAGARPA (Secretary of Agriculture, Livestock, Rural Development, Fisheries and Food)
Minister Rafael Pacchiano Alamán	Minister José Calzada Rovirosa
PROFEPA (Federal Agency of Environmental Protection)	INAPESCA (National Fisheries Institute)
CONANP (National Commission of Natural Protected Areas)	CONAPESCA (National Commission of Aquaculture and Fishing)
INECC (National Institute of Ecology and Climate Change)	Pesca (INAPESCA + CONAPESCA)

police, handles violations of environmental and wildlife law and is authorized to make arrests. (When Ps2 was collected off the beach, she was taken to the PROFEPA office in Mexicali and held on ice until necropsy.)

CONANP (*KO-nanp*) is the agency that Paco works for. It oversees environmental communications, offering community outreach and education with a focus on conservation and sustainability. CONANP administered the PACE-Vaquita program. INECC (*EE-nek*) is Lorenzo's domain. Despite being a decentralized public agency of the Federal Public Administration, INECC maintains a strong connection to SEMARNAT.

On the industry side of the divide is José Calzada Rovirosa, Mexico's minister of agriculture. Minister Calzada is a member of the PRI political party and the supervisor of SAGARPA, which stands for *Secretaría de Agricultura, Ganadería, Desarrollo Rural, Pesca y Alimentación.* In English, that's Secretary of Agriculture, Livestock, Rural Development, Fisheries and Food. As such a name implies, Calzada's office focuses on advancing revenue-earning cultivation of land and water.

Among other ag-related agencies, Calzada is responsible for Mexico's two aforementioned fisheries agencies, INAPESCA and CONAPESCA, which work hand in glove and are commonly referred to together as Pesca (*pesca* is Spanish for fishing). Whatever conflicts exist higher up, it is Pesca that finds itself smack in the center of the vaquita controversy. SEMARNAT may have jurisdiction over endangered species like vaquita and totoaba, but poaching is a Pesca problem.

INAPESCA is the research branch of Pesca. It is supervised by General Director Pablo Arenas Fuentes and charged with the development of alternative fishing gear as well as scientific studies, including stock surveys. As to stock surveys, Octavio Aburto-Oropeza and colleagues wrote in a 2016 *Conservation Letters* paper, "Curbing vicious cycles in which one resource is depleted after another should be a primary goal of fisheries managers in the [Upper Gulf of California]."

CONAPESCA, Pesca's management branch, issues fishing permits and regulates fishery law. It is led by Commissioner Mario Aguilar Sánchez, who controls the "promotion of fishing and aquaculture activities." Commissioner Aguilar is considered one of the most vitriolic enemies of vaquita. And here is an important piece of the puzzle: while federal ministers like Pacchiano and Calzada come and go, Pesca always retains the same core group of people—even if those people shift positions. Aguilar is a perfect example, possessing various titles within Pesca since 1993.

Another example is Luis Fleischer. Fleischer has worked within Pesca since 1980, holding a range of jobs from scientific investigator for INA-PESCA to representative for CONAPESCA. He is currently the Mexican Fisheries Attaché for international affairs. Although Fleischer is promoted on Facebook as a whale expert who has (translated) "contributed to the population recovery of [the gray whale] and to the conservation of the ecosystem it occupies," *Eye of the Whale* author Dick Russell maintains that Fleischer "espoused allowing gray whaling"—that is to say, he promoted legalized hunts for the exact species he claims to have helped.

Fleischer actually lost his role as the Mexican delegate to the International Whaling Commission because of bad press on his prowhaling rhetoric. It was 1993, and Japan was (as always) pushing for a resumption of commercial whaling. "Japan had offered $234 million in economic aid to various countries to secure IWC votes toward just such a resumption," wrote Russell. Fearful of what a turnover in law would mean for struggling whale populations, distinguished writer and environmental activist Homero Aridjis wrote to Mexico's president. His letter specifically argued that Fleischer "was always on the side of the Japanese" and presumably could not be trusted to maintain antiwhaling policies.

Around the same time, the Group of 100, an Australian establishment of chief financial officers, published an international press release declaring the same concern. "When Fleischer returned to Mexico," wrote Russell, "he was replaced as its IWC delegate."

Fleischer still works for Pesca.

With staunch rivals in power for decades, it's no surprise that the vaquita recovery program has been steadily sabotaged. As Eric Dinerstein wrote, "In the absence of constant vigilance, a few individuals can make decisions against the best interests of a nation."

Indeed, officers of Pesca are not only not helpful; I'm told they move in opposition, blatantly snubbing conservation directives. Most significantly, they refuse to recognize that gillnets are killing porpoises. Fleischer and colleagues actually wrote a paper stating that zero vaquita mortalities occurred in analyzed finfish, shark, or shrimp fisheries and claimed that other causes of decline need be examined.

That stand is now echoed by fishermen. Sunshine Rodriguez, president of the Federation of Coastal Fishermen in San Felipe and flagrant opponent to conservation initiatives, was quoted in 2016 as saying, "They should just declare (the vaquita) extinct because fishermen are not killing it." He went on to blame other factors like red tide and predators. (As previously mentioned, vaquita deaths have not yet been linked to red tide. And although it is conceivable that some degree of shark predation occurs, accounts remain rare and anecdotal.)

Even after the necropsies of Ps2 and her kin, fisheries officials would not accept the cause of death as entanglement. Why would they deny such a thing? Well, in Upton Sinclair's timeless words, "It is difficult to get a man to understand something, when his salary depends on his not understanding it."

I was told about a confidential conversation in which a high-ranking officer from Pesca disclosed a practical point regarding the fisheries' opposition to protecting *Phocoena sinus*. "Why do you think Pesca doesn't want to save vaquita?" he had asked. "Because if they accept that there's bycatch, then they will be accountable for bycatch of other species. If they give up vaquita, then they will have to give up dolphins, whales, sea turtles. And they will never do that."

The Upper Gulf artisanal shrimp fishery has been valued at almost $6 million per year. That's the fishery Javier Valverde's *chango* is designed for—the gear he's never been allowed to use. With the gillnet ban now in effect, one might expect Pesca supervisors to push for alternative equipment, but they won't. There is a consensus that they have no interest in seeing *chango* succeed. Production continues to drag, approval is balked, and deliberate physical interference is allowed on the testing grounds. Without good development and unbiased assessment, the future of vaquita-friendly gear remains in limbo. And that's just where Pesca wants it.

The hope is that *chango* could eventually prove successful enough to make shrimp gillnets obsolete, if only it would be allowed fair trial. But Aburto-Oropeza and colleagues described the switch to alternative shrimp trawls as a "'quick-fix' . . . in which longer-term environmental degradation is not addressed, vast sums of money are invested, and social well-being left unconsidered." The proposed system, they wrote, is "by no means sustainable" because it "does not provide the fishers with a viable future livelihood, compared to their historic fishing activities."

It's hard to know without knowing. The quandary of INAPESCA's wavering is but half the matter. CONAPESCA's permit dispensation also shows clear bias against vaquita conservation. Issuing fishing permits to convicted poachers while withholding them from alt-gear fishermen—talk about tipping the scales!

When I spoke with Zak Smith, a senior attorney with the Natural Resources Defense Council, he said, "There are people involved who are not coming to the table in good faith. I believe that if one looked at the actual evidence, they could reasonably conclude that CONAPESCA has an unstated interest for the vaquita to go extinct as fast as possible, and then fisheries can get back to doing their business the way they always have."

Fisheries agents, I'm told, have many times recommended rounding up all the vaquitas and dispatching them to Sea World "to get rid of the problem." They have also applied nefarious strategies to eliminate the porpoises from their habitat. Historically they transferred permits to gillnetters in Guaymas, asking them to come fish in the Upper Gulf. In a more recent scheme with similar intent, members of Pesca supposedly held private meetings with like-minded fishermen and said, "Go fishing! Go fishing! Finish vaquita."

A 2007 *Nature* article testified that "fishing industry advocates sometimes speak openly about wiping [vaquita] out." And a 2015 *McClatchy DC* article concurred that "some of the fishermen blamed for the vaquita's dwindling numbers would cheer a declaration that the creature is extinct."

Can that really be true?

I was told that Pesca doesn't give interviews, but I lucked into a meeting with a former Mexican supervisor of fisheries. Luis Tiznado says he's been out of Pesca for more than a decade, but he was "in" for twenty-four years, long enough to know the culture. As I sat in an Ensenada cafe, fanning away cigarette smoke, Tiznado openly acknowledged, without contrition, that were the outside world not pushing so hard, Pesca would simply let the vaquita go extinct.

He stated unequivocally, "Nobody—not the fishermen, not the Mexican government, not the Mexican people—would be doing anything if there wasn't so much international pressure." He described the pressure as both emotional (conservation organizations) and financial (potential boycotts and embargoes).

He declared vaquita a lost cause, doomed to extinction by its own evolution. He argued that any effort to alter that course is a tragic waste of time and resources. He also informed me that gillnets, although they occasionally entrap vaquitas, are "only a very small part of the problem." The real problem for the porpoises, he argued, is the reduction of fresh water from the Colorado River. (That assertion would soon be scientifically debunked.)

"From that standpoint, the vaquita's critically endangered status is no fault of the fishing industry"—he said as he stubbed out his cigarette—"so I cannot appreciate the need to 'save the species' by placing artificial constraints on the fishermen."

Luis Tiznado is a PhD oceanographer.

~

For someone who embraces halcyon time and peaceable relationships, dealing with so much political conflict was like having my nerves dragged over sandpaper. Luckily, I was scheduled for a boat trip into Alto Golfo to meet some legendary conservationists. A famous band of sea dogs had arrived "in defense of the highly endangered vaquita porpoise, a species on the brink of extinction."

I could hardly wait to get out on the water, away from *terra firma* and her societal trappings. Maybe in the realm of living vaquitas I would find a flicker of hope that had thus far eluded me. I had, of course, accepted that I would never actually see one with my own eyes; with fewer than sixty of the timid animals surviving across more than fourteen hundred square miles, spotting a penny in a cornfield would prove easier.

That didn't mean it wasn't worth trying.

CHAPTER 6

Pirates on Patrol

It was 8 a.m. when Fernando Schnitzer slid the Zodiac onto the beach. The tide was low, so Gustavo and I had to walk barefoot over a stretch of wrinkled sand to meet him at the surf line. In a previous life, Fernando was a high school history teacher in Puerto Rico. He now served as a deckhand for Sea Shepherd Conservation Society and also drove its Zodiac, the *Wolf.* Captain Wolf was his nickname.

Pant legs pushed high, we tossed our gear into the inflatable boat and quickly climbed over the rubber siding, which felt something like whale skin. Twenty-six-year-old biologist Elizabeth Brassea Pérez jumped in with us. Eli, as she's called, was wrapping up her master's degree in marine mammalogy at Mexico's renowned Center for Scientific Research and Higher Education at Ensenada—CICESE (pronounced *SEE-se-say*)—the same institution where Gustavo is working toward his doctoral degree. Gustavo wanted another set of trained eyes to search for vaquita, and Eli brought not only her trained eyes but also the cheerful vigor of a devoted student.

Fernando swung the prow away from San Felipe, revved the motor, and launched us into the Vermilion Sea. The *Wolf* ran full speed for a mile before our destination came into view: the M/V *Farley Mowat*. The decommissioned US Coast Guard cutter was the larger of two ships sent by Sea Shepherd to protect vaquitas, and it looked far more majestic than I'd expected: one hundred ten feet of plated steel held between shimmering silver water and white-gray sky. The R/V *Martin Sheen*, an eighty-one-foot sailboat, floated nearby as we motored abeam the *Farley* and climbed a rope ladder to the main deck.

Fingers reached to take our bags and grab our hands. What seemed a silent mass of metal from afar suddenly teemed with life as a happy jumble of crewmates welcomed us aboard. Most of them were volunteers—quitting their jobs, selling their homes, they had arrived from countries far and wide to help vaquita. I would soon learn just how doggedly Sea Shepherd volunteers work to aid marine life in crisis.

Despite what detractors say, they didn't look much like pirates.

∿

My first exposure to Sea Shepherd Conservation Society came from a couple of half-watched episodes of Animal Planet's *Whale Wars*, a reality series shot in the Southern Ocean Whale Sanctuary. We don't have cable television at home, so I've only ever caught pieces of the show, which follows Sea Shepherd founder Captain Paul Watson and his crew as they face the dramas and dangers of confronting Japanese whaling ships in the cold, isolated waters off Antarctica.

Commercial whaling was banned in 1986 by the International Whaling Commission, yet three countries—Norway, Iceland, and Japan—still insist on violating that ban. Japan continues its annual hunts under the pretense of "scientific research," a farce that received particular public reproach after whale meat, carved into giant filets on bloody ship decks, was tracked to Japanese hospitals and school cafeterias.

Because most of Japan's citizens quit eating whale a long time ago, the meat is primarily marketed to institutions by the country's Fisheries Agency. That's why Sea Shepherd's founder isn't fooled when he's approaching a gruesome slaughter and Japanese workers dutifully raise a sign stating something like: We're collecting tissue samples. Captain Watson knows that those "tissue samples" are destined for kindergarten lunch plates.

Using Sea Shepherd's now-famous direct-action tactics, its ships have obstructed, stymied, and infuriated Japanese whalers since 2005. Meanwhile, *Whale Wars* has taken the crusade into living rooms, rallying public outcry for the protection of Earth's largest mammals.

After years of sweat and struggle, it must have been a great relief for Sea Shepherd representatives to stand in a courtroom in March 2014 and hear the International Court of Justice's twelve-to-four ruling: "In the case concerning whaling in the Antarctic . . . [Japan must] revoke any extant authorization, permit or licence [sic] to kill, take or treat whales in relation to JARPA II and refrain from granting any further permits in pursuance of that programme."

A defeated Japan agreed to abide the ruling. Victory at last.

Sadly, but not surprisingly, Japan reneged on the deal. When Japanese whalers returned from a four-month poaching expedition spanning the austral summer of December 2015 to March 2016, they winched 333 whale carcasses from their holds. Two hundred and thirty were females, and 90 percent of those mature were reported to be pregnant.

Alas, the battle continues.

～

Although Sea Shepherd remains best known for its whale work in the Southern Ocean, it runs other campaigns, too. Sharks, sea turtles, coral reefs, dolphins, bluefin tuna, seals, and sea lions have all benefited from the nonprofit organization's mission "to end the destruction of habitat and slaughter of wildlife in the world's oceans in order to conserve and protect ecosystems and species." The vaquita campaign, aptly named Operation Milagro—*milagro* is Spanish for miracle—launched in early 2015.

That was a dire time. When Captain Oona Layolle, campaign leader and director of ship operations, sailed into Alto Golfo at the helm of the *Martin Sheen*, she came upon miles and miles of gillnets. The maze of watery webs was so dense that she could barely navigate her ship through the tangle.

Antagonistic fishermen added to the fray. Oona and her crew were blocked, followed, and harassed. They were told that they were wasting their energy. "Vaquitas don't even exist," the fishermen shouted.

By the time of my visit in 2016, however, Sea Shepherd had formed an alliance with the Mexican government and was operating alongside its Navy as part of the official ban-enforcement team. Oona was now captain of the *Farley Mowat*. With twin five-thousand-horsepower engines that can propel the ship to speeds of up to twenty-eight knots, the *Farley* had joined Operation Milagro in December 2015 as a quick, muscular mate for the *Martin Sheen*. Both ships were actively patrolling the Gillnet Exclusion Zone.

Having become a high-profile spokesperson for the vaquita conservation program, Oona attended every diplomatic conference. And her V-logs—captivating online video updates from the field—were garnering quite a bit of attention.

The first time I met Oona was for dinner in San Felipe at La Vaquita, the restaurant owned by disbeliever-turned-advocate Jose Maria Cuevas. As we relaxed on the open-air patio under a pretty string of lights that reminded me of stars, she spoke of her background. She was raised in Colombia by a French mother and Brazilian father. Both are mariners.

"I traveled with my family for six years on a sailing boat," Oona said with her lilting accent, "and I realized how the beautiful undersea landscapes were disappearing. A lot of beautiful places with marine wild-life were dying. So I wanted to do something to stop that."

I appreciated her passion for conservation.

"The thing is that it is a really critical moment for this species, *la vaquita*," Oona continued. "She's almost, almost extinguished." (In the gendered language of Spanish, *vaquita* is feminine, so many native speakers refer to the species as "her." It's a charming and admittedly contagious style.)

Oona has a quiet grace that belies, or perhaps demonstrates, her profound drive to change the course of things. With a keen ability to listen and consider the perspectives of others while fluently communicating her organization's message—in four languages if necessary: French, Spanish, English, and Portuguese—she is an effective diplomat for conservation policy. In a world of Latin machismo, it also doesn't hurt that along with her Master 500 mariner license, Oona possesses both charm and good looks. One can only imagine how many hearts she has stolen from Mexican officials, especially those who have watched her pilot a 160-ton pursuit vessel.

Mexico's minister of environment, Rafael Pacchiano, met Oona in Mexico City in the spring of 2015. That was when they brokered their unique alliance that allows Sea Shepherd to patrol the Upper Gulf—Mexican waters under maritime law—and confiscate unlawful fishing gear in vaquita-protected zones.

"Before I came," Oona told me, "I thought the illegal fishing boats would only come out at night. Being illegal, you try to hide. It was very surprising to see that they were really not hiding at all. The refuge was full of illegal gillnets everywhere, day and night. And the fishermen were very confident."

Oona paused to dip a chip into her salsa and then said, "Now, during the daytime, there is not much fishing activity. The illegal fishermen go at nighttime to set their nets."

She clarified, "The nets are still here. They're just hidden under water."

~

After storing our dry sacks in the forward crew cabin, Gustavo, Eli, and I were given a brief tour of the *Farley Mowat*. We visited the bridge, messroom, and galley, peeked into the engine room, and got the ever-important briefing on how to use the head. Our guide was US Army veteran Corey Dahlquist, who holds a bachelor's in English and a master's in science law and who served two tours in Iraq. As a deckhand and medical officer, he spoke sincerely about his months with Sea Shepherd and the importance of its mission to protect the ocean life that we all depend on.

On the back deck, Corey led us to a massive snarl of rope and twine: gillnets.

"These are the problem," he said, lifting up a length of netting and stretching the strands into big open squares. "If the openings are greater than 15.2 centimeters [six inches], like this one, the net is for totoaba, and we can confiscate it."

"We also destroy longlines," Corey continued, exchanging the netting for a handful of hooks. He explained that when longlines are found in the patrol area, the crew carefully drags them in and cuts the monofilament to pieces. So far, they'd appropriated nine longlines, each stretching at least a mile long and bearing hundreds of deadly hooks. The hooks gave me the creeps. They looked like something used in bizarre body-modification rituals in which people are pierced and suspended by their skin. Corey wore gloves to protect his hands from the razor-sharp barbs, and the steel curves clattered like prison chains when he dropped them back into their bucket.

The following day, five Mexican marines would come aboard to collect the confiscated items for disposal. In addition to the longlines, Sea

Shepherd had already turned over almost thirty gillnets. There were undoubtedly hundreds more to find, but locating them had become a wicked game of cat and mouse.

Bucheros had taken to hiding their gear. At first they replaced their marker buoys with floating trash—old soda bottles, empty gas cans— which might go unheeded. So Sea Shepherd started examining every piece of questionable flotsam. Then poachers took to trapping live sea- birds and tying them to their illegal nets. The poor birds, unable to fly away, would appear to be casually sitting atop the water, but were, in fact, living buoys. (Greed and cruelty know no bounds.) Once the bird exploit was exposed, *bucheros* started attaching anchors. Anchors are both invisible to patrollers and heavy to pull out, making confisca- tion more difficult.

Oona had said during dinner, "We've been retrieving so many nets, now they decided to put bigger anchors. And sometimes they put even two anchors on each end."

If nets can no longer be spotted at the surface, how does Sea Shepherd locate them?

Farley's boatswain, a Brit who goes only by his last name, Conniss, had cleverly engineered a net-catching gadget from a barrel bottom. The crew calls the device a "phantom ray." The flat contraption, which indeed resembles a rusty stingray, is attached by a chain and trawled be- hind the ship at various depths. The length of the chain determines how deep the phantom ray will dive and remain while in tow—the longer the chain, the deeper the depth. Welded to the phantom ray is a sturdy hook to snag the netting. It's an ingenious contraption.

I couldn't help being impressed by Conniss's intense work ethic. As boatswain, he cared for all aspects of the ship aside from the engines, which were managed by chief, second, and third engineers. Barely atten- tive to anything outside his sphere of influence, Conniss toiled away in the ship's open-air machine shop on the back deck with saws, hammers, power drills, and sanders, producing a near-constant racket. In addition to daily projects for ship maintenance and improvements, he and his deck crew had managed to hone one phantom ray for each Sea Shepherd vessel, including the *Wolf.* He had also recently given one to the Navy to try.

Fostered by increasing acts of trust, Sea Shepherd's relationship with the Mexican Navy had been growing stronger, their vaquita-protection efforts more intertwined. In fact, just the day before, both parties had participated in a spectacular media event in the Bay of San Felipe. While a flock of thirty-plus press members scribbled notes and snapped photos, Mexican marines in stately white uniforms stood at attention on the decks of their Navy ships. A military helicopter flew in low to impress the crowd. The Sea Shepherd crew, donning their spiffiest campaign shirts, invited reporters to tour the *Farley Mowat.*

When the press conference moved to the naval base for announcements, Oona sat at a long table near Minister Pacchiano, who later posted a summary on his Facebook page. "In San Felipe, Baja California, we have followed the Vaquita Conservation Program for almost one year since implementation. During this time, ninety-four vessels have been secured and we have arrested seventy-two people doing illegal fishing activities. In the Government of the Republic, we are committed to continuing efforts that allow us to conserve this species," he wrote in Spanish.

For decades, vaquitas have been dying as bycatch in the gillnets of commercial fishermen. Now linked with the dramatic totoaba-trafficking story, its crisis is garnering extensive media attention. As more and more news outlets—BBC, CNN, the *New York Times*, *The Guardian*, and *Science*, among others—publicize the grave and urgent situation playing out just south of the US border, public awareness for this vanishing cetacean is at last emerging.

When Oona stepped to the conference podium, she wore a tailored dress suit and the air of someone who knows her way around politics. "It is an honor to be able to work with the Mexican government. The collaboration between Sea Shepherd and the Mexican government is an example to the world of how we can join forces to protect our planet. Actions that lead to the extinction of any living creatures are crimes against life and should be treated as a serious felony," she said. "The situation is dramatic, taking into consideration the amount of vaquita left and the illegal fishing activity happening at night. But we cannot lose hope."

Hope and reality can be tricky allies.

It was Sea Shepherd that found Ps1 on March 4—a bundle of white, rotting flesh, floating in the supposedly protected waters of the Vaquita Refuge, next to a totoaba that was missing its swim bladder. Eleven days later, on March 15, Ps2 was found lifeless on the beach. Exactly nine days after that, one week post press conference, Sea Shepherd would recover the body of Ps3, and Oona would write in an article: "We found a third dead vaquita on March 24 at 17h36, position 31°03.2513 N – 114°49.0371 W. . . . Finding three vaquitas in three weeks is finding one dead vaquita per week. . . . If we continue losing the vaquita at this rate, it will be extinct by this December."

~

I was looking forward to talking more with Oona during my time on the *Farley Mowat*, but she was not acting captain during our stay. She had too many diplomatic responsibilities ashore—an unending slew of meetings and paperwork—so Captain Woody Henderson, a confident Californian with moppy blond hair, had taken the helm. Woody was no stranger to the *Farley*. He was the one who had delivered the ship to the Sea of Cortez in the first place, piloting from Tampa Bay, Florida, through the Panama Canal and up the Pacific coast of Mexico.

Woody was thrilled to have Gustavo aboard. None of the current crew had ever seen a vaquita (alive), and that made Gustavo, who had logged about ten *Phocoena sinus* sightings, somewhat of a celebrity. A special two-day outing had been planned to celebrate his visit and learn from his experience. Gustavo had been generous to invite me along.

As everyone prepared to get under way, I stopped by the bridge and found Woody and Gustavo hovering over a navigation map like wizards plotting a feat of magic.

Could they conjure a vaquita?

Time would tell.

A rush of anticipation surged through my veins as a jangle of metal chain signaled the pull of anchor. Deckhands to deck, Woody set course while his first mate and communications officer adjusted knobs and levers amid the ship's blipping electronics. Minutes later, on an overhead screen, I watched as the black marker for our ship crossed into an upside-down pentagon in the middle of the Gillnet Exclusion Zone.

We were entering the Vaquita Refuge.

As the eastern sun ratcheted off the horizon to the thump and grind of Conniss's sander, I climbed to the observation deck, some twenty-five feet above the water. Ocean air skittered up my nose, a briny bouquet of phytoplankton and benthic sediments, familiar notes of rot and renewal.

Beneath a rigid sunshade, Eli was preparing our sighting log as Gustavo climbed the last steel rungs to arrive on the platform behind me. The day was blushing with the promise of calm water and excellent visibility. The milky sky was dissolving to a lovely robin's-egg blue, and Heermann's gulls floated by like sooty angels.

This was my chance. Steadying my weight against the smooth cadence of the ship, I prayed for luck and lifted my binoculars to the turquoise sea.

Dear vaquita, are you there?

CHAPTER 7

Searching for Vaquita

At once, a huge, dark shape was flung skyward as though spit out by the sea. With our eyes locked on and binoculars focused, we reveled the sight: a breaching humpback whale.

Surrounded by a spray of white water, the black behemoth—long pectoral flippers held wide, tail fluke twisted to the left—seemed to momentarily freeze against the sun-drenched sky. It was a perfect postcard snapshot. When gravity regained dominion and the whale dropped, it rocketed a geyser of water thirty feet in the air. Crystalline droplets hung for several seconds before following the cetacean back into the sea.

The ship's crew cheered.

So did we. Logging such a spectacular first sighting felt auspicious.

For centuries, encounters with whales and dolphins have blackened the pages of mariners' journals. They have been carried on the voices of elders and celebrated in every age of art. Stories became legends and legends, lore. Think of Paikea the Whale Rider, Natsilane, Jonah, and Moby Dick. The ancient Greeks believed that Orion took shape as a constellation after being carried skyward on the back of a dolphin. In northern Australia, there is the tale of Ganadja, a kindly and brave *ind-jbena*, or dolphin spirit, who is mother to all modern-day dolphins. The Amazonians believe that the pink river dolphin, or *boto*, takes human form and lures lovers to the underwater world of Encante.

Alas, there is no legend centered on vaquita. That's not because the desert surroundings, scoured by waves of sun and sand, are too desolate for legends to take root. Rather, it is because nobody even noticed the little porpoises until eighty years ago when gillnets began plucking them, dead, from the delta.

Myth would soon follow, but never legend.

If vaquita is lacking in legend, it is surely flush in names. The animal has been called cochito, gulf porpoise and Gulf of California harbor porpoise, desert porpoise, and, sweetly, panda of the sea. *Vaquita marina* means "little sea cow" (*vaca* is cow in Spanish). The species' scientific name, *Phocoena sinus*, is derived from Greek to Latin, with the most direct translation being "big seal of the gulf." To assuage any doubt, porpoises are not members of the seal family. And even though porpoises were historically called mereswines—from Proto-Germanic *mari* (sea) plus *swīną* (pig)—they are not in the oinking Suinae family either.

Porpoises form their own taxonomic family, Phocoenidae.

There are only seven phocoenids: Dall's, harbor, spectacled, Indo-Pacific finless, narrow-ridged finless, Burmeister's, and vaquita. Geographically speaking, vaquita's nearest cousin is the harbor porpoise, whose globe-wrapping range includes the upper Pacific side of the United States. That explains why vaquita was once dubbed the Gulf of California harbor porpoise, the assumption being that land and evolution divided the two. Recent genetic studies, however, have revealed that vaquita's closest genetic relative is actually the Burmeister's porpoise. Endemic to the coastal waters of South America, the Burmeister's is recognized by its backswept dorsal fin.

Most of us know very little, if anything, about porpoises. Perhaps it's because the word *cetacean* commonly means "whale or dolphin," categorically excluding the third and only other member of the cetacean clade—the porpoise. Lacking the imposing size of whales and geniality of dolphins, porpoises are cast to the corners of human interest, where their elusive lives garner little attention. In 2016, most people had never even heard of vaquita, one of the least recognized of all seven underappreciated porpoise species.

As one might expect from appearance, porpoises are closely related to dolphins. In fact, they look so dolphin-like that people commonly assume that they are just a smaller version of the same animal. They are actually quite different. Anatomically, porpoises tend to be shorter and more robust around the middle than dolphins. Lacking a beak, porpoises bear a rounder countenance, and their teeth are shaped like tiny spatulas rather than the conical dentition of their Delphinidae cousins. Vaquita's teeth are found only at the front of the mouth.

Although a porpoise's dorsal fin is typically small and triangular compared with a dolphin's, the difference is not overly dramatic with vaquita. *Phocoena sinus* has the largest dorsal fin relative to body size of any phocoenid. Averaging about seven inches tall, it rises conspicuously above the water, but only for a few seconds at a time.

It was a dorsal fin we searched for as we peered through our lenses from the highest deck of the *Farley Mowat*. The water in Alto Golfo can be quite choppy, but as luck would have it, the surface that day was smooth. What's more, Gustavo had directed Captain Woody Henderson into the southwestern quadrant of the Vaquita Refuge, where underwater acoustic monitoring devices have recorded the highest presence of porpoise activity. We couldn't ask for better circumstances to spot our subject.

Biologist Eli Brassea and I moved to the open platform forward of the observation deck. The shelf not only offered unobstructed views, but also access to the Big Eyes. Bolted to the platform, this set of jumbo military binoculars swivel on its mount. At 25 × 150 magnification power, the Big Eyes allow visual clarity at exceptional distances, and Eli and I had fun trying them out.

Sitting behind the massive apparatus, which looks like a pair of conjoined telescopes, I spied objects a full mile away. I zoomed in on Roca Consag, a 286-foot geological formation jutting up from the water like a jagged tooth and whitewashed with layers of bird guano. Supporting an abundance of underwater marine life and hosting a healthy California sea lion rookery, it is a major attraction for San Felipe tours boats.

Rotating the Big Eyes eastward, I spotted another humpback stitching its way across the gulf. The humpback's scientific name, *Megaptera novaeangliae*, means "big-winged New Englander" because New England is where the species was first identified. With every breath, the ocean traveler rose like a black submarine and released a bushy umbrella-shaped plume. First one blow, then two, and with a final inhale, the whale rounded its namesake back. An arrow-shaped dorsal fin arched into view followed by several feet of spine and then those iconic flukes. Its mighty tail, raised like a sail, with its white underside as distinct as a fingerprint, was the last thing to disappear as the animal dove for the deep.

During Sea Shepherd's patrols, someone from the crew usually remains stationed at the Big Eyes, so when a deckhand named Rodrigo came to take his shift, Eli and I scooted off to the side and resumed our search through our personal binoculars. Rodrigo Gil Kuri, a contemporary musician from Cozumel, had written in his online bio: "I am happy to be on Operation Milagro, an effort to save our very own *vaquita marina* of Mexico. As a Mexican, I'm very proud to see an effort from my government to stop crimes against nature in the Sea of Cortez."

I asked him if he enjoyed serving as ship's lookout. He answered that he did, but he explained that although, like us, he loved seeing ocean animals, he could not get sidetracked from his main focus: criminal activity. His job was to look for floating trash that might mark a gillnet. If he spotted anything suspicious, he would radio down to Woody on the bridge, who would angle the ship over to investigate. Using hand-held poles and nets, the refuse would be hauled in for assessment and then properly discarded; any attached netting would be confiscated.

Rodrigo said he was on alert for questionable boats, too. I pointed to several pangas bobbing in the distance. What were they doing in the refuge?

He double-checked through the Big Eyes and shrugged. "Those are just clam divers."

Clam divers are allowed to work in the restricted area, and once you know what to look for, they're easy to identify. Their pangas float motionless, with hoses hanging over the side. While one fisherman remains at the surface as a safety, the designated clammer dons a leaded belt and drops into the silty depths. He holds a knife in his hand and has a bag tied to his waist. Breathing through a hookah, the clam diver collects mollusks by feel, rising to unload his catch whenever his bag is full.

It's supposedly hard to fake clam diving as a cover-up for poaching because the air system takes up much of the boat; there is not enough space for nets, too, especially not the big, heavy nets required for totoaba. I studied one of the clam-diving boats through my binoculars, thinking maybe I could observe someone come up or go down, but I quickly bored of the unchanging scene. The safety man just sat there, enveloped by blue—sky above, water below—with his wide-brimmed *sombrero* holding back fierce rays of sun like a shield.

The only other nearby craft was the *Martin Sheen*. Always within view and a worthy spectacle, my gaze often returned to its outline. With its cobalt hull, elegant masts, and sheet-white sails, it gave me the impression of a model ship inside a bottle, perfectly poised on a teal bend of glass.

Hour by hour, the morning ticked by. Rodrigo held to his post and we to ours, eyes glued to the water. The aquatic environment was nothing short of spectacular. "Alto Golfo de California" is one of the Baja California to Bering Sea Region Marine Priority Conservation Areas. The official B2B report describes this region, designated PCA 25, as "a unique oceanographic area. This area has some of the largest tides to be found anywhere in the world, with vertical displacement of as much as six to nine meters (20 to 30 feet)." The report also states that "due to trenches and basins nearby, this area experiences intense upwelling, along with strong tidal mixing, which creates one of the most productive areas in the Gulf of California . . . characterized by endemic species, among them 22 endemic fish species, including the critically endangered totoaba. A wide variety of seabirds, such as brown booby, black skimmer and [Heermann's gull and elegant tern,] nest on the islands in the area. The green sea turtle uses [resources] for feeding, and juvenile loggerheads are also occasionally seen . . . following possible migratory paths from as far away as Japan."

The vaquita is cited as the only marine mammal endemic to this B2B area, although eight other nonendemic species are also found, including fin whale, *Balaenoptera physalus* (the second largest animal on the planet, behind the blue whale); gray whale, *Eschrichtius robustus*; and killer whale, *Orcinus orca*. When a Bryde's whale, *Balaenoptera brydei*, chugged past the *Farley*, puffing like a fifty-foot steam engine, Gustavo happily added the sighting to our log. It was my first time seeing a Bryde's in person, and I felt the kind of jolly satisfaction a birder experiences when spotting a particular avian from his or her life list.

At one point, Eli went gaga when a mass of fur-covered muscle popped up on the port side. An adult California sea lion, *Zalophus californianus*, appeared. The bulbous lump on his noggin—an enlarged sagittal crest—gave away his gender. In a playful manner typical of the species, the sea lion twisted and flipped at the water surface, repeatedly returning to a head-up posture, taking us in with his curious gaze. As a marine mammalogist, Eli's passion is pinnipeds ("fin-footed" seals and sea lions), and she cooed at the 650-pound predator as if he were an oversized puppy.

Eventually, the seascape, tinted like gemstones, shifted from aquamarine to sapphire, and long, soft waves began to form. Still there were no vaquitas. Despite our initial optimism, it was no surprise. For all the time Oona had spent piloting ships around Alto Golfo, she had only been graced with a single sighting. When she described this deeply moving experience to me, her voice was so richly animated, it resonated like pure light.

"It was pretty crazy because we spend like two months looking for them," she recalled. "Then the president came and announced the gill-net ban. For two days after, the Navy was arresting all the pangas during the day, and so the area was way more quiet. It was one of the first days that we witnessed the Vaquita Refuge without illegal fishing activity. And we were enjoying navigating without stressing out about illegal fishermen surrounding us and telling us to leave. And then . . . *la vaquita* was around us. There were actually four of them, and they stayed maybe thirty minutes, or one hour. It was unbelievable. Like magic!"

At the time, Sea Shepherd was wrapping up its first season—totoaba were migrating south toward Isla Ángel de la Guarda, and the captain and her crew were preparing to depart Alto Golfo for the summer months. The encounter stirred Oona's spirit and made the whole campaign feel personal. "It was like her coming to say thank you, please come back."

Oona kept her vow to return.

~

Around noon, Gustavo, Eli, and I took turns going down to the mess hall. There, the ship's cook, Sheila Hanney, had prepared a gorgeous spread of noodles, mushrooms, and vegetables. There was no meat—Sea

Shepherd maintains a corporate policy of serving cruelty-free food on its vessels. It happened to be deckhand Fernando Schnitzer's birthday. In observance, Sheila had decorated the announcement board with colored markers and had baked a homemade chocolate cake—vegan, of course. (Her secret substitute, which I have since tried with great success, is to mix and add one tablespoon of ground chia seeds with three tablespoons of water for each egg.)

The meal was delicious, but Fernando's celebration was bittersweet. After a year of dedicated service, it was his last full day aboard the *Farley Mowat*. He readily admitted that it would be an adjustment to return to normal life in Puerto Rico, but he was keen to get back to the everyday pleasures of friends and family. As we ate, I looked around at the cultural and professional diversity of those who would miss him. There was Mark Crowder, a deckhand from England; CB Nolan, an engineer from the United States; John Paul "JP" Geoffroy, a diver and videographer from Chile (who would later be targeted by the Mexican cartel); and others.

Oona's words came to mind. "It's amazing because you get people from all around the world, and each person brings their own experience and skills," she had told me, "and completely different kinds of personalities that at the end are all fighting for the same cause. It is beautiful to see."

Curious to know more about life as a Sea Shepherd volunteer, I asked my lunch mates to share their most moving experiences during Operation Milagro. Several chimed, "The whale rescue!" As everyone clamored to add their favorite bits of the story, Mike Sine, the second engineer, pulled up the video on his computer. Surrounded by smiles, I watched the drama unfold.

In February 2016, Sea Shepherd came across a young humpback whale with a stretch of gillnet and a tether of rope looped around its head. The air-breathing mammal was struggling to swim. As it huffed with exhaustion, pulled down by an unseen measure of net, Oona radioed PROFEPA and the Navy to assist. A rescue team quickly converged. Working from inflatable boats, the rescuers moved steadily closer to the whale.

The team exercised extreme caution. A whale's powerful tail could cause grave injury to a human if it were to accidentally or defensively strike a small boat. Fortunately, the humpback, although visibly distressed, seemed to understand that the humans were trying to help. It allowed itself to be reined in close to the *Rescate Marina* Zodiak and continued to surface as gently as possible.

As the humpback grabbed ragged breaths through its double blowhole, the team pulled, plotted, fidgeted, and finessed. After four hours, the whale was free, but the most poignant part was yet to come. Instead of diving away in a panic, the young humpback seemed to savor its liberty, swimming lavishly at the surface. It even rolled onto its broad back and flapped its white pectoral flippers, as though waving thanks to its rescuers. I chuckled at the video.

For every cheerful story, however, there is a sad one to counter it. On April 6, the Sea Shepherd crew would discover a less-lucky humpback. Washed ashore, the dead whale showed clear signs of entanglement, including a piece of netting still attached to a barnacle on its rostrum. "This latest death shows how important our work here is," Woody would be quoted in a blog. "We will continue patrolling and fighting side-by-side with the Mexican Navy and authorities to stop illegal fishing and better protect all species in the Gulf of California, especially the critically endangered vaquita."

During my stay on the ship, crew members supplied many accounts of animals suffering as bycatch. They had heroically liberated rays and sea turtles, totoaba and sharks—all kind of marine species—from the steely grip of gillnets and longlines. But for every animal saved, they were forced to mourn the deaths of so many others.

For example, the crew had recently hauled up a gillnet clutching a tremendous great white shark. The poor, drowned animal hung limp, with bloody water gushing from its mouth. Because of its size, it took judicious maneuvering to cut it free. Finally unbound, unleashed, the once-mighty, once-essential apex predator artlessly flopped with a splash and descended into the void. A valuable life doomed to rot.

The *Farley*'s communications officer told me another chilling story. Roy Sasano had come from the Royal Canadian Navy, and his captain's license allowed him to take the controls when Woody was away from the bridge. One day, while he was piloting the ship, he saw what appeared to be fins surfacing in every direction. At first, Roy thought they were dolphins, but he quickly realized that they were rays—hundreds of them. Their sable wingtips flapped up like tiny pointed pennants as the immense school journeyed just beneath the surface.

"It was a magical experience," Roy said. "Everyone ran out on deck to take in their beauty."

But later that night, the crew was called to pull up a longline. Tug by laborious tug, they reeled in a chain of sagging, lifeless bodies—rays— the same splendid creatures they had relished just hours earlier.

Roy shook his head at the heartrending memory. "We saved some, but most were already dead," he said. "We've pulled so much stuff out of the water here. The nets, the longlines, they just kill everything. And I'm just sad about it."

I thought about Pesca. The heads of the fisheries don't want to acknowledge bycatch because it could damage their business. They're just like the leaders of the chemical companies who refuse to admit the effects of exposure toxicity, or the sugar industry executives who purposely conceal data showing the grave effect of glucose loading on the human body. People in power often go to remarkable lengths to preserve market share. Indeed, there seems to be this idea that commerce must be upheld at any cost, no matter the consequences to human health, animals, or the environment. It is still, as Rachel Carson wrote in 1961, "an era

Hammerhead shark entangled and drowned in a gillnet set for totoaba, one of the countless victims of bycatch in the Gulf of California. (Courtesy of Sea Shepherd)

dominated by industry, in which a right to make a dollar at whatever cost is seldom challenged."

In certain Alto Golfo fisheries, namely industrial shrimp trawling, bycatch has been reported to account for up to 90 percent of what lands on deck. That's simply mind-boggling.

My heart ached for Roy and for the whole crew. I often wonder how any of us who work in conservation, who care so profoundly about the world and all its inhabitants, march forward against such a barrage of dreadful challenges. How do sympathetic souls combat compassion fatigue when faced with so much senseless death?

Part of the answer must lie in the type of people who work for stewardship organizations in the first place. Sea Shepherd seems to attract volunteers who are characteristically optimistic. I was, as so often I've been through the years, encircled by people who believe that things can be better and who recognize their role in manifesting constructive change. It's not that they are always or inanely happy; rather, they just know how to compartmentalize angst and set it aside to focus on a bigger objective. When you put individuals like that together, solidarity strengthens commitment. The result? A powerhouse of action.

As a team, Sea Shepherd volunteers maintain a pact, both to one another and to vaquita. They cheer each progressive step and celebrate hard-won accomplishments with vivacious and unified energy. Regardless of difficult moments, they manage to keep their eye on Operation Milagro's published mission "to help this shy and elusive porpoise beat the odds, bringing about a miracle to restore the vaquita population from the brink of extinction."

~

Protected by the sunshade of the observation deck, I stared across the water. The desert air was hot and dry. The distant mountain landscape had changed from the peach hues of morning to the drab tan of an escaping afternoon. As the sea gathered into ripples—becoming less and less suited for spotting dorsal fins—we were fortunate to log more whales, mostly humpbacks. Each was a treasure to see. Their blows, distinct billows of vapor, rose like white apparitions against the now-emerald ocean.

Unexpectedly, Gustavo pointed, and we swung our binoculars to port. A megapod of long-beaked common dolphins, *Delphinus capensis*, came barreling toward the ship. As the cetaceans—upward of two hundred and fifty of them—embraced the *Farley Mowat*, churning the waters with their enthusiastic greeting, Eli and I scurried down from the observation area to get a closer view. Suddenly the ship was a hullabaloo of running feet and gleeful shouts as the whole crew, even Sheila, came rushing out on deck to enjoy the experience.

Such a gregarious interaction perfectly exemplified the difference between dolphins and porpoises. Porpoises would never behave like that.

I remembered Lorenzo telling me that CNN had approached him to do a piece on vaquita, but they wanted them leaping out of the water. He had to say, no, vaquitas don't do that. So, CNN never came.

At the bow rail, I cozied in with several crewmates. Our cameras amassed countless shots of the commotion. My close-up images would portray a carnival of splashing water and gray-torpedo bodies with white sides, floating over the Vermilion Sea, as airborne as acrobats. Common dolphins are residents in the Gulf of California and are one of the most frequently sighted species. Megapods, however, are rare. "We have only seen about three big pods of dolphins since last fall," someone near me reported, but I was too enraptured to take notice of who it was.

I couldn't help wondering if whale watching—as long as it remained outside the refuge—might provide seasonal income to local fishermen with out-of-work pangas. Could that be successful? Or would ecotourism merely provide another opportunity to exploit the waters? It's hard to believe that whale-watching boats would abide by rules any better than fishing boats. After all, it would be the same men at the rudders.

Just after dinner, I climbed alone to the observation deck, closing my jacket against the evening breeze. The sun was low on the horizon. Melting like butter, it dripped down the craggy desert mountains and puddled in the bay before soaking into the landscape. Shadowed waves, lifting and falling all around the ship, became a million phantom dorsal fins, a megapod of imaginary vaquitas.

I sat listening to the rhythmic slap of water against steel until night overtook the gulf. Soon, moonshine reached across the ocean like an astral yellow-brick road, and once-dark waves, now illuminated, flickered like candles in a concert of stars. I marveled at the magnificence of nature.

Then it came to me. Somewhere in the darkness, a *buchero* was casting his deadly net under the same exquisite light.

~

The forward cabin is triangular due to the angle of the bow, with three narrow bunks stacked against each wall like drawers. By the time I tottered in, a couple of volunteers were already asleep. Someone's knees poked out from behind a bunk curtain; a length of durable fabric afforded a modicum of privacy in these shared quarters.

I stole into the middle bunk on the starboard side. Crawling between the soft, clean sheets, I snuggled down and stuffed my earplugs into place. My mind wandered back on the day, gradually winding down like a spinning top slowing to a teetered roll.

Gustavo and Eli were in the mess hall getting ready to watch a movie with a few other night owls. Woody had retired to his captain's quarters, and his Spanish first mate, Paloma de Castilla, was now manning the bridge. Possessing a mariner license, Paloma, like communications officer Roy, took shifts piloting the ship. Throughout the night, someone stationed at the radar would maintain constant vigilance for any dot flashing in the Vaquita Refuge. The ship's high-end radar system not only detects potential pangas; it can also accurately track speed and direction. If, after a period of observation, a dot didn't disappear (most did), the *Martin Sheen* would go on reconnaissance with the *Farley* as backup. Paloma would call the Navy if needed.

Exhausted and grateful to be in the care of such a dedicated crew, my eyes fluttered shut. Sleeping on boats is something I've always enjoyed, and I was quickly lulled to dreamland. Set idle against the heavy waves, the ship swayed through the night like a giant rocking cradle. I slumbered like a babe, though at times the roll was so extreme that I had to bend my knees ninety degrees to keep from rolling out of bed.

Moments before dawn, I slid down from my bunk. Snagging my jacket and binoculars, I tiptoed from the room and climbed to the deck to watch the sun rise. In the purple glow of daybreak, brown pelicans swept by nose to tail, and the feathered procession dipped and yawed over the calm water like ballet dancers across a steel-blue stage. It would be another day of good visibility, another opportunity to see *la vaquita*. I smiled at the thought.

At breakfast, an exhausted Eli pushed back her long, wavy hair and rubbed her eyes. Between the "nauseous rocking" and the "symphony of snores," she had barely caught any sleep. Chatter filled the mess hall as the crew poured in. Dunking his spoon into a bowl of cereal with soy-milk, Fernando announced, "Last night I dreamed we found the white shark. I kept wondering what was holding it up. Then I realized it was surrounded by dolphins. They were acting like buoys."

Everybody nodded as if it made perfect sense. They all understood strange dreams of sharks and dolphins and buoys.

I was beginning to understand, too.

～

The second day on the observation deck unfolded much as the first day had. As Woody motored around the refuge, Gustavo, Eli, and I scanned a seemingly endless field of blue. We searched with our naked eyes. We searched with our binoculars. We surveyed waters close in and far out, shuffling forward and aft, from starboard to port, always hoping to spot a dark triangle, a vaquita dorsal fin, poking out of the water.

Thankfully, we never got bored. The gulf was full of cetaceans. We logged several more sightings of breaching, tail-lobbing, or traveling humpbacks. We spotted Bryde's whales and some kind of rorqual that we encountered too briefly to identify. When another (or the same) megapod of long-beaked common dolphins showed up, Roy deployed the drone for an aerial view. The two-foot-wide, four-legged minihelicopter captured remarkable footage of our ship traveling amid an army of dolphin escorts. It was quite the sight.

Remote control in hand, Roy looked like a kid with an expensive toy, but I knew that this kind of amusement was a treat. The drone, which can travel a remarkable three miles from its controller and is equipped with infrared light for nighttime vision, is more commonly employed to spy into pangas exhibiting sketchy behavior. Fisherman had apparently taken to holding up their corvina permits to the drone's eye like citizens of a sci-fi city.

Some pangas harbored illegal gear, and Roy had caught several *bucheros* red-handed, casting or retrieving totoaba nets. What might seem to be demonstrable proof of poaching regrettably is not. In a typical twist of Mexican law, drone footage is not considered firsthand evidence and is therefore inadmissible in court.

In the afternoon, Paloma found some time to hang out on the observation deck and told us the story of a recent run-in with fishermen. In addition to her busy job as first mate, she was often asked to handle interactions with Mexican nationals, which sometimes meant addressing adversaries. Recently, the *Farley* had tailed a panga seen rushing away from the refuge. When the ship caught up, Paloma said hello to the fishermen and apologized for taking chase.

"Sorry we came fast," she told them in Spanish. "We just wanted to make sure you are not inside of the refuge of the vaquita." Although the men presented corvina nets and permits, the Sea Shepherd crew was fairly sure that they were poachers because, during pursuit, they had caught sight of a gillnet with totoaba wrapped in it. The bundle appeared to have been hastily dumped. Nobody could say for sure that it was these fishermen, but the timing was awfully suspicious. For that reason, the Navy was called out to investigate.

Paloma spoke with the fishermen while they waited. "They were not disrespectful," she told us, "but they were nervous, and they started speaking loud to protest. Why we were bothering them when the vaquita didn't exist anymore? One was saying the vaquita only comes here to reproduce, and after that they leave. Which of course is not true. And they also said the problem is the cutoff water from the Colorado River, which was the source for feeding the vaquita." That's also not true.

Paloma did her best to educate the fishermen about how gillnets, not changes to the river, are decimating the rare porpoises. She told them, "As human beings, we cannot do nothing when we know a species is disappearing. And this species is really disappearing."

The men said to her, "You take care of the vaquita, but we have to take care of us. We have to eat, and our families have to eat. And [even though it's prohibited], we have to fish corvina inside the refuge because the corvina is there."

"Of course, as human beings we have to feed ourselves," Paloma had empathetically responded. "But the problem," she explained to them, "is that the fishermen do not respect the laws. And a lot of fishermen are hiding the nets [for totoaba] with this permission they have for corvina. And the control is not good. So now we have to stop the vaquita from extinguishing. And the only thing we can do is what we are doing."

Hearing this story, I had to agree. What Sea Shepherd was doing— assisting Mexico in patrolling for poachers and safeguarding the Vaquita Refuge—was the most tangible plan I'd seen so far. Campaign Operation Milagro certainly appeared to be helping. In fact, the crew's strength, compassion, and sensibility gave me a shot of hope, like a provisional vaccine against the bleak state of affairs. Two years earlier, the Upper Gulf was packed with boats and strewn with gillnets. Now, despite it being high season for totoaba, the water was quiet to the eye. We had not pulled up any illicit nets nor seen any signs of poaching.

I asked Paloma what happened to the corvina fishermen.

She said the Navy released them without charge.

~

At three o'clock, Woody turned the *Farley Mowat* toward shore. Despite two full days of searching, sunrise to sunset, traversing the most acoustically active regions of the refuge with three dedicated observers and a fifteen-person crew, we'd failed to find a single vaquita.

Still, I could not complain. We had tallied almost twenty cetacean sightings, including the humpbacks and Bryde's whales and two megapods of long-beaked common dolphins, not to mention charismatic sea lions and handsome seabirds.

Now that I knew what vaquita habitat looked like, I was excited to turn my attention to the scientific research being conducted by INECC. Lorenzo's colleague Armando supervises a study that uses underwater monitoring devices, called c-pods. Gustavo, who has been working with the acoustic expert since 2008, invited me back to help set up and deploy some units. I could hardly wait to see that process and find out what the researchers were learning.

Off the bow, solid earth awaited our return and signaled our dispersal. Gustavo was due back at his office in Ensenada. Eli had a ticket for an eight o'clock bus to Hermosillo, Sonora; she would endure the sixteen-hour ride for a much-anticipated week with her family. I would ready my car for the trip back to Arizona. And while the rest of the Sea Shepherd volunteers remained in Alto Golfo to hunt gillnets, Fernando would be making his way home to Puerto Rico.

As San Felipe loomed closer, its details and colors returned to focus: the crescent-shaped beach pebbled with hotels, the festively colored *malecón*, the lighthouse, and the shrine to the Virgin of Guadalupe perched on the hill. As I studied the tiny pink and yellow sail of a catamaran in the bay, I found my mind shifting gears, preparing for my drive home, when suddenly—

Dorsal fins!

My binoculars raced into position. They revealed approximately thirty dolphins charging our way. Within moments, the cetaceans were leaping this way and that, carving our wake like world-class surfers. These were not common dolphins. They were bottlenose. My heart skipped with delight as I watched them frolic, so reminiscent of my days in Golfo Dulce. There was even a baby in the bunch, and I cheered as it darted and jumped in sync with its mama.

My friends, charmed by my exuberance, agreed that it was a fantastic finale.

When at last the dolphins fell back, turning in search of some other adventure, Sheila clambered onto the observation deck. She was carefully balancing a bowl in her hand, which held an afternoon treat of hand-dipped fruits—apple, pear, fig, apricot, wrapped in blankets of mouth-watering dark chocolate.

"*Cerrar con broche del oro*," exclaimed Eli with infectious good cheer.

Gustavo and Paloma laughed and repeated the saying, a toast to the day. "*Cerrar con broche del oro!*"

Close with a gold pin. It means to end with a flourish.

We certainly did.

CHAPTER 8

Hearing Is Believing

"Okay, are we almost ready to start?" asked Gustavo, sitting in front of his laptop at the kitchenette table. Across the room, Ivan Jaramillo was dropping ten new D batteries into a twenty-six-inch-long tube of gray PVC pipe. On summer break from university, twenty-one-year-old Ivan had arrived in San Felipe with Gustavo to help prepare INECC's underwater acoustic monitoring devices. I'd come down from Arizona to do the same.

The devices, called c-pods, are officially described as "self-contained ultrasound monitors that select tonal clicks and record the time, duration and other features of each click to 5-microseconds resolution." Simply put, they record the high-frequency sounds that vaquitas make while navigating and foraging in the Vaquita Refuge. C-pods are vital not only to discovering where the little cetaceans spend their time, but also, as I would soon learn, to estimating how many of these porpoises are still alive.

C-pods are typically deployed from mid-June to mid-September, when legal fisheries are historically between seasons and fishermen are off the water seeking shade to mend their nets. Illegal fishing is also reduced at that time because most totoaba are southbound for their annual migration. With everyone off the water, c-pods are relatively safe from being scooped away by nets or industrial trawlers. They are not, however, totally safe.

Disappearing equipment is a serious problem for the acoustic research team. Since 2008, well more than a hundred c-pods have vanished, a loss calculated in both financial terms (about $3,400 per unit) and scientific terms (priceless). Although equipment can be replaced, data cannot, so even though the devices are designed to function up to five months at a stretch, Gustavo is now switching them out every two weeks for download. When I arrived in July, he was halfway through the monitoring season.

Every summer, INECC rents a condo for their study period, and our two-room work space offered a much-appreciated respite from the outside heat. After Ivan inserted batteries in the forty-six c-pods that we were readying for deployment, I slipped a silica-gel pack into each one to absorb unwanted moisture. It's a testament to the brutal humidity in the area that the packs had to be dried for two hours in the oven at La Vaquita before use. In the condo, even with the door tightly shut, it was at times unbearably muggy, and I silently thanked the tiny wall-mounted AC unit for spitting cool air into the flow of the ceiling fan.

At the table, Gustavo studied a map of the refuge marked with waypoints to indicate where each of the c-pods would be positioned. Every unit is labeled with a factory number. Keeping track of placement is crucial for resulting data to be properly analyzed.

Soon c-pods stood across the floor in rows, like cylindrical dominos. Maneuvering cautiously to avoid toppling them, I handed the first one—number 2609—to Gustavo. With the base of the tube resting on the tile and the open end securely between his knees, he demonstrated the best technique for finagling the clip that locks down the batteries and makes the electrical contact. Then he installed the unit's memory.

Every c-pod gets a four-gigabyte memory card that corresponds to the number printed on its tube. Whenever the tube is retrieved from the field, its card is downloaded using dedicated software and then systematically reformatted to ensure that all the specs are fresh and up to date before the next rotation. As Gustavo slipped 2609's memory card into its slot, he warned against prematurely activating the unit. When he finished, I took that c-pod away and handed him the next, 2612.

One by one, battery clips and memory cards were added to each c-pod—2625, 2481, and so on.

Once all forty-six units were equipped, Gustavo, Ivan, and I worked in unison to activate the c-pods in batches. Each managing three tubes at a time, we clicked the memory cards into place and—on Gustavo's cue—pressed the internal start buttons to set the time stamp. Next, while Gustavo recorded the time stamps for each batch, Ivan and I added tiny data sheets into the tubes and applied Vaseline to their O-ring seals. As the units were capped with screw-on lids and tightened with a torque tool, I couldn't help chuckling. Each plastic lid is stamped with a web address for wayward devices—www.phonehome.com.uk—revealing the manufacturer's sense of humor.

We completed the whole job in three and a half hours. That pleased Gustavo. When he works alone, it can take eight to twelve hours, and that's just the prep stage. Dozens more hours of labor are required to deploy and retrieve the devices and then to dismantle them and download their memory cards. The whole process is repeated every two weeks.

It's a lot of work, but Gustavo never complains. Keeping the data safe is worth every effort, he said. Besides, he knows that collecting acoustic recordings wasn't always that easy.

~

There is a proverb: "Seeing is believing."

Humans are visually cued animals, so much so that we can supposedly decode a visual scene in just thirteen milliseconds. Of course, we employ other senses, too, but with such a richly developed visual cortex in our curious brain, the vast majority of us rely predominantly on sight to explore our world.

Vaquitas would surely modify our proverb to "Hearing is believing." Porpoises are highly acoustical animals that depend on echolocation, or sonar, to navigate their surroundings. Sound, which travels about five times faster and farther in water than in air, plays a vital role in aquatic habitats, especially ones with limited visibility like the murky waters overlaying the Colorado River delta.

Like bats and dolphins, porpoises make high-frequency clicks that bounce off objects and echo back, giving them an auditory "image" of scenes and objects. The fatty crown on the porpoise's head, called the melon, emits and focuses clicks like a sound lens, while incoming reverberations, received through the thin, lipid-coated bones of the lower jaw, are directed to the inner ear.

Vaquita clicks are typically between 128 and 139 kilohertz. Although resonating well above the range of human hearing, which is 20 kilohertz max, they can be recorded with specialized equipment and analyzed through rigorous scientific processes. Sonar recordings have contributed a lot to what we know about Mexico's panda of the sea.

"Vaquitas make narrow-band clicks," acoustics expert Armando Jaramillo Legorreta once told me. Armando is Mexico's head scientist for vaquita-sonar research (as well as Gustavo's boss and Ivan's father), and he is wonderful at explaining acoustic science in a way that makes sense. "Dolphin clicks contain a much wider range of frequencies," he said. "Dolphins also make whistles and other sounds, some of which can be heard by the naked human ear. Porpoises do not." So, vaquitas are unable to produce audible chatter of the Flipper variety.

Deploying acoustic detectors in Alto Golfo since April 1997, Armando has built an impressive library of data, stored in the coastal hills of northern Ensenada. INECC is housed at the Center for Scientific Research and Higher Education, which overlooks Mexico's Autonomous University of Baja California and the cerulean bay below. Somewhere inside Armando's office, held for posterity, is the first acoustic research tool he ever used: the porpoise box.

Designed in the United Kingdom to filter, identify, and store phocoenid sonar, the porpoise box consisted of a hydrophone attached to 328-foot cable that plugged into a box of electronics, which then hooked into a computer connected to a GPS device. Given that the system had been tested with several porpoise species and that Gregory Silber, the first scientist to capture vaquita clicks (in 1986), wrote that "*Phocoena sinus* acoustic signals are similar to those described for other members of the Phocoenidae," Armando was confident that the porpoise box would work with vaquita.

Designers of the box suggested dragging the hydrophone behind a boat while traveling along a line grid, systematically searching the waters much as a visual survey might do. Armando did not have much success with that method, though. Knowing the exceedingly shy nature of vaquitas, he worried that the boat noise was scaring them away. After a few days of motoring around the Upper Gulf with poor results, he decided to disobey the recommended protocol. Instead, he picked a spot, stopped his panga, shut off the motor, hung his hydrophone, and waited.

Like magic, vaquitas appeared.

The first time Armando saw vaquitas with his own eyes and simultaneously watched the porpoise box pick up their acoustic signals, he was thrilled. "For sure we were hearing vaquitas!" he told me. He and research partner Lorenzo Rojas quickly adjusted their methodology to utilize fixed points randomly selected around the distribution area, and location by location Armando began recording.

Although the simplest unit of acoustic emission is a click, clicks do not occur in isolation, he explained. Rather, they are made in groups called trains, and trains are grouped into events. "Using the porpoise box, an 'acoustic event' was diagnosed as one to several trains," he said. "A single event was determined by the time gap that came between trains. That gap was about fifteen minutes. So, if a train ended, and then quietness ensued for over fifteen minutes before a new train started, the porpoise box divided the data into two acoustic events. Two separate encounters."

The INECC scientists recorded numerous encounters between 2001 and 2007, a period during which Armando tried to conduct three acoustic surveys per year. Every time he observed vaquitas while simultaneously collecting acoustical recordings, it revalidated the competence of the system. By 2008, he had collected eleven years of data, and the findings appeared profound.

From 1997 to 2007, the acoustic detection rate—the number of times per day that vaquitas were detected—dropped 58 percent. Based on those results, Armando reasonably concluded that the population of *Phocoena sinus* had been reduced by more than half. Those findings were confirmed by two large-scale visual surveys conducted within the same time period, one in 1997 and another in 2008. The shipboard data demonstrated the exact same decline.

So, the news was terrible. But the acoustic data were good.

Officially confirming that acoustic techniques were reliable and that Armando's data could be trusted was a big step forward, scientifically speaking, namely because INECC had collected several times more acoustic events than sightings with human eyes. The only problem was in trying to increase the sample size. The porpoise box was not entirely automated. Someone had to sit on a boat, monitoring the computer in real time. So, if the scientists wanted to record more encounters—and they did—they needed more boats equipped with porpoise boxes working out on the water. The cost of those additional vessels, with gas and maintenance, not to mention labor, quickly raced outside their meager budget.

Thankfully, by 2008, technology developers had come up with first-generation passive acoustic monitoring (PAM) devices. With PAM, researchers could now deploy devices in their study areas, wait a period of weeks or even months, and then go back and retrieve their data. To appreciate such utility for a quickly disappearing and difficult-to-detect species like *Phocoena sinus*, one simply has to juxtapose the logistics and limitations of a large-scale visual survey.

During a visual survey, a ship travels along transect lines, a grid of close, parallel tracks that traverse the distribution area. Never deviating from the prescribed path, onboard observers look for vaquitas. At every sighting they note group size, location, and distance from boat. Then, based on how many porpoises are seen, a density estimate can be calculated.

Here's the challenge: the boat only briefly approaches any given location before passing by. If a dorsal breaks the surface within the observers' line of sight—and the observer is skilled or lucky enough to spot it—the sighting is logged. However, if the animal surfaces too far from the boat, is somehow missed by the observers, or comes up after the boat has passed, it goes uncounted. To make matters more challenging, vaquitas are said to react to a ship's passing within half a mile, so sightings often occur at a fair distance.

Strategically placed, tethered in position, and working every hour of every day, a PAM device is unlikely to miss a vaquita arriving into the area as long as the porpoise emits at least one click train. And while a ship may be further limited by environmental conditions such as bad weather or shallow water, acoustic equipment can withstand the ocean elements at nearly any depth. The advantages cannot be overstated.

PAM turned out to be a scientific game changer.

～

Gustavo was hired by INECC in 2008 to help coordinate field operations. He was charged with managing the new PAM devices—getting them into and out of the water as well as downloading their data for Armando to analyze. At the outset, to determine which kind of passive acoustic monitoring device to commission, the team tested three different varieties: the c-pod, the t-pod, and the a-tag.

They liked that the c-pod could record vaquita clicks from a distance of up to thirteen hundred feet with internal circuitry that garnered several important elements relating to each recorded click, including time, duration, center frequency, intensity, and bandwidth; it could even extrapolate a frequency trend. During their trial study, Armando and Gustavo deployed devices at more than sixty sites in and around the refuge. Analyzing data from their trials, the team agreed that the c-pod was the best choice. After negotiating a collaboration with designer Nick Tregenza at Chelonia Limited Inc. in the United Kingdom, the c-pod was adopted as Mexico's official vaquita monitoring tool.

With the new system, the INECC scientists revised their acoustic parameters, shifting the unit of evaluation from trains back to clicks. "Clicks, which the c-pod excels at organizing, have better statistical characteristics," Armando explained, "and the statisticians who work with us found that looking at individual clicks and the number of clicks emitted, as opposed to more generalized trains, allowed more precise analyses to be made."

In addition to garnering greater detail, capturing data in this new way dramatically increased the study's sample size. Whereas the old porpoise box required someone to be physically present during the recording period, the autonomous c-pods could remain static in the field, functioning full time, unattended. There was, and still is, one critical caveat: only human eyes can count. Modern acoustic tools like c-pods can neither identify individual vaquitas nor gauge group size. Distance and direction are problematic too.

Victor Orozco (on left) and Rafael "Gordis" Sánchez, two Islas del Golfo Co-Op contractors, exchange c-pods in the Vaquita Refuge. (Brooke Bessesen)

So much has been learned, though. First, the distribution of vaquitas is not homogenous across the distribution area. They prefer waters less than one hundred feet in depth and tend to stay within about sixteen miles of shore. Within that range, there are certain areas where clicks are heard relatively frequently and other areas where there are no clicks at all, although the majority of areas fall somewhere in between. Looking at an early chart of acoustic encounters, I could not help noticing an area where lots of little dots overlapped into a blue blob. Was that a vaquita hot spot?

Yes, Gustavo told me. He confirmed that a markedly higher density of acoustic encounters has been recorded in the southwest corner of the Vaquita Refuge, the area we searched from Sea Shepherd's *Farley Mowat*. To give an idea of the disparity, the scientists were getting at least one to two acoustic encounters per day in that active zone in 2015, whereas c-pods in less active areas might record only one encounter every ten days.

Why do vaquitas make more clicks in certain areas? The most obvious hypothesis is that areas with more acoustic activity are foraging grounds where the animals are echolocating for food, but nobody knows for sure. It has been shown by other scientists that porpoises can interpret one another's sonar, and there is also some evidence that when porpoises are foraging together, only one of them actively echolocates; the others just passively receive the bounceback. Presumably, the resounding clicks give everyone in the group the information needed to catch prey while eliminating a confusing cacophony of sound ricocheting in every direction.

Such organized teamwork is exciting to consider. Who decides who will be the clicker? Do they take turns? Is it based on seniority? Skill? Some other factor?

Although porpoise phonations are not yet categorized into, say, feeding clicks versus social clicks, c-pod designer Tregenza has suggested from experience that when porpoises are in the presence of prey, they click at higher rates. That would make sense. It's true of bats—their standard cadence becomes faster as they approach an insect and want more information about its shape, speed, and direction of movement. As analyzing algorithms improve, researchers will most assuredly gain insight into the behaviors of vaquitas.

But that will happen only if there are vaquitas alive to analyze.

～

The word *acoustic* is defined as "relating to sound or a sense of hearing," so it's incredibly strange, even a bit disturbing, for a newcomer to learn that the study of vaquita acoustics involves no sound whatsoever. The data are completely silent. During my first visit to San Felipe, Gustavo showed me the software he and Armando use to evaluate sonar recordings, which are nothing but blips and dashes on a computer screen. As peaks of color zipped across the screen like a 1980s equalizer, I had to resist the urge to reach over and turn up the volume.

Humans aren't the only animals who can't hear vaquitas. Silber noted that "phocoenid porpoises are able to remain undetected while searching for food, because the sounds also exceed the hearing of their prey." Such is the adaptive benefit of echolocating at high frequencies.

When I asked Gustavo if it bothers him that, as a researcher of vaquita sounds, he has never actually heard one, he laughed aloud. Apparently, the absurdity had never occurred to him. I personally found it quite difficult to grasp the meaning of the data lines without any associated sound. Perhaps, I suggested, if I could hear something, even for a moment, the seemingly random marks would begin to make sense. I knew the recordings of blue whales could be sped up to make them audible. Couldn't vaquita recordings be slowed down to the same effect?

I asked. Gustavo gave into my doggedness and told me that Armando had, in fact, slowed down a vaquita click train. I waited with obvious anticipation as he shuffled through his computer files like a miner searching for a gem. At last he located the audio clip and clicked play.

First was silence. Then, out emerged a long, wet sputter. It sounded so much like flatulence that I stifled an embarrassed titter before Gustavo's knowing look sent me tumbling into a belly laugh. One can only hope that vaquita sounds are better appreciated at their normal frequency.

Returning to the hard data on the screen, Gustavo reminded me that c-pods record a frequency range of 20 to 166 kilohertz, so in addition to porpoise clicks, the devices pick up other noises. He drew my attention to two lines of acoustic input, which appeared dissimilar. "This one is the sonar of a vaquita," he said, pointing, "and that is a dolphin."

As Armando had described, their sonar signatures look distinctly different. Such differences are key to Gustavo's new doctoral research—he's examining the acoustical characteristics of eight nonvaquita sounds, such as wind, boat motors, and various dolphin clicks. Not only will the study help Armando more easily remove bias in their vaquita data, but as comparative details come clear, Gustavo hopes to someday be able to identify separate dolphin species by the characteristics of their clicks.

Imagine that.

~

"Has anyone ever attempted to photograph vaquitas with underwater camera traps?" I once asked Gustavo.

Camera traps are used to study many elusive land species. For example, I know a biologist who counts jaguars in the rain forests of Costa Rica using images snapped by motion-activated cameras. The researcher has never met one of his two-hundred-pound study subjects in the wild, yet he is able recognize photographed individuals based on their unique rosette patterns.

It turns out that Gustavo has been helping Antonella Wilby, a doctoral student from the University of California at San Diego, who is attempting to do the same with vaquitas. Antonella is a National Geographic Young Explorer, described as "a passionate roboticist, explorer, and photographer, [who] hopes to unify technological innovation with exploration and storytelling." Seeking to be the first person to capture an underwater photograph of a living vaquita, she has been working on an aquatic camera trap that will be acoustically triggered by porpoise sonar clicks to record the animals in their refuge.

It's a provocative plan, but Antonella is facing a plethora of problems. So far, her NASA-style machine—the SphereCam, a fiberglass ball with bubble-shaped windows—has been fraught with too many technical hiccups to know whether it could ever function for its designed purpose. Her 2015 deployment failed due to glitches in the system, as did her 2016 trials.

Gustavo worries that *Phocoena sinus* is a poor subject for camera-trap studies. Even if the equipment works, the odds of photographing a vaquita are slim; the water is just too murky. And because Antonella would need cameras in at least as many locations as there are c-pods, the cost of such a program would be prohibitive. Building on the cheap, the university prototype cost $5,000 in materials and construction. The same unit on the retail market, with all the engineering factored in, would cost five times that amount.

When I finally met Antonella, she was at the docks in San Felipe, poking around in the metallic guts of her SphereCam. She had driven down from San Diego only to discover that her camera was again out of commission. Red curls whipped across her freckled face, and a grimace held her features. "Trying to build and work with these kinds of electronics in the field," she fretted, "a million little things can go wrong."

I admire Antonella's tenacity and truly hope she succeeds. But notably, I find her ongoing struggles with waterproofing, inadequate analog sensor chips, and a lack of sufficient long-term power output to be an oblique demonstration of the exceptional design of the c-pod. The tubular unit may not take pictures, but it works like a charm for collecting acoustic data.

~

With our cache loaded in the back of the truck, Gustavo, Ivan, and I motored into town and delivered forty-six c-pods to be exchanged by nine Islas del Golfo Co-Op fishermen. I recognized some of the men from my *chango* primer in Javier's yard, men with amusing nicknames like Mala Cara (Bad Face), Gordis (Chubby), and Muelas (Molars). Lacking alt-gear permits, INECC contracts have been lifesavers for these fishermen and their families.

A set of field supplies—a clipboard, data sheets, waypoint map, handheld GPS, plus a voucher for the gas station—was provided for each of three teams. I agreed to meet everyone at the marina at 5 a.m.

Work concluded, Gustavo, Ivan, and I headed to La Vaquita for a bowl of guacamole. After, we took an evening stroll on the *malecón*. Despite the pervasive heat, the beach was lined with camping tents. Families were barbequing, chatting in lawn chairs, or just sprawled happily on the sand. Cars, motorcycles, and all-terrain vehicles jammed the road, and people packed the sidewalk where Saturday-night vendor carts tempted passersby with street corn, candy, fresh churros, and mango on a stick carved open like a flower and sprinkled with chili powder.

Weaving through the lively crowd to the mixed rhythm of a dozen competing bands, I savored the music of Mexico. People were crooning and high-stepping to trumpets and guitars, snare drums and saxophones. Wandering too close to a swinging ensemble, Gustavo was nearly knocked over by a giant blue tuba.

As much as I enjoyed the fiesta, my eyes kept tracking out to the moonlit ocean where, oblivious to the clamor, waves rolled up the summer sand at their own unhurried pace. I could hardly wait for the next morning. Come sunrise, I would be riding the waves in a fisherman's panga, racing out to exchange c-pods in the Vaquita Refuge.

CHAPTER 9

Science in the Sea

Even in Mexico, July 4 felt like a holiday as we jetted at thirty-five miles an hour across the blue Sea of Cortez. There wasn't another boat in sight. Roca Consag's silhouette adorned the eastern horizon, and the mountains behind us glowed amber, like the arched backs of ancient dinosaurs. Although the water was fairly calm, a capricious breeze hinted at rougher conditions ahead. The day's forecast predicted ten mile per hour winds by eleven o'clock. We would need to be finished by then; fishermen hate a surging sea.

Our team's exchange area was in the western range of the Vaquita Refuge, where Gilberto Ruiz, better known as Giby, an introspective fellow with sinewy limbs and a gray goatee, had been hauling up c-pods for Paco to swap out. It was a pleasure to see Paco again under happier circumstances than our meeting at his office the day Ps2's body was discovered. With three c-pods exchanged and fourteen to go, I was carefully examining the field log so that I could assist our team by taking over as scribe. Paco's brother Alán Valverde, our convivial driver, was thwarting the sun with comedic movie-star sunglasses as he monitored the GPS device, navigating the three miles to the next waypoint.

Moments later it came into view: *Sitio* (site) 32. A red marker flag bobbed on a low, smooth wave, tethered to an orange buoy. Beneath the buoy—which was painted with the waypoint number and crowned with a flashing light for night detection—a sturdy rope descended into the darkness. Giby's muscles strained as he tugged the line, eventually pulling a dripping c-pod aboard.

Paco unhooked its carabiner and called, "Two-six-four-oh."

I jotted down the number on the log sheet.

"Two-oh-four-eight," I said, handing him a fresh tube from the bin at my feet.

He clipped 2048 onto the line and slipped it overboard.

As we watched it sink, Paco described its mooring, explaining that the c-pod hangs vertically thirty-three feet above the bottom. Below that, the main rope splits and runs down to two heavy anchors. Securing the devices in their prescribed locations was quite a challenge at first. Unlike other marine environments with solid seafloors, the Upper Gulf has been shaped by the influx of fresh water from an enormous river. Although the water is not terribly deep (at one point Alán checked our depth reader: seventy-two feet), sediment creates complications. Silt, suspended in the water, becomes more and more dense as the water deepens, and the muddy stratum at the bottom is many feet thick. Because the c-pod's factory-designed mooring didn't work, Armando and Gustavo had to devise a special system, which required diving down to examine the seafloor.

"I can tell you, it's only mud," Armando once said of the experience. "At only five meters [sixteen feet] below the water surface, you are unable to see your hand." He told me that clam divers, who pump air compressors, carry lead weights, and drop in like moonwalkers, have to work by feel. And they are at constant risk of drowning, hypothermia, and decompression sickness.

In that same habitat, inhospitable to humans, porpoises dash about with easy grace. They don't mind the muddy water because their marvelous sonar—*click-click-click*—furnishes them sight. Perfectly adapted, vaquitas paddle, play, eat, grow, live, and love, just as their kind has done for millennia. True ancients of the ocean, they have been thriving in the Upper Gulf of California since well before man emerged from the evolutionary clay.

The earliest prewhales reportedly returned from land to sea some fifty million years ago. *Basilosaurus*, which lived in the Eocene epoch, is thought to be the antecedent of modern-day cetaceans. Fossils and phylogenetics show that toothed whales—systematically named Odontoceti—took form about thirty million years ago. By about fifteen million years ago, the family Phocoenidae had split off as porpoises.

Then, three and a half million years ago, the Baja peninsula broke from the mainland along the San Andreas Fault, forming an inlet nearly seven hundred miles long. A group of porpoises from the South Pacific traveled up that corridor to fill the niche and, arriving at the northerly limits of the embayment, adapted to the aquatic landscape conscribed by the river delta. In a breath of time, the unique species *Phocoena sinus* surfaced as an apex predator in a newly formed and fertile bionetwork.

I once asked Armando about the features of vaquita's underwater world. Apparently, silty ridges prevail, and mounds rise from the ocean floor, sometimes reaching fifteen feet tall. In the northern part of the refuge, closer to the Colorado River where the bottom tends to be flatter and the water extremely shallow, occasional peaks break their watery bonds during low tide to catch a gulp of air. To the south and west, though—in the regions with the greatest acoustic activity—underwater contours appear much more complicated.

Exactly how topography plays into the ecology of vaquita is yet unknown, but an adult porpoise surely recognizes every bump and curve, like a farmer knows the turns of his land. The tiny, black-eyed cetaceans must also know the behavior of their prey within that environment. At least twenty marine species, including bronze-striped grunts, gulf croakers, small crabs, and squid—mostly bottom-dwelling creatures—make up a vaquita's diet, and this gastronomic mélange is located and captured over slopes of mud and silt.

Fishermen know every good ridge and valley in Alto Golfo, too. Many argued against the decision to designate the Vaquita Refuge simply because one of the best shrimping sites falls inside the polygon. Indeed, for several years c-pods deployed in the three best fishing spots kept disappearing. No matter how many times they were replaced, units at those locations were never recovered. Despite signs of tampering, cut ropes, and things like that, Armando isn't sure whether the missing c-pods were purposefully removed or accidentally netted. Either way, those three unproductive research locations were eventually abandoned.

As Paco, Alán, Giby, and I sped to *Sitio* 33 to swap the next device, I thought about all the years Armando had invested in vaquitas. It has been his entire career. It was surely bad enough to witness their steady decline from 567 to 245, but when the totoaba crisis arose in 2012, he saw the population suddenly plummeting at a ghastly rate of 34 percent per year.

～

Expedition 2015 was the most recent CIRVA-recommended vaquita survey. As in 1997 and 2008, the study was a joint project between SEMARNAT and NOAA, primarily funded by Mexico—this time to the tune of $2.25 million. It combined visual and acoustic data to estimate the population size of *Phocoena sinus*.

Working sixty-four days between September 28 and December 4,

2015, the 170-foot R/V *Ocean Starr* traversed waters deeper than 66 feet throughout the known range of the species, now contained in the Gillnet Exclusion Zone. The ship carried a dozen experts from Mexico, the United States, the United Kingdom, and Germany, led by Lorenzo and Barb Taylor as the chief scientists. Six sets of Big Eyes binoculars allowed observers to spot porpoises up to three miles away.

Despite traveling more than a thousand miles of track line in waters as far south as Puertecitos, the visual team recorded only fourteen vaquita sightings, representing twenty-six individuals. Moreover, the distribution range of the species seems to have contracted farther, as there were no sightings outside of the Vaquita Refuge.

"We knew from the acoustic data that there were some vaquita out there but that they had declined drastically," Barb had said. "I can't tell you what a relief it was to see them."

The scientists hosted a Fishermen Day when several traditional fishers from around the region were invited out. Some even saw vaquitas. Cameras from the CBS show *60 Minutes* were also on ship during a sighting and captured quite a bit of footage. The resulting segment, "The Last Vaquitas," aired in late May 2016. It captivated a broad American audience and helped launch the haunting story of Mexico's endemic porpoise into mainstream news, contributing to what would soon become an international media bonanza.

On the acoustic side of the effort, Armando and Gustavo did their standard summer sampling between June and September. Then, once the visual survey commenced, they added more c-pods to the north and west so as to cover all the shallow areas that the expedition ship could not enter. They deployed 135 devices in total. Eighty of those were lost between September and December, mostly due to commercial shrimp trawlers. Even with replacements, a dozen sites were still missing equipment by the end of the survey. Nevertheless, Armando said the acoustic sample size was huge compared to the visual sample size.

When a team of top scientists and statisticians from around the world arrived in San Diego, California, in April 2016, they were met with both sets of data. After a lot of math and modeling, the expert panel projected that fifty-nine individuals remained.

Fifty-nine vaquitas. That's what the survey revealed.

"The difficulty of obtaining precise abundance estimates for rare and cryptic species plagues conservation biology," wrote Taylor and colleagues in a subsequent *Conservation Letters* paper. "Nevertheless, our study objective was to obtain such an estimate of the number of vaquitas remaining at the beginning of the two-year gillnet ban. We achieved this objective, despite the catastrophic decline, by drawing on the strengths of an international, multidisciplinary team."

Curious to know how the acoustic and visual information were synced up and compared, I asked Armando to explain the science as simply as possible. He told me that the acoustic data had to be "calibrated" against the visual data. During Expedition 2015, the Vaquita Refuge was the calibration area—where the ship and sixty-nine c-pods overlapped—and calibrations derived from within that polygon were used to convert data in the shallow regions, essentially equating acoustics to number of animals.

The metrics, complicated by several factoring components, were extremely complex. Armando explained the basic concept with an example. Imagine that there are one hundred vaquitas visually confirmed in the calibration area, and at the same time the acoustic rate for that area averages five hundred clicks per day. That means that five hundred clicks equal one hundred vaquitas. If the acoustic rate later decreases to two hundred and fifty clicks per day, the number of vaquitas has presumably dropped to fifty.

He made clear that these models are used for estimating populations, not to provide an exact census. Although acoustics can always be used to mark general trends in abundance, more precision can be accomplished with calibrations correlating visual and acoustic data. That is the frontier of cetacean research. Armando said that a lot of scientists involved in bioacoustics believe that once they obtain exact calibration factors to estimate abundance for their particular species, visual surveys will no longer be needed. Having matched visual and acoustic data over multiple studies, that might be proving true for vaquita. With too few animals to justify another visual survey any time soon, it's exceedingly helpful to know that acoustics are a reliable proxy.

Armando told me about a fascinating hypothesis he formed while analyzing the data from Expedition 2015. For every sighting that provided both visual and acoustic data, he measured the clicking rate, the number of clicks per second in each train, and found that the clicking rate appeared to correspond with group size. When there were more animals in the group, the clicking rate was higher. Going back to the earlier idea of one porpoise acting as "clicker" for everyone in the group, then, we might conclude that if there are more individuals in that group, the clicker must make more clicks. Because Armando's been unable to see the animals while they are clicking beneath the ocean surface, he does not yet know if this finding can be scientifically demonstrated and cannot test his hypothesis with raw data. Still, it's a trail worth following.

Another noteworthy finding was the amount of acoustic activity detected in the shallow regions of Alto Golfo. It was unexpectedly high. Using the porpoise box for the 2008 survey, Armando and another researcher had to stay awake to manage the hydrophone from a shallow-hull sailboat. For all the time they invested, only one vaquita was detected in the northern waters.

But when using c-pods in 2015, they heard vaquitas over several days in the northern region, closer to El Golfo de Santa Clara. "There are vaquitas frequently visiting those waters," Armando said, adding that this discovery has real significance for the species' conservation plan.

When the population estimate from Expedition 2015 was released in spring 2016, the media announced about sixty surviving vaquitas. But at least three had perished since the actual survey, a point made abundantly clear when Lorenzo left the statistics meeting to go necropsy Ps2 and her conspecifics.

With statistics showing a 90 percent decline since 2011 and a greater than 97 percent decline since 1997, Taylor and colleagues concluded, "If the vaquita population could grow at its maximum intrinsic rate, it would not reach 2008 levels (> 250 vaquita) until 2050."

Can the porpoises—and can we humans—stay the course?

~

"*Dorsales!*" Giby shouted against the wind.

It was unusual for me to hear Giby speak, much less shout. Alán pulled back the throttle and idled the boat. Had Giby seen dolphins?

There was a wreck of seabirds flocking and diving at a distance, and our downwind nostrils were assaulted by the associated fish smell. Perhaps some bottlenose dolphins were circling a bait ball, enticing the birds to forage with them. We all scanned as the seconds ticked by. My watch read 6:55 a.m.

"There!" Giby pointed to the left.

Spinning my head, I caught sight of a single dorsal fin just as it disappeared into the inky blue. But almost immediately thereafter, with my eyes still locked on the spot, two vaquita dorsal fins broke the water surface in unison—dark gray triangles rising and falling in a tightly synchronized arc.

A surge of reverence stole my breath, and an unexpected flash of heat filled my eyes before wetting my cheeks. Thrilled by my extraordinary good fortune of seeing such wondrous beings, I wiped my face and pushed back the tears. Now was no time for clouded vision.

Although the porpoises were not right next to our panga, they were easily seen and unmistakably identifiable with our bare eyes. Paco broke the trance with a call for cameras; frozen in awe, none of us had snapped a single photo. We rummaged through our pockets and bags and got our telephoto lenses ready, but despite drifting for ten or fifteen minutes more, watching quietly in all directions, no more *dorsales* were spotted.

We never saw the vaquitas again.

I marked the GPS location in my notebook like the X on a treasure map: N 31°6.94′, W 114°40.06′. Had we seen a mother and calf, or perhaps a mating couple? Vaquitas are most commonly sighted as pairs, but unless one is substantially smaller than the other, it's difficult to conclude the relationship. A slight size difference is not enough because the species exhibits sexual dimorphism—males are smaller than females. Even that can be confusing, however, because the male's dorsal fin is wider and taller than the female's, which can give a false impression that he is bigger.

No matter their sex or status, it felt like a miracle to witness two of the last wild vaquitas. What a gift to see *Phocoena sinus* in living flesh!

"For every vaquita that's out there . . . every year there's a 50 percent chance it's going to die in a fishing net." The memory of Barb's words suddenly gutted me. Would this beautiful duo soon be dead? Would they, like Ps2, suffer the agony of asphyxiation in a gillnet? Would they be labeled for necropsy as Ps4, 5, or 6?

The truth of their tenuous situation ate at my insides. Thankfully, I was cheered by the fishermen, who for the rest of the day made a fuss, repeating how lucky I was. They said that only one other person who ever went out with them had spotted vaquitas.

After *Sitio* 35, where Paco released c-pod 2607 from its mooring line and then connected and lowered 2620 into the water, he shared an amazing story.

He and his CONANP colleague Ramon Arozamena had gone out to exchange c-pods in the fall of 2011 and saw two vaquitas in the refuge, one big and one little. Meanwhile, Alán and their dad, Javier, radioed to say that they were watching four vaquitas, so Paco and Ramon headed over to meet them. Eventually, there were nine vaquitas milling around the two pangas. For a species nearly always alone or in twosomes, it was a remarkable sighting, the largest group ever encountered. The men stayed with the porpoises—or, rather, the porpoises stayed with the men—for two full hours.

Paco proudly showed me video of the event. "People say vaquitas don't jump," he laughingly interjected as I watched one lurch out of the water. As silly as the maneuver appeared, sloppy and low, not at all like a dolphin's graceful leap, it did qualify as a jump. Taken by Paco's easy manner, friendliness, optimism, and knowledge, I asked him more about his life as a biologist.

"I'm born here. Born in San Felipe. All my grandfathers and fathers and brothers, my friends and cousins are fishermen," he said. "*Como pescador soy nacido.*" I am born a fisherman.

But Paco's real passion is science. Like me, he is fascinated with the ecological twisting and folding of assorted lives within a single habitat. He told me what he knew about Alto Golfo before the fishermen came in the 1920s. Back then, he said, schools of totoaba churned the waters, giant sea bass charted the deep, manta rays sailed en masse, and black-and-white killer whales and sharks of every shape and size circled an abundance of prey.

"Already there is far less life here," Paco told me. "Less and less every year."

Another story followed, this one passed down from his grandfather about a full-grown blue whale, *Balaenoptera musculus*, that had gotten caught in the chains of a big shrimp trawl. Apparently, the hundred-plus-foot whale, entangled and frightened, was dragging the vessel and its occupants through the waters of Alto Golfo. Repeating what he'd been told, Paco said, "The fishermen from nearby boats rushed over and worked together to cut the chain." The next morning, they found the whale dead on the beach with the chain in its mouth and around its body.

And so it went. C-pod by c-pod, we fell into a rhythm of waypoints and stories. By ten o'clock, the wind had kicked up, and the ride began to feel more like a rodeo than a drag race, with every robust wave causing a crash and rattle of fiberglass. Despite the bumping and jarring, Alán never gave up his speed—or his humor. Behind us, he could be seen yelling out jokes, his smoker's teeth brandished in an enthusiastic smile. Even though nobody could hear a word of his comedy due to the wind rushing over our faces, he let out big belly laughs, slapping his hand against the steering wheel in self-amusement. I giggled at him, knowing that I, too, was enjoying my own private celebration.

That pair of *dorsales* was forever burned into my memory.

July is the season of fireworks, even in Mexico, but that night's pyrotechnics—glorious as they would be, shooting from the beaches of San Felipe and bursting in splendid brilliance over the moonlit Vermilion Sea—could never compare to my internal fireworks after glimpsing two healthy, free-living vaquitas.

In the weeks and months following my return home, promise unfolded like a flag. Organizations and institutions around the world began vigorously voicing support for vaquita. As more and more international measures were announced, monthly news breaks generated a palpable sense that, at long last, the species' trajectory toward extinction might be diverted.

Totoaba were getting more protection too. By August 2016, Sea Shepherd was engaged in a powerful new campaign, Operation Angel de la Guarda. Like a guardian angel, the *Farley Mowat* was tracking totoaba on their migratory loop. With the Mexican Navy as backup, the crew was prepared to confiscate nets and investigate questionable pangas, applying pressure to midgulf poachers as they had in the Upper Gulf.

On the political front, the Center for Biological Diversity was seeking trade sanctions, urging the Obama administration to "certify Mexico for failing to enforce a ban on totoaba trade . . . [and] ban the import of Mexican seafood and other wildlife until the illegal totoaba trade ends."

In addition, UNESCO, the United Nations Educational, Scientific and Cultural Organization, was calling for a permanent gillnet ban in the Upper Gulf of California. To make its intentions clear, the United Nations was considering pulling its designation for the Sea of Cortez as a World Heritage Site, an action that could weaken Mexico's tourism industry.

In a subsequent report, UNESCO declared that "the Integral Strategy for the Protection of the Vaquita that is implemented as an emergency measure since April 2015 has not delivered the expected results. . . . Illegal fishing of the totoaba continues with few illegal fishermen actually being prosecuted due to complex inter-institutional responsibilities to detect, determine, halt and prosecute illegal activities." That report also stated that "CONAPESCA and INAPESCA, responsible for the establishment of a viable alternative fishing program and permits, have been largely absent in the implementation of the Integral Strategy for the Protection of the Vaquita thereby contributing to its failure."

So, when Mexican president Enrique Peña Nieto sat down with US president Barack Obama on July 22, 2016, the pressure was on. In the wake of that transnational tête-à-tête, an exciting announcement was posted on the White House website: "Mexico will make permanent a ban on the use of gillnets in all fisheries throughout the range of the vaquita in the upper Gulf of California."

A permanent gillnet ban. All fisheries. It was fantastic news.

In September, at the 2016 World Conservation Congress, more than ten thousand delegates of the International Union for Conservation of Nature voted on an array of vital conservation initiatives. Among them, Motion 13 dealt with the plight of *Phocoena sinus*. After a lengthy justification, outlining specific concerns regarding the potential extinction of a critically endangered species, IUCN members urged Mexico to "hasten the implementation of gillnet alternatives" and to "review current compensation programmes to ensure full compensation to fishermen and communities supporting vaquita-safe alternatives." Motion 13 further implored seafood importers to promote fishing methods that preserved the lives of vaquitas and prevailed on the Convention on International Trade in Endangered Species (CITES) and the International Police Organization (better known as INTERPOL) to assist all involved governments and organizations "in combating the illegal international trade in totoaba products."

Shortly thereafter, CITES took the baton. Its seventeenth meeting of the Conference of the Parties, called CoP17, was held in Johannesburg, South Africa. There, Mexico, China, and the United States—the three countries most enmeshed in the criminal smuggling of totoaba swim bladders—were tasked with opening up cross-department communications regarding all criminal detainments and seizures of contraband. CITES leaders made clear that a more unified trinational effort must come to bear if vaquita is to survive.

When the International Whaling Commission met in Portorož, Slovenia, in October 2016, it was asked to address an emergency Resolution on the Critically Endangered Vaquita. Submitted by twenty-one nations, the resolution pointed to a history of inaction. "Noting that the Commission first passed Resolution 1994-3, which acknowledged the immediate need to eliminate incidental catches of vaquita throughout the entire range of the species" and "recalling IWC Resolution 2007-5 which urged members of the IWC and the world community to support Mexico's efforts to prevent the extinction of the vaquita by reducing bycatch to zero in the immediate future and assisting in providing financial resources and technical as well as socioeconomic expertise" and "the repeated recommendations of the IWC Scientific Committee, CIRVA and IUCN that gillnets must be eliminated from the vaquita's range in order to reduce bycatch to zero consensus," the drafting committee "expresses deep concern that the vaquita numbers less than 59 animals and is facing imminent extinction."

Not surprisingly, the whaling nations of Japan and Iceland attempted to block the resolution, claiming that the IWC doesn't have jurisdiction over *Phocoena sinus* because it's a small cetacean, yet despite debate, the resolution passed. It pushes Mexico to "eliminate any exemptions to the [gillnet] ban" and urges all IWC governments "to support Mexico's efforts to prevent the extinction of the vaquita."

By November, Lorenzo had garnered the necessary funds and authority to initiate a new strategy that he had mentioned to me over the summer: a multi-institutional ghost net removal project. The objective is to extract derelict gear from the waters in and around vaquita habitat, which will not only make Alto Golfo safer for the remaining porpoises, but will also make the region more conducive for testing alternative fishing gear. Trials have always been stymied by a slew of vagrant nets; freed of submersed obstacles, new and more effective testing can readily commence.

The ghost net project is a collaboration comprising several Mexican governmental institutions, including SEMARNAT, INECC, the Navy, the environmental police, CONANP, and the secretary of national defense; several large nongovernmental organizations, including Sea Shepherd, World Wildlife Fund, and Museo de la Ballena; and forty-five artisanal shrimp fishermen from Pesca ABC, including those from Islas del Golfo Co-Op. The coalition was already searching out and removing unattended fishing equipment in and around the Vaquita Refuge. It was arduous work. From mid-October to mid-November, the team retrieved twenty longlines and fifty-eight nets. Some of those gillnets were old ghosts—*redes fantasma*, wayward souls, lost or abandoned at sea—but most were recently set totoaba nets.

Then, December 2016 came like the cherry on a sundae. Mexico's legislative branch was finally poised to reform the Federal Penal Code against Organized Crime, imposing two to eighteen years of imprisonment for poaching *Totoaba macdonaldi*.

What's more, China sponsored its first Totoaba Enforcement Workshop. "About 100 enforcement officers from fisheries, market control, customs and coast guard in Guangdong province attended the workshop, where they learned the conservation status of Totoaba and Vaquita (*Phocoena sinus*) and to identify Totoaba maw," reported the CITES-China website. The event "featured information sharing sessions with representatives from Hong Kong SAR, Mexico and the U.S., who shared their hands-on experience and efforts to combat the trafficking."

Anyone reading this news would be heartened. I certainly was.

Unfortunately, I would soon discover that things had been sliding downhill in the place that mattered most. As international declarations of protection were being ceremoniously documented into human history, the situation in the Gulf of California was rapidly deteriorating.

Sea Shepherd had withdrawn from Operation Angel de la Guarda due to cartel threats and a no-show Navy. When the gillnet ban prevented shrimping season's normal start in September, a protest rally in San Felipe reportedly drew a thousand fishermen. The assembly proved nonviolent, but the community was clearly growing restless. And INECC, which had increased the number of c-pods from forty-six to ninety-three with plans to maintain them year-round, had to retrieve all those devices. Even with all legal fisheries closed, there were too many boats on the water and too much risk of data loss.

As the mighty totoaba, unaware of any societal goings-on, rounded the most southern point of its migration path and carved up along the mainland shores toward its annual spawning grounds, outlaws in Alto Golfo were ready and waiting to seize a new bounty of *buches*. They were soon casting nets and grabbing endangered fish like drunkards at a beer fest. Many pangas were completely lacking numbers on the hull—nobody was even bothering to try to look legal. Emboldened men wearing balaclavas plundered the sea in broad daylight.

"The poachers are much more threatening than they ever were before—they are not afraid of anyone," stressed a conservation manager. With new Navy commander Marco Pescina Ávila in charge, there is no longer a visible military presence in San Felipe as there was earlier in 2016. Despite the brazen increase in illegal activity, streets and beaches are patently unattended. And whispers of corruption run through town like restless mice.

"It's scary. And it's happening because enforcement is terrible, so there's no power to stop them," the manager told me. "This is a matter of national security."

CHAPTER 10

Witnessing Extinction

A BABY VAQUITA HAD WASHED UP on the beach twenty miles south of San Felipe.

She was not just a baby. She was a premie, with her umbilical cord still dangling. Lacking any marks on her fragile skin, she had presumably been expelled while her mother flailed to death in a gillnet.

I heard the news from Armando. Having just arrived at the INECC condo for another visit, I was helping him prepare a few c-pods while Gustavo was out running errands with the new field coordinator. As I dropped batteries into the long tubes, Armando asked if I'd heard about the baby and showed me a photo on his computer. My heart pitched into my throat.

The tiny, black form looked deflated, pressed almost flat against the sand, as if the gravity of existence were simply too much to bear. The photo was taken on March 12, 2017, practically a year to the day of my first visit and those gruesome images of Ps2.

I would later read a *Tech Times* article that said, "Mexico's minister for agriculture, Jose Calzada, asserted that the government is doing everything to protect the vaquita. He claimed an 'ambitious program' is in the pipeline to salvage them." The article explained that "the baby vaquita's corpse would be sent for examination at a lab in San Francisco to test for toxic substances and pathogens."

Again with the red tide.

I thought back to scientist Omar Vidal's report of a premature fetus among the dead he examined in 1995. Through the years, how many infants have expired before they could make a single sonar click or take their first sip of milk? Lives cut short. The forfeiture of so much potential.

Here's how it should have gone. We can calculate that the mother of the neonate became pregnant in the late spring of 2016. Carrying her developing fetus for approximately eleven months, two months longer than a human child, she would have given birth to her daughter sometime in late March 2017. That little girl would have arrived into the watery world looking something like a shiny gray watermelon. She would then have nursed for six to twelve months, drinking nutrient-rich milk from the mammary slits on her mother's abdomen. In time, she would have grown into a stout, active juvenile and then a sleek, healthy sub-adult. She would not have reached sexually maturity until after her third or possibly up to her sixth birthday; thereafter, she would have become a mother herself, perhaps delivering a new son or daughter every other year through her adult life. With any luck, she might have reached a life span of more than twenty years before passing away of natural causes, leaving a vibrant lineage of offspring and great-offspring.

Instead, she was dead before her first breath.

It is to such devastating consequence that vaquitas generally give birth between February and April, a period that coincides with the high season for totoaba. Now, with so few individuals left, the loss of this single unborn calf—the slaughtered promise of her life—seemed a blow beyond all reckoning. Yet I knew that anyone focused on the big picture of bycatch would see the premie as mere statistic.

Spring poaching was rampant, and the toll to marine life was stagger-ing. Just since the New Year, I was told that ten dead whales, countless dolphins, and one sea turtle had washed up along the shores near San Felipe. It is a disturbing reminder that vaquita is not the only species to be concerned about.

Some of the victims possessed obvious signs of entanglement. One beached whale carcass seen by a local man named Dale Vinnedge "had a totoaba net in the back of its mouth and wrapped around its body." Another, a legally protected Bryde's whale found floating in the Upper Gulf of California by Sea Shepherd, was bound in a deadly tangle of knots that spoke of a desperate struggle. The great animal had writhed and twisted, gasping for air before the trussing stole its last breath.

On February 11, 2017, alone, Sea Shepherd added fourteen long-beaked common dolphins to the death toll. The animals were reported by the organization to be afloat in Alto Golfo, some "with net marks on their bodies." (Poignantly, February 14 is World Love for Dolphins Day.)

Sometime in January, a photo of a dead vaquita had arrived at CONANP from a trustworthy source. Although the animal's body was never recovered, it was considered the first verified porpoise victim of the season. Woefully, it wasn't just the decimation of Alto Golfo marine life that made matters so grim. At least one human had also recently died in the water.

On January 25, 2017, while Sea Shepherd was running its standard patrols, the crew spotted a panga with four men fishing illegally. Caught in the spotlight of the *Farley Mowat*, the poachers immediately fled, but after igniting their motor and zipping into the dark, their panga lurched to an abrupt stop, as if the propeller caught a net. A splash agitated the icy, black waters. When the *Farley* moved closer, a blue sweatshirt was seen thrashing in the sea.

Man overboard!

The Sea Shepherd crew jumped to action, quickly tossing two life rings, one of which the drowning man was able to grab. He was too cold and exhausted to climb the ship's rope ladder, however, so a crane was used to haul him on deck, where medical personnel began emergency care. That is when the event turned truly chilling.

Lolling onto his back, the fisherman sounded desperate. "*Hay otro amigo abajo!*" There is another friend down!

There's another person in the water?

"*Sí, sí!*" he replied.

It was a tireless night followed by a heartbreaking day. Despite a nineteen-hour search with all the local resources of the Mexican Navy and Sea Shepherd—ships, Zodiacs, and drones—the second fisherman, the friend, was never found.

Local communities were hurt and angered by the news. In several subsequent online comments, they blamed Sea Shepherd, the government, and everybody else working with vaquita conservation. They said that they were tired of people putting the lives of animals over the welfare of humans. I could appreciate their position, but the resentment seemed somewhat misdirected. Weren't totoaba poachers putting money over the welfare of the people? Couldn't it be argued that avarice had sent that poor fisherman to his death?

I do not mean to imply that every cooperative is run by cartels, but as Oona once told me, "The leaders of the cooperatives, they're the one who own the pangas, the engines, and the permits. So they have huge power. And the other people in the communities are kind of like slaves to them because they can put a lot of pressure on them to go and fish. And that's why it's not the fault of the fishermen that are at sea but really the bosses that are sending them. The fishermen do not have much choice."

Fishermen were being pushed toward the dangers of poaching by the oppressive thumb of organized crime, and without any legal work or political recourse, their bitterness was rising to the surface. Misdirected or not, the first round of violence came as I was packing the car for my March trip to San Felipe.

~

Social friction, which had been coiling like a viper, struck with ferocity on the evening of March 8, 2017. A *La Voz* article wrote (translated), "Last night virtually all the people of El Golfo de Santa Clara made a violent demonstration."

The Obama administration's claim that no gillnets would be allowed in Alto Golfo notwithstanding, corvina was still exempt, and the season was due to commence. The uprising came on the heels of an announcement that no corvina permits would be issued because fishermen had failed to produce their environmental impact study, called an MIA, on time. MIAs, long compulsory but never enforced, provided a legal loophole for SEMARNAT to delay the fishery.

Regardless of being pledged another $4.5 million in federal compensation to offset any financial loss, the community was anything but compliant. Fifteen vehicles were damaged or overturned, including several government trucks and patrol boats set ablaze. Smoke filled the streets "among cries against the insensitivity of the Federal Government that for two years has not let them work," stated the *La Voz* article. Several officials were physically attacked, and three PROFEPA inspectors were said to have been beaten before their escape. "Municipal police who were to start their night shift had to return to their homes as they were not allowed into the village," the article continued.

San Felipe fishermen were also affected by the corvina delay, and the riots in El Golfo de Santa Clara seemed to put everyone's nerves on edge. When I arrived on March 12, I found myself tamping down feelings of apprehension. I had come to participate in the ghost net project, which, suspended since December, was scheduled to recommence. After a safety meeting with participating institutions, though, the effort was again postponed. The fishermen contractors for the project believed that it was too risky to be out on the water.

When I ran into Javier on the street, he said that things had definitely gotten worse, the dangers more palpable. He told me that during the ghost net project last fall, their boat was surrounded by four to five pangas, which he believes came from El Golfo de Santa Clara. The men were wearing masks and approached in a menacing manner. Although Javier gunned the motor and slipped away before any confrontation, he was still furious. "The Navy, they are supposed to be with us at all times. And they were not with us," he reported. "We will not go out again until they get the *bucheros* out of the water. We live here, we are taking their nets. It is not safe."

When I thanked Javier for his courage under such strain, he smiled nervously. "I just hope I don't end up like a Bible character that is killed for doing what's right."

He wasn't overreacting. Other people were nervous, too.

Friends of the Vaquita had recently changed its Facebook status to secret. That group was originally founded by US expat Dale Vinnedge in the spring of 2016, with the goal of uniting El Dorado Ranch residents into an action committee. Early on, local members held meetings and invited speakers. They even discussed plans for a vaquita festival. Eventually, though, it became clear that openly crusading was not a realistic option in San Felipe given the obvious strain on the fishermen and their families. By the time of my visit that March, the group was essentially defunct, mostly due to safety concerns. A now-private Facebook page, the last vestige of intent, displayed a comment under a totoaba net photo that read, "Be careful, Dale."

Things had worsened for vaquita, too, and dramatically so. Based on the summer acoustic data, the population was now half the previous figure: just thirty porpoises left.

The media was going berserk. In a press release from the Center for Biological Diversity, international program director Sarah Uhlemann said, "This shocking new report shows that vaquitas are on the verge of vanishing forever. We will lose this wonderful little porpoise from our planet—and soon—unless Mexico finally gets serious about banning gillnets and actually enforces the law."

A World Wildlife Fund report would propose that "wherever they are found (in water or on land) or however they are used (fishing, storage, selling or buying) . . . all gillnets in the Upper Gulf should be seized by authorities and destroyed. Any proof of possession or use of gillnets should be accepted as evidence in court."

The solution could not be stated better.

Still, it looked as though things might actually go in the opposite direction. The permanent gillnet ban was not permanent after all. Despite the agreement Mexican president Enrique Peña Nieto had made at the White House, he never published the decree in the *Diario Oficial de la Federación*, so nothing was set in stone. Permits could soon be reinstated.

Everyone seemed overtaxed by the crisis, including the acoustics team from INECC. Gustavo said, "Despite all the investment that we are making, it feels like we cannot do anything. It creates such sadness and frustration." To meet the demands of the moment, the scientists had "secretly" deployed six adjacent c-pods in the southern part of the Vaquita Refuge where active poaching overlaps two of the most acoustically active sites. With the ghost net project on hold, I was invited to assist the next exchange, and that's how I came to be helping Armando at the condo.

"This is not a regular sampling season for us," Armando explained, "but given the current situation, we decided to look at what's happening acoustically. We need to use moorings with no sign at the surface."

Because the data had to be retrieved pretty much weekly and Gustavo was swamped with other work, Mauricio Nájera Caballero, a gentle, spectacled marine biologist from Mexico City, had taken over as field coordinator. Mauricio and I would eventually be charging across the wild blue in the wee hours of the morning, with Rafael "Gordis" Sánchez and Victor Orozco, two Islas del Golfo Co-Op contractors. Victor, I would learn, did not believe in vaquitas until five years ago when he accidentally caught one in his net. Now he's dedicated to their safety.

As the twinkling lights of San Felipe lit the black horizon, we pulled our coats tight and began the six c-pod exchanges. The cold water lay flat and still, like an accomplice sworn to secrecy. Working furtively without buoys or flags to guide us, Gordis relied solely on GPS and read coordinates off the field log by the light of my cell phone. At each of the waypoints, a grappling hook was dragged around until it snagged an anchor line. It was a slow and taxing affair. Even so, I was privately grateful to be doing something familiar. With so much community unrest, it seemed prudent not to be collecting nets.

Of course, prudence is not in the vocabulary of Sea Shepherd. As the sun rose in a blush of crimson, we could see the silhouettes of its ships in the distance. Still on patrol for Operation Milagro, Sea Shepherd's latest cast of volunteers was towing phantom rays and bravely confiscating whatever gear they could.

~

Oona was late.

Without cell reception, there was no option but to wait for her, so I sat in my car outside a community of rental homes in San Felipe, staring at sand berms quietly baking in the sun. After twenty minutes, she arrived by foot, winded and clearly stressed.

"Are you okay?" I asked.

"I'm sorry, I lost track of time," said the captain, pushing several strands of loose hair from her face. "It's been totally crazy. I've been on the phone nonstop because we have a . . . a situation," she said, pausing to choose the right word.

She explained, "One of our ships found an active gillnet with sixty-seven totoaba. And the Navy hasn't shown up yet. It's been three hours!"

It's no wonder she was stressed. Sea Shepherd is dependent on the Mexican Navy for protection, and sitting in Alto Golfo with well more than $1 million in uncut *buches* was like standing in a Juárez alley holding a duffel bag of stolen cocaine. Later that evening, I picked Oona up at the docks and took her back to Sea Shepherd's rental house, which is made available for crew members sleeping ashore. There, she filled me in on the details.

Originally there were sixty-eight totoaba, but one corpse was lost as they pulled in the five-hundred-foot net. One fish still alive was released back to the sea. Eventually, the Navy showed up, and the remaining bodies were taken into evidence—their swim bladders carved out and destroyed by the environmental police. Although no one would ever stockpile their organs in a Chinese safe or slurp them in fish maw soup, the sad fact remained that sixty-six lives came to nothing but an over-stuffed incinerator.

"What happened during Operation Angel de Guarda?" I asked as Oona stirred maple syrup into a pot of hot green tea. I had heard that Sea Shepherd's plans to follow and protect totoaba had also turned into a . . . situation.

She told me that they had to abandon the campaign because their efforts were ineffectual. "The Navy was supposed to meet us down there, but they never showed up," she said. Her face was drawn, and she lacked the cheerful spirit I remembered from last year.

She said that the *Farley* was working in waters notorious for poaching as well as piracy. The situation got dicey. In early September 2016, during a refueling trip to the Upper Gulf, a crew member named John Paul Geoffroy—whom I'd met during my stay on the ship—received

Sea Shepherd crew with sixty-six dead totoaba on the deck of the Farley Mowat *with the Mexican Navy Defender alongside. (Courtesy of Sea Shepherd)*

a threatening phone call from a man claiming to be a cartel member. "They knew my name, mother's and daughter's name, what I looked like, a home address in Chile," JP was quoted as saying. "They knew the boat's name, its movements and said if we go back south my daughter and I will be dead."

The ship didn't go back south. It wasn't worth the risk.

I asked Oona if she was planning to try again this year. "I don't know yet," she answered, staring into her teacup. "I hope it will be possible. But we need to know if the Navy will be around. Or PROFEPA. Because just us in the middle of wildlife trafficking and cartels—it's not going to work."

～

A week after I spoke with Oona, another dangerous situation made headlines.

I would hear the story from Mauricio, who happened to be in town when a vehicle with a megaphone drove through San Felipe announcing that the following day there would be a peaceful meeting on the *malecón* to discuss the situation with Sea Shepherd.

The next day, March 26, a storm of people showed up. Several pick-eters raised handmade posters. One sported a picture of netted fish and said: *El mar es de quien lo trabaja y lo navega.* The sea belongs to those who work and navigate it. Another showed the Sea Shepherd flag with a red circle and a slash: *Fuera el gobierno.* Outside the government. The main attraction, however, was an enormous green banner. It stretched along the sidewalk for a full block with several names written in big, black block letters: BARB TAYLOR, LORENZO ROJAS, OMAR VI-DAL, OONA LAYOLLE. (Armando sardonically joked about his name being left off.) For a meeting purported to have peaceful intent, the scene certainly appeared ominous.

When Sunshine Rodriguez, president of the Federation of Coastal Fishermen in San Felipe—an alleged crime leader with political aspira-tions—took center stage, he incited the crowd with fury-fueled rhetoric. Once spectators were whipped to a jeering froth, Sunshine proclaimed that two hundred pangas would radicalize on March 30 to drive Sea Shepherd out of the region, adding that if the conservationists refused to depart, the fishermen would burn their organization's ships. To em-phasize his threat, a panga with "Sea Shepherd" scrawled along its side was set on fire in the middle of the street. Around the fireball, cheers of solidarity carried orange flames and black smoke skyward.

The Mexican government immediately intervened. The titanic na-val warship *Armada Durango* was sent to ride alongside Sea Shepherd for several days, and a restraining order was issued against ringleader

Sunshine and his angry band of fisherman (although no one was ever arrested for the unlawful pyre).

When would-be terrorists arrived at the marina on March 30, police were on high alert, and the vast majority of pangas were prevented from launching. The protesters, it turned out, were mostly all bark, and after lurking around for several hours, hostility wore to boredom, and everyone wandered home. Violence had been pacified, and Sea Shepherd was safe. But the fears that drove the fishermen's demonstration were not as easily dissipated as a street full of protestors.

"I was thinking all afternoon to publish this, the situation that I live, as well as thousands of families in the port of San Felipe BC . . . that like mine depend on the Fishing," wrote resident Ross Miranda in a Facebook post. "There are no sources of Work in San Felipe, what will each of the fishermen do, where are they going to be used ?? . . . Many young people like me could be left without the opportunity to realize our dreams. . . . I am absolutely sure that an Environmentalist would not have the time to answer this, but . . . What would they feel Them when they get home and not have to offer their children?"

Poverty and conservation can never coexist. Why, then, doesn't Mexico's million-dollar government compensation program fund alternative-career education and vaquita-friendly gear, which could earn men their income instead of lining the pockets of a few fishing moguls? With job options available, this entire conflict might have been avoided.

"Sea Shepherd is not in the area to oppose legal fishing activities," Oona later said in a *Maritime Executive* interview. "Sea Shepherd's actions are focused on illegal fishing, and the only fishermen who have any reason to be angry with the Sea Shepherd ships are those whose illegal activities are being disrupted and shut down by Sea Shepherd crews."

Unfortunately, no one fares well on the cusp of scarcity.

~

Biologist Eric Dinerstein's book *The Kingdom of Rarities* explores the natural histories of several wildlife species that reside in small numbers. Some were driven to scarcity by human activity, whereas others came by it naturally. Dinerstein describes two types of rarity: geographic rarity (inhabiting a limited or narrow range) and population rarity (being "hard to find even in its favored habitat"). Using the author's words, vaquita is "twice rare."

It is this rarity that prompts some people, even a few scientists, to argue that the species is doomed to evolutionary extinction. They assert that because *Phocoena sinus* was never abundant, even prior to gillnets, limited genetic diversity is threatening its survival. Inbreeding, they say, has brought vaquita to the end of its natural existence, and the species is destined to disappear in as few as ten to twenty years.

"I have to call bullshit," Lorenzo retorted when I brought it up to him. Then, resuming his usual composure, he added, "There is no biological indication that the species is heading for extinction. To the contrary, vaquitas reproduce. We have seen calves, and they are healthy. They feed properly. They have a flexible diet, so they have the chance to choose what they are going to eat. Of all the vaquitas killed as bycatch in gillnets, we have never seen one that looked sick or had an empty stomach." In addition, necropsies have never revealed disease or lethal parasite loads.

"Vaquitas are very resourceful animals," he said. "Stop killing them and they will recover."

Early on, Lorenzo and Barb ran several statistical models to try to gauge the pregillnet population size of the species. Unfortunately, there are no records in Mexico to assist such an endeavor. The best model, made by Armando—using all available data, including landing weights for gillnetted fish, which were not regularly reported, along with piecemeal mortality statistics—suggested three to five thousand individuals.

Another model showed the number upward of twelve thousand, but Lorenzo says that seems too high.

Dinerstein wrote that certain species may fundamentally exist in small numbers, which was likely the case with vaquita. Accordingly, if their population was around five thousand in the 1920s, one should not presume that it had historically suffered a decline from, say, twenty thousand. It is quite possible that the habitat only ever supported about five thousand porpoises.

"And their genetic composition shows that," said Lorenzo. He and Barb coauthored a scientific paper demonstrating that the limited genetic variability found in *Phocoena sinus* is not cause for concern because it came from historical fixation rather than recent decline. Lorenzo explained, "Because vaquita probably always lived in small populations, they probably purged their lethal alleles, and that's how they adapted for survival."

Alleles are inherited genetic material that determine an organism's characteristics. A lethal allele is a mutant that causes premature death. The lethal alleles revealed by inbreeding are recessive, meaning that you need two copies for the deadly effects to manifest. So, when a population crashes and there is no choice but to mate with close relatives, more lethal alleles are exposed. Generation by generation, the species' biological fitness is reduced—it's called a population bottleneck. Even if the tribe recovers, it remains at risk. On the other hand, in yet another marvel of nature, populations that are naturally small seem to tolerate inbreeding because over thousands of years, the lethal alleles have been exposed and purged.

The argument for evolutionary extinction, however, can also be based on shifts in the environment. Some people contend that the population is dying out because of climate change. It's true that instabilities in water temperature may affect ocean ecologies in truly dire ways, but because vaquita is adapted for life in the Upper Gulf, where warmer waters and

WITNESSING EXTINCTION   157

dramatic seasonal fluctuations are the norm, the species should be at no greater risk than any other facing the challenges ahead. It certainly cannot be argued that the perils of climate change make salvaging vaquita a moot cause.

Not to be deterred, many Pesca officials opine that vaquita is in dire straits because of environmental changes wrought when the Colorado River quit pouring into Alto Golfo. With the completion of the Glen Canyon Dam in 1963, the United States gained control over the southern watershed, and by regulating drainage and extracting resources for agriculture, the water in the lower riparian area was essentially turned off, like a faucet gone dry. However dramatic the aesthetic transformations of the surrounding landscape, though, the diminishment of fresh water did not seem to hurt vaquita—or totoaba, for that matter.

In a 2017 scientific paper that comprehensively reviewed published research on the topic and cited several hundred references, Richard C. Brusca and colleagues wrote, "The marine ecosystem of the Northern Gulf remains rich in nutrients, high in biodiversity and productivity, and appears to continue to be healthy, except for the impacts of historical and current fisheries." They went on to state, "There also is no evidence that reduced Colorado River flow has negatively impacted the health of the critically endangered vaquita porpoise, and assertions that it has done so deflect attention from the actual cause of decline—bycatch in legal and illegal gillnet fisheries."

That the evolutionary-extinction theory appears unfounded does not stop opponents from taking other angles of attack. Some rivals have now put forth a truly absurd supposition: that great white sharks are gobbling up all the vaquitas. Others say that INECC is falsifying the rapid decline of the species and that the acoustic data are not sound.

"They never trust our acoustic monitoring program," Lorenzo once told me. "When we presented the first 34 percent decline in 2014 at the presidential commission in front of the minister of environment, they said they could not accept the data." Luis Fleischer has consistently argued that it's impossible to assess cetacean populations using acoustics. Yet another official maintained that Armando's data were simply not reliable because he had failed to do any calibrations on the vaquita's swim bladder.

Swim bladder? Porpoises are mammals, not fish. They don't have swim bladders.

That official nevertheless insisted that vaquitas would need to be placed in a pool to measure the response of their swim bladders to acoustic pulses. He clearly didn't grasp that c-pods record cetacean sonar clicks, not sounds bouncing off organs.

INAPESCA even proposed doing the 2015 vaquita survey itself. How frustrating it must be for experts like Lorenzo to attempt productive communication amid such folly.

Having spent twenty years studying and working on behalf of vaquita, Lorenzo remembers the days when there were more than six hundred of them in the Gulf of California. He has endured a lot of frustration and seen a lot of death since then. "Basically, when we started, the population mortality was about 8 percent per year," he recalled. "The goal was always to eliminate gillnets, and that didn't happen. But by pushing hard and negotiating and keeping the vaquita on the agenda of the federal government, we were able to reduce that decline to something around 4.5 percent. And we kept down the fishing effort, the number of boats, for some years."

He said if the totoaba-smuggling scheme had not blindsided everyone in 2012, the population might actually be stabilizing now instead of plummeting toward extinction. "When I was a bachelor's student discussing vaquita with my professors, what was killing them was bycatch in totoaba nets. There had been an illegal totoaba fishery for years, everyone knew about it. But this explosion was totally unexpected. Never in my wildest dreams would I have imagined that we would come back to that when we were doing so well."

~

Looking at the photo of the premie on Armando's computer, I felt despair sweeping into my heart. It had been a year since my first visit to San Felipe, and it seemed that nothing had been fixed. Despite all the resources brought to bear, almost half the remaining vaquitas had been killed.

The population had gone from sixty to thirty, and the figure of thirty was actually derived from the summer monitoring season—the c-pods I'd exchanged with Paco more than six months ago. Given the age of the data and the current state of poaching, thoughts of the future could scarcely be endured.

On March 29, 2017, the tiny fetus would be labeled Ps5 and placed on a stainless-steel table at the Tijuana Zoo. She stretched just two feet and weighed five and one-third pounds. Her itty-bitty dorsal fin was still creased and folded, as it would have been in her mother's womb. To perform the examination, veterinarian Frances Gulland donned yellow gloves that extended to her shoulders. She handled the baby with gentle compassion.

Attending the necropsy was CIRVA member Robert Brownell, the first biologist to fully describe *Phocoena sinus*. It has been thirty-five years since the publication of his landmark paper describing the exploitation of vaquita, in which he wrote, "If good enforcement capabilities are available, this indefinite [totoaba] ban will decrease the number of porpoises killed in the totoaba fishery." That was 1982. Three and a half decades later, he is still standing witness to the slaughter of vaquita as bycatch.

Ps5 was not alone that day. She was to be joined by two other casualties, Ps4 and Ps6.

Ps4 was found on March 19, a week after Ps5, but he was first to be necropsied, which explains his number. When Sea Shepherd discovered the eighty-two-pound male in the Vaquita Refuge, he was covered with deep knife wounds, the kind of damage potentially made when cutting away monofilament—or stabbing a body in hope it sinks.

Ps6, an extremely decomposed calf, was retrieved near the port of San Felipe. The corpse, which was missing its head, actually turned out to be a long-beaked common dolphin. The cause of its death could not be determined.

Another vaquita, Ps7, would show up on April 20. This yearling was spotted adrift in the refuge with crosshatched markings marring her skin like totoaba-net tattoos. Yet another juvenile victim would turn up on April 25, and like so many gone before, the cause of death for Ps8 was "trauma, entanglement."

So, at least five porpoises, two adults and three young, would perish in four months. As I sat with Armando, prepping c-pods, I simply had to ask. "How many vaquitas do you think are still alive?" Armando is a scientist, and his penchant for data-substantiated precision makes him uncomfortable with speculation. I pressed gently, "I know it's just a guess, but . . . "

He sat utterly still for a few painful moments as a dampness found his eyes. His answer was almost inaudible.

"Maybe fifteen."

CHAPTER 11

Saving Bigfoot

I woke up on a Puerto Peñasco beach, north of town. The sun was still hiding below the horizon, but the stars knew their shift was over. Already dimming, they were but a few delicate freckles on the face of the cool, gray sky. I yawned and stretched and sat up on my sleeping bag to take in the seascape. The tide was coming in. Long licks of water reached toward me over polished fragments of shell. There was no crash and roar as with the arching waves of the open Pacific, just a rhythmic hush, a steady pulse, as low and compulsory as a heartbeat.

I slipped out from under my sheet and felt the sand conform to my soles. A long walk took me over and around boulders of black stone, namesakes of Rocky Point. Scattered between, seaweed and fish skeletons waited to be reclaimed by the sea.

Having time alone to breathe and think among the workings of nature always settles my spirit, and this morning was no different. The spinning details of contentious politics and dwindling populations were momentarily laid aside as I scooped up shells and examined the soft hues of pinks and whites and browns that tumbled in my palm. Every shell is a life in representation, a life that came and went. Millions upon millions of lives, layered, stacked, and polished to an oily shine, formed the moist foundation on which I now stood.

The water stretched westward into a distant mist where I envisioned it lapping the shores of San Felipe. Between this beach and that one, I thought, are the last living vaquitas. Just knowing that they were swimming beneath the same morning sky filled me with reverence. But, oh, how their watery world has changed since the time when the shells at my feet were whole, moving, alive. The story of vaquita is no longer one of ancient waters swarming with life, of pristine habitats and balanced ecologies. It is no longer the story of original design.

Now it is the story of humans.

Who are we? What has meaning? Where is our place in the fragile lives of porpoises?

If I wanted to get to the root of my quest to understand why vaquitas are dying in gillnets, I needed to take a broader view. I needed to delve into the mind of *Homo sapiens* and investigate the tricks and convolutions of our perception. Shifting baselines, for example, are but one hiccup in the advancement of human intelligence.

Baselines are foundational reference points. Against them we measure rate and degree of change. They are not merely tools of science. We all intuitively establish baselines, which we use to gauge change around us. Baselines are what prompt older people to state generalized perceptions such as television shows are more violent, the world is less happy, or technology is more complicated than it used to be. Youngsters lacking equivalent baselines inevitably fail to recognize the difference.

For example, if a chocolate bar costs $1 when I am a child but over the course of my life goes up to $8, I will spend my old age lamenting that the price of chocolate is too expensive. On the other hand, a young boy buying the same candy will not balk at the $8 price because it's all he knows. My baseline is $1. His baseline is $8. The baseline has shifted.

If we apply this concept to the environment, a frightening comprehension emerges.

Ask a graybeard for a fish story, and you are bound to be regaled about a childhood catch that was "this big!" Any listening kids will giggle. They'll think that he's exaggerating or that his memory has failed—after all, no fish is that big.

Actually, fish really were that big. In fact, fishing preferentially removes larger specimens, causing a steady decrease in overall size. When the old man passes away, so does his baseline. Every generation naturally accepts the planet as it is, with ever-smaller fish, fewer birds, and less ice. That's how humans as a whole unwittingly overlook drastic and devastating changes to the environment. The unfolding declines are broken into a series of baselines—ever shifting—so the overall loss is never felt by a single generation, never suffered by a single soul.

Totoaba used to be seven-foot behemoths that migrated in schools so enormous they churned the sea. Thousands of vaquitas used to swim in the Gulf of California.

Not anymore.

What's the most upsetting part? We don't really miss them because we never knew those days. Intellectually appreciating loss is not the same as personally experiencing it.

As one might expect, shifting baselines are not always about declines. Take our human population, which has skyrocketed from five hundred million in 1500 to three billion in 1959 to our current seven and a half billion. Much to our downfall, the consequences of such conquering growth will never be fully grasped.

While big-scale changes elude us, there is another fickle trick of human perception that tangles our goals of benevolence. We even have a phrase for it: out of sight, out of mind.

〜

Although the myth that vaquita doesn't exist is categorically false, it's not entirely far-fetched. Like Bigfoot, vaquita is elusive. And with its numbers so low, the vast majority of fishermen from Puerto Peñasaco—and many from San Felipe and El Golfo de Santa Clara—have never glimpsed one. Think of how long it took before scientists could describe the physical appearance of *Phocoena sinus*. It was thirty years after the species was named. In many ways, the mystery of vaquita continues, and it leaves me wondering, can people ever really care about an animal they cannot see?

I often recall a conversation with my friend Maria Johnson at a cozy Arizona coffeehouse on a winter morning. Maria had just returned from doing field research based at the Kino Bay Center, about a five-hour drive south of Puerto Peñasco. Her focus of study was bycatch. As we sipped warm drinks, she described the demoralizing experience of mucking around in piles of dying fish and plunging her hands into flaccid, slime-coated bodies to carefully count gasping animals.

The official Spanish terms for bycatch are *captura incidental* and *fauna de acompañamiento*, but a lot of fishermen just call it *basura*. Trash. Hammerhead and angel sharks, cownose rays, endangered loggerhead sea turtles, shovelnose guitarfish, and, of course, juvenile totoaba become *basura*. In all, the long-running Kino Bay bycatch project has documented more than two hundred marine species caught in industrial shrimp trawls. Gratefully, no vaquitas have been found; the study area is too far south for them. But Maria does know of one very unexpected find: a seahorse.

This darling fish is recognized for its pointy snout, protuberant potbelly, and curlicue tail. It also has chameleon-like camouflage—armored plates with delicate protrusions, cryptically colored in goldenrod, orange, mottled pink, or brown to match the environment. The particular species found was a Pacific seahorse, *Hippocampus ingens*. Reaching a foot tall, it is the largest of all seahorses. And, as a vulnerable species, rare to the waters off Kino Bay and supposedly protected by law, its presence as bycatch was both sad and significant.

A poignant truth is that compassion for gilled vertebrates is low. Maria says that's because compassion stems from connection, and most people have never "connected" with a fish. When we do connect—with other humans and certain animals—we issue them value in our minds and then respond to that value. We act upon it. Just imagine seeing a family member, a beloved dog, or even a baby harp seal clubbed to death in a pool of blood. What's the normal gut response? It's horror and anger derived from deep and abiding compassion.

Knowing this truth, Maria spends time thinking up ways to foster compassion for fish. In her effort to change people's mind-sets about bycatch, she has discovered that certain interactions correlate directly with attitudes of concern. She's come up with four levels of connectivity equating to four degrees of compassion.

Level one is talking. Because most people have no knowledge of bycatch, any information is a start. If Maria just talks to people about bycatch, however, she rarely finds a sympathetic listener. No matter how compelling her descriptions of death, changes in mind-set are minimal. I'm loath to admit that while Maria spoke of her experiences on commercial fishing vessels—scenes far removed from the comforts of our velveteen chairs—I found myself admiring her silver earrings. Perhaps my attention to jewelry was a way of escaping the atrocities she bared.

Pictures apparently seem to help. That's level two. When Maria shows photos of bycatch, people suddenly relate a little more—they express better understanding and some degree of concern. We really are visual creatures. Seeing is believing.

The jump from photos to video, from level two to level three, is even more significant. Humans readily connect with moving images, which can trigger mirror neurons. Mirror neurons are believed to empathetically connect us to the movements and experiences of others. Maria told me that she can see the shift on people's faces as they watch fish thrash in agony. However, she says, even video rarely fosters long-term change. Although viewers may feel temporarily distraught, such emotions are fleeting. By living in a moviegoing culture, frequently exposed to projected violence, perhaps we have trained our brains to shake off disturbing footage.

Level four is the highest level of connectivity: firsthand experience. If Maria can take people out on a boat and let them not only see but also smell and touch the wreckage, they immediately "get it." Direct encounters can change mind-sets in permanent ways. Experience is the sword of change.

Unfortunately, it's just not possible to tap into level four on a regular basis. "If only we could grab people by the hand and take them out to see what is happening," said Maria, "we could fix so many problems. But of course we can't, so we are left trying to bridge a chiasmic gap—trying to talk and show photos and post videos in hopes of affecting whatever change we can."

One might assume that people would feel more compassion for vaquitas than fish. But without level four (we can't go out to see them), level three (there is no underwater video), or even level two (the only full-body photos of the porpoises are dead porpoises), there is a serious challenge with connecting.

Barb once told me, "You'd think that with the most endangered marine mammal on Earth, that you'd be able to get someone like *National Geographic* or *Animal Planet* to be interested. But they won't touch it. They want full-frame underwater video, and if they can't have that, tough, the species gets to go extinct."

Lorenzo said the same. When a major news organization called him, wanting to see live, charismatic vaquitas, he told them, "The only photos we have are dead vaquitas or just a small dorsal fin." The reporter lost interest. "I remember, the guy told me, 'It would be very cruel for the American public to see only dead vaquitas.' And I thought, you're having the Iraq War and people are being shot and killed and you're telling me that three vaquitas in a gillnet are too disturbing for the public? Jesus Christ."

So, for twenty years, there were no photos, no video, and no marketing. The destruction of vaquita (and other species in the Sea of Cortez) might have forever remained in the shadows if not for some creative thinkers who have found other ways to raise consciousness and inspire action in the world.

~

In addition to being a bycatch researcher, Maria is a fine artist who creates anatomically precise drawings of wildlife with riveting esoteric themes. When other avenues of connectivity fail her, artwork serves as a bridge. Her black-and-white stipple drawing of the seahorse—a simple rendering of *Hippocampus ingens* pickled in a jar of formaldehyde—has a deeply stirring effect.

Maria recently joined doctoral student Eric Magrane to develop an exhibit called *Bycatch* for the University of Arizona Museum of Art. Eric wrote poems to go with several of Maria's drawings, and the pairings were presented on plain white walls. Part of the poem next to the seahorse read as follows:

> This one specimen bleached white and is that your front pouch filled with little replicas of yourself, you the male who carries the babies, hundreds of little horses preserved forever in non-life . . . never to emerge.

If the collaborative series was designed to elicit empathy for the aquatic victims of the food industry, it worked. On opening night, the entire exhibit room was hushed by sadness.

Barb is another scientist tapping into the power of art. She has an online gallery of beautiful vaquita paintings she's created through the years. One I find particularly compelling juxtaposes China's panda and China's endangered drum fish, the bahaba, with Mexico's vaquita (panda of the sea) and totoaba—four species whose lives have become oddly intertwined. Another favorite shows three vaquitas swimming through a blue desert sky, flanked by ravens and spires of cactus—the desert porpoise. Barb also makes vaquita-themed pottery and jewelry; in fact, Oona wears a gorgeous copper wrist cuff that Barb crafted. The scientist-artist even fashioned labels for a VAQUITA wine, bottled by Fallbrook Winery in Southern California.

"Vaquita has a marketing problem," said Barb. "That's the reason that I got into producing vaquita artwork. People are so inundated with the stuff on their phone and computer that getting somebody's attention is a formidable task."

It's true. In a world deluged by technology, art can still get attention.

Guillermo Munro Colosio—better known to his fans as Memuco—is a Mexican artist and environmental activist. He has created more than thirty murals around Puerto Peñasco, many featuring vaquita. Among his works is an underwater world painted on the conjoining walls of a street corner, and both sides of the cascading steps near Playa Bonita are covered with his imaginings. Not surprisingly, Memuco's work stirs up some controversy. "I did a mural in City Hall in 2007," he told me, "and they completely destroyed it. All the fishermen went to complain and protest, and they vandalized it. The next mayor coming in just covered it all in white."

Luckily, the new town mayor is Memuco's cousin. Now, with municipal support, the environmental artist not only creates public installments, but also visits schools. His art-themed presentations—always free of charge—raise kids' awareness about the little porpoise native to the waters near their home.

"I teach children how to draw them and paint them. But before that,

I ask, 'Do you guys know what's a vaquita?' And from a group of twenty to thirty kids, only one or two will raise their hand. Tells you a lot. There's no education by their parents or by the schools or by the government. So it's just me going into the schools to do that."

Environmental outreach through the appeal of art is not a bad strategy. Consequently, I was thrilled to discover a giant mural while visiting Alto Golfo's tiniest village. What lone-wolf artist had decorated El Golfo de Santa Clara with oversized vaquitas? I immediately stopped to find out.

Leonardo Gonzales Rodriguez is a middle-aged father, a man of faith, and a quiet but confident conservationist who recently turned his house into an eco-canvas. When I met Leo, he had been painting for three months, a little each morning. Above our heads, where the roof beams form a peak, an Earth icon hovered beneath the eye of God. It gave a feeling that his enchanting porpoises (not to mention our serendipitous acquaintance) were being watched from on high.

As Leo's young wife tended their infant daughter, surrounded by puppies in the yard, I asked if promoting vaquitas ever made him nervous. No, he said. His community is neutral on the subject. "*No mala, no buena—no importante.*" Not bad, not good—not important. His neighbors have no mind for an animal they believe is "*fantastico*" (imaginary), and they don't care enough to worry whether the myth is right or wrong. Fishermen sometimes even stop to ask what kind of animal he's painting.

Needless to say, Leo is a believer. His brown eyes sparkled as he expressed his thoughts about the divinity of nature, and they opened to saucers when I shared the story of my vaquita encounter during the c-pod exchange. Indeed, as we talked and talked, he seemed genuinely excited to connect with a like-minded soul, and I was reminded of a saying they have in Mexico: *Dios los cria y ellos se juntan.* God makes them and they find each other. It's kind of like saying birds of feather

Artist-conservationist Leo Gonzales Rodriguez with a vaquita mural he painted on the side of his house in El Golfo de Santa Clara. (Brooke Bessesen)

flock together, except the literal translation is so much sweeter. It was a gift to find Leo.

∼

Art is not limited to paint and graphite. When it comes to promoting an elusive species, books have a role to play too. Writers are like magicians; they can conjure imageries from a hatful of letters and foster feeling without a single external prop. Indeed, through the art of story, vaquita comes alive in any location or time.

Memuco's father, Guillermo Munro Palacio, is an author. Among his titles, he has two about vaquita. One is a miniature-sized nonfiction piece, *Érase una vez: Una Vaquita Marina*, which translates to *Once Upon a Time: A Vaquita*. The other—a novel titled *No Me Da Miedo Morir*, or *I'm Not Afraid to Die*—is centered on Sonoran cartel activity, with vaquita in the subplot.

I also discovered Spanish comic books created specifically for young fishermen. Titles like *Milagro en el Alto Golfo* portray vaquita as the victim in an age-old battle between good and evil. In the end, grimacing poachers are always defeated by courageous (and indisputably handsome) fishermen, who stand strong for the future of their community. These conservation-themed comic books, published by Defenders of Wildlife in collaboration with other nongovernmental organizations, are disseminated around the Upper Gulf by a variety of local groups, including PROFEPA and Pronatura.

When I went looking for books about vaquita in the United States, I only found a few. All were self-published and written for, or by, children.

To write and illustrate *Vinny the Vaquita*, geophysicist Jen Gabler collaborated with her then-three-year-old son Sander. When a discussion about blue whales, the world's largest cetacean, prompted an internet search for the smallest one, the mother-son duo discovered vaquita—and the tragedy of gillnets. After hearing the meaning of "endangered" in the simplest possible terms, Sander insisted through his tears that they do something to help. Thus, a picture book was born.

While Jen managed a full-time job, sometimes writing through the night, Sander offered up rhyming couplets and assisted in directing the story. "He had very specific ideas about what colors I should use in the illustrations," Jen said of the experience. After the printed paperbacks arrived at their Texas home, Jen ordered sixty plush vaquitas—the number estimated to be alive at the time—and packaged up and sold Vaquita Adoption Packs, with profits going to conservation. It was such a clever idea that many people, myself included, quickly bought them out.

The only nonfiction book about vaquitas was written by Aidan Bodeo-Lomicky, who, at age thirteen, scribed *The Vaquita: The Biology of an Endangered Porpoise*. Aidan isn't just some kid who wanted to see his name in print. He's the real deal. It states on Amazon that 100 percent of Aiden's profits go toward vaquita conservation. Actually, by the time that he published his fifty-page introduction to *Phocoena sinus* in 2013, he had been posting news, poems, and artwork about the imperiled species for two full years.

How did an eleven-year-old boy from Bethlehem, Pennsylvania, become immersed in the plight of a porpoise in Mexico? That's when the goals of several individuals, of science and social media, began folding together into an exciting grassroots movement.

As the story goes, Aidan first learned of the endangered status of vaquita while browsing the Save the Whales website in 2011. Upset that people knew nothing of the species, he decided to launch V-log, short for Vaquita-blog. Aidan also emailed Save the Whales and was consequently connected with a biologist named Tom Jefferson. Tom is the director of VIVA Vaquita, the only organization exclusively dedicated to the species.

On one of my trips to California, Tom and I met at a cafe in the suburban outskirts of San Diego. He arrived in a blue vaquita T-shirt that read, "Without conservation, I have no porpoise." As a graduate student in the 1980s, Tom was a field assistant for Gregory Silber—the first scientist to record vaquita sonar clicks—and although he did other work thereafter, Tom has forever remained interested in *Phocoena sinus*.

During the 2008 vaquita sighting survey, he secured independent funding to do a photo expedition and identified four individuals based on natural dorsal fin markings. (Those animals were never sighted again.) He said his remarkable close-up images as well as the subsequent population decline announced by CIRVA—567 vaquitas down to 245—received lackluster appreciation in the media.

"After the initial flurry of activity, things just kind of stopped," said Tom. "That's when I realized what was really needed was a focus on environmental education, raising public awareness." He turned his attention to outreach efforts, establishing VIVA Vaquita in 2009 as the joint project of three US organizations: American Cetacean Society, Cetos

Research Organization, and Save the Whales. That's how Aidan's email ended up in Tom's in-box.

Aidan self-published *The Vaquita*, and Tom was his editor. That same year, the young author had been contacted by Muskwa Club, a student-driven organization founded by three California middle school students. Muskwa members had started hosting vaquita awareness booths in their communities and, after reading Aidan's V-log, thought there might be potential for collaboration. After Aidan joined Muskwa—which then became a partner organization with VIVA Vaquita—the teens established International Save the Vaquita Day, or ISTVD, to be celebrated annually on the first Saturday after the fourth of July.

When Tom mentioned ISTVD, I chuckled. "Honestly, I get a giggle out of it," I told him, "because it's International Save the Vaquita Day, and everybody's like, 'What's a vaquita?'"

"I know, exactly!" Tom laughed aloud. "That's why we need an International Save the Vaquita Day!"

On July 9, 2016, I attended an ISTVD event at the Museo del Caracol in Ensenada, Mexico. Under a small outdoor tent hosted by VIVA Vaquita, I found coloring books, stickers, and informational pamphlets. As children explored a craft table with the help of volunteers from a local marine mammal organization, PROCETUS, the biologist directing the event, Fernanda Urrutia—who coincidentally did her master's thesis on *Phocoena sinus* under Armando—fielded questions from the public. Around noon, a couple of short documentary films were shown, attracting a gaggle of camp kids. I couldn't help noticing that the audience was far more engrossed in (Maria's level 3) moving pictures than the (level 1) discussions about vaquita around the craft table.

Fernanda told me that the Ensenada event was originally planned for San Felipe, but she didn't want to push a save-the-vaquita theme on a community she knew would not be receptive. As a matter of fact, there were no official ISTVD events around Alto Golfo, although the fishermen of Islas del Golfo Co-Op did meet on the *malecón* in matching vaquita shirts and posted group photos to Facebook.

ISTVD has taken root, growing bigger every year. In 2017, there were thirty-eight events in seven countries. Cofounder Aidan Bodeo-Lomicky is now seventeen and planning to become an environmental lawyer. Although he's the president of Muskwa and still active with VIVA Vaquita, he hasn't blogged in many months. When I spoke with him by phone, he told me, "V-log was intended to give the vaquita attention. But a lot more people have heard of it now. Like if you just walk around the city and ask people, it's very, very different than it was three years ago."

He said it's also a different issue than when he started. "It's just kind of crazy now. There are just so many complexities with the fishing communities and the Mexican government and the US government and the NGOs. And the totoaba black market adds a whole other layer."

"It's the vaquita vortex,'" I offered. "That's how Frances Gulland describes the people and the politics and the kind of 'madness' around it."

"Yes!" agreed Aidan. "I never could have imagined that one species that nobody ever heard of had such an enormous amount of complexity. I wonder if every native species has a similar situation once you really dive into them. As far as I know, this is one of the most complicated species-recovery missions of all time."

Undeniably, it is a historical time for vaquita conservation. And even though Aidan is no longer blogging, events continue to be chronicled.

$\sim$

Film is a persuasive form of storytelling, but when it comes to documenting the vaquita story, filmmakers don't have it easy. Without much footage of *Phocoena sinus* to work with, they must capture visuals that don't include an actual porpoise, all the while skillfully pointing to their missing lead character.

For many years, there was but one film about vaquita, a nine-minute short produced by Chris Johnson. After the Australian filmmaker managed to capture a clip of video while out on Tom Jefferson's boat during the 2008 survey, he launched a five-year film project. With an active website and blog, plus sponsorship from an array of organizations, *Vaquita: Saving the Desert Porpoise* shaped much of what an early audience would know about *Phocoena sinus*.

Of course, the totoaba boom had not yet come to light.

Recently, the Environmental Investigation Agency produced a five-minute video to augment its 2016 report detailing "how illegal trade in totoaba swim bladders is driving the vaquita to extinction." Filmed mostly on location in Guangdong Province, China, *Collateral Damage* exposes the sale of fish maw in public markets, taking a closer look at the Asian side of the crisis.

The first feature-length film about vaquita is currently in production. Wild Lens filmmakers Matthew Podolsky and Sean Bogle began shooting *Souls of the Vermilion Sea* in May 2015, just after Mexico announced the temporary gillnet ban. Their full documentary is expected to be released in 2018. In the interim, they have been producing short films to keep viewers keyed in, gaining an impressive following through blog posts and podcasts.

"The film is not just about vaquita," Sean told me, noting that one of their main goals is to offer a balanced perspective. "It's about how one single species can affect so many people. This includes the fishermen, the scientists, the people that are there. This includes the people in the US, the customers who are buying shrimp. The people in China buying swim bladders."

Sean and Matt are both biologists who care deeply about the safety of vaquita, but they don't want fishermen made out to be bad guys. "They're not," said Sean. "They're people. They have to support their families. They have to feed their children. And fishing is the only thing for them to do there. So when you put a gillnet ban and you say, 'You can't fish anymore,' well, what is the alternative? They need guidance. They need a different infrastructure."

Presenting a film that will resonate with both fishing families and environmentalists is a fine line to walk. Obviously, fishermen should not be allowed to obliterate entire ecosystems. Neither should conservation measures collapse communities. But where, exactly, is the midpoint? Where on the sliding scale is the compromise deemed fair? At this juncture, neither side is satisfied.

The day I arrived in San Felipe after the violence in El Golfo de Santa Clara, I planned to attend Matt and Sean's screening. A thirty-minute version of *Souls of the Vermilion Sea*—or rather, because the film was to be projected in Spanish, *Almas del Mar de Bermejo*—was scheduled to play at the cultural center at 7:00 p.m. The guys were in town, and I was eager to meet them and see their show.

Strangely, though, nobody else I knew was going. There was nobody from INECC, nobody from Sea Shepherd, and nobody from El Dorado Ranch. Even the men from Islas del Golfo Co-Op, who have supported the filmmakers and appear on camera, opted out. Why?

As one person put it, "The energy is too high right now, and someone might want to make a point. There is nothing to be gained by going."

When I met Matt and Sean that afternoon at the Taco Factory on the *malecón*, they admitted that the timing was unfortunate. They said they had to cancel their screening in El Golfo de Santa Clara. "We are not afraid of the fishermen. We consider them friends," Sean said. "But some of our sources suggest that it would only escalate the issue there."

My nerves were on edge as I climbed the stairs of the cultural center that evening. Should I linger by the door and keep an eye out for suspicious attendees? Such worries were wasted. The room was soon filled with local families, many toting children. As everyone shoveled popcorn into snack bags and chatted with their neighbors, I watched Sean and Matt visibly relax. After the screening, written questionnaires inquired whether the film represented the reality of the people, whether it seemed to blame a particular party, or whether it triggered certain emotions.

The survey was followed by a group discussion. Those who stayed seemed pleased to have a forum for communication. Things weren't easy, several admitted; the fishing restrictions and unfair compensation program had put their community under terrible stress. But hope rang in their voices as they spoke about the value of education and the importance of providing a better future for their children. Several said that they were sorry things had gone so poorly for vaquita and expressed a sincere desire for the species to be safeguarded.

That these families had sympathy for the lives of porpoises when their own lives were so destabilized filled me with appreciation. So much had changed since my first visit. Everyone was openly acknowledging that vaquita was real and the situation dire. Seated in that circle of chairs, progress was being be made.

I admire Matt and Sean for riding the middle line, for embracing humanity over agreement. After all, the unification of divergent minds is vaquita's only chance. I am further inspired by Maria and Barb, Memuco and Leo, Guillermo, Aidan, and Jen, who have stepped beyond the ease of daily routine, sometimes into the line of fire, to make positive personal statements with their artistic talents. Their work is helping us stitch together a stronger, more knowledgeable world.

～

On May 1, 2017, tourists videotaped a pair of vaquitas swimming off San Felipe. That the people recognized the animals and knew their significance was quite incredible. No longer oblivious to Mexico's disappearing species, supporters around the globe are now awake to the predicament of *la vaquita*.

Amid this growing awareness, Leonardo DiCaprio, the American actor and environmentalist, posted a tweet to his 17.5 million followers:

@LeoDiCaprio: "The vaquita is the most endangered marine mammal in the world. Join me + @World_Wildlife and take action. http://wwf.to/2poDGkh" 6:52 PM - 10 May 2017

The link, which led to an online petition asking Mexico's president to make his temporary gillnet ban permanent, triggered Enrique Peña Nieto to respond with a tweet of his own.

@EPN: "I welcome @LeoDiCaprio and @World_Wildlife 's concern regarding the Vaquita Marina." 7:40 PM - 11 May 2017

Over the next six minutes, Peña Nieto continued in a verbose string of tweets, writing:

Mexico has focused all its efforts to prevent the extinction of this species. Since Feb/2015, we have eliminated one of its main causes of death: the shrimp and scale fishery, establishing a two-year ban on the area. Our government has also extended the protection zone to a surface three times larger than the original. Mexico's Navy has more than 300 marines, 15 boats and unmanned aircraft systems watching over this area.

He proudly concluded, "Mexico's government is making a major effort, doing what should have been done decades ago to save the Vaquita Marina." This last tweet prompted World Wildlife Fund to ask one simple question.

@World_Wildlife: "Thanks @EPN. Will you commit to permanent gillnet ban by May31 & provide community fishing alternatives?" 9:56 AM - 12 May 2017

At this point, DiCaprio jumped back in with a hashtag to Aidan Bodeo-Lomicky's V-log, adding, "With fewer than 30 vaquita left, the time to act is now."

This whole Twitter exchange might have seemed nothing more than snarky social jousting, but the tweets were so much more. They were the opening statements of what would become major negotiations for vaquita. DiCaprio would soon be flying to Mexico City to team up with another forerunner for the WWF petition—Mexican billionaire Carlos Slim—to form an alliance with President Peña Nieto.

Their goal?

To finally get gillnets out of the water.

CHAPTER 12

Sending Out an SOS

With May's copious sunrays pressing on my shoulders, I listened to a cacophony of sounds: the hum of the winch, the grinding of rope over the deck rail, and the grunts of sweaty workers, noises that were underpinned by the crackle of hundreds of crabs, conches, and other shelled sea creatures spilling onto the deck of the *Farley Mowat*.

As another algae-laden ghost net was painstakingly hauled aboard, a sea jelly—not translucent and flimsy, but solid and yellow—came up strangled in twine. Its gelatinous bell was shaped like a well-worn sunhat under which densely congealed tentacles formed a ruffled flamenco skirt. Despite their strenuous toil, the crew's compassion never wavered. Still alive, the invertebrate was gently released from its yoke and returned to its watery home.

Captain Luisa Albera, an experienced mariner from Italy who was presently at the helm of the *Farley*, watched from the bridge window as, hand over hand, six deckhands raised another hundred feet of gillnet from the teal waters of the Upper Gulf. The next bycatch victim was not as lucky as the jelly. We all gasped for air when the stinking corpse of a cownose ray was lanced free, slithering around in its own goo until it could be effectively hooked and dumped overboard.

Lifting my eyes from the gruesome scene, I took in the magnitude of the entire operation.

Across the waves, the *Narval* waited at the ready. The 135-foot boat, owned by Museo de la Ballena, had traveled north along the Baja peninsula from La Paz to San Felipe. Like the *Farley Mowat*, it was serving as a retrieval ship—its able crew would seize and process the next net to be located.

Between us, forty otherwise-out-of-work shrimp fishermen from the nongovernmental organization Pesca ABC could be seen trawling for gillnets. Eighteen pangas were there, each dragging a grappling hook. Traveling side by side along parallel transect lines at speeds less than five miles per hour, the lineup looked like a slapdash marching band. Another panga, zipping about, was driven by a fisherman named Armando "Muelas" Castro. Whenever a trawler hooked a net, it was Muelas's job to go attach a marker buoy and then relay location coordinates to either the *Farley* or the *Narval*.

Following at the back, a twentieth panga was running side-scan sonar, sponsored by World Animal Protection as part of its Global Ghost Gear Initiative. I'd been given a primer on the apparatus. The EdgeTech 4125, referred to as a towfish, looked like a four-foot-long silver bullet designed to be towed underwater by a cable. Owner Jared Berg and his associate Andy had recently arrived from Monterey Bay, California, to deploy the $50,000 system in hope of locating derelict gear that might otherwise be impossible to pinpoint.

As WAP's Elizabeth Hogan explained, side-scan sonar "uses multiple acoustic signals positioned at an oblique angle to the seafloor in order to provide a broad digital image of the area." The submerged towfish sends a video feed to an on-boat screen, which is monitored by the technicians. It's a clever way to search for gillnets missed by the grappling hooks.

Two military crafts hung at the fringes of the action. The orange Navy *Defender* was acting as security, and a Zodiac from PROFEPA carried two government inspectors charged with authenticating recovered nets and any marine fauna, especially endangered species, found in the gear. They rounded out an impressive flotilla, twenty-four vessels in all.

The ghost net project is logistically managed by Sara Amozurrutia. As the project's coordinator, she is funded by World Wildlife Fund through a contract with Mexico's Commission for the Knowledge and Use of Biodiversity, or CONABIO. Associated with the project since October 2016, Sara understands the challenges of the job. In addition to dealing with endless texts, ever-shifting schedules, and hefty reports, she acknowledges that she could face potential hazards.

When she went out to help Mauricio exchange the six c-pods, they saw quite a few *bucheros*. "We were careful," she told me, explaining that people know she oversees the program that confiscates poachers' gear. "We did not use binos or cameras, and we avoided eye contact. It is not worth the risk because they can see my face and later recognize me in town."

She admitted that Javier's panga being accosted by masked men was unnerving, as was Sunshine Rodriguez's main-street boat burning. Still, Sara considers her work "a huge opportunity." The thirty-year-old biologist actually turned down her dream job—doing research from a sailboat in the Galapagos Islands—to return to her current position. "Yes, Galapagos might be the adventure of my life," she told me, "but this is vaquita. It's my duty as a Mexican to take care of her. She's so special!"

Sara was standing next to me on the *Farley Mowat* as the last section of ghost net was wrangled in. Great swathes of rotting rope soon traversed the bow before us, stretching to and fro into a massive blanket of mud and marine life. Patricia Gandolfo, the net retrieval coordinator for Sea Shepherd, was with us, too. Her afternoon would be spent dismantling the gear with the deck crew, a grueling effort that would take several hours. All the netting was to be cut up, all the buoys were to be drilled, and anchors and plumbs would be stacked for scrap metal.

On the back deck, I'd noticed several colossal white bags filled with chopped-up rope and monofilament from previous nets. They were marked PARLEY. "What does Parley mean?" I asked Patricia.

The supervisor finished logging some figures on her laminated chart and answered, "Parley for the Oceans. They recycle the netting into shoes. Adidas makes them, and they're really expensive." I would later learn that a pair of limited edition *Adidas x Parley* tennis shoes costs nearly $200.

Overhearing our conversation, Sara chimed in. "Yesterday, I transferred nets from the office of PROFEPA to shipping containers for Parley," she said. "We needed a truck and a crane because it was sixty-one bags. Fifteen tons!"

Fifteen tons is the equivalent of ten hippopotamuses. And that's just one load.

In addition to serving the multi-institutional ghost net project, Sea Shepherd crews are still towing phantom rays from November to June. As a result, they are responsible for extracting the majority of gear. In fact, I'd seen more stuffed Parley bags on the deck of their second vessel—which was no longer a sailboat. When the cartel situation got sketchy, the *Martin Sheen* was replaced by a bigger, stronger, and more intimidating sidekick, the *Sam Simon*, a 180-foot quadruple-deck behemoth painted gray-and-black camouflage with a shark mouth at its bow and the words ANTI-POACHING on its outer plating.

Whereas the *Farley* works as a retrieval ship, the *Sam Simon* focuses full time on Operation Milagro. It can help the ghost net project when extra muscle is needed, but is otherwise committed to regular patrols.

Sea Shepherd crewmates Patricia Gandolfo (right) with volunteer Connie Sanchez begin the arduous task of cutting up a ghost net on the deck of the Farley Mowat. *(Brooke Bessesen)*

Right now, I could see its imposing frame searching the waters near Roca Consag.

Earlier in the week, I had spent a couple days aboard the *Sam Simon*. Oona, now captain of that ship, was once again landlocked with other duties, and Captain Thomas Le Coz was in charge. He had shared some interesting news. As media updates indicated, Sea Shepherd was no longer just dealing with hidden nets; now, the number of poachers working out in the open, breaking the law with complete impudence, had increased to a shocking level. Even though it was the end of totoaba season, the ships' crew had just documented ten poachers on one night.

Thomas let me watch the drone footage. It was quite disturbing. Not only were *bucheros* tossing multiple totoaba to their floorboards, but they were doing so without a wit of concern that a camera was hovering overheard, filming their activities. When I expressed surprise, Thomas cued another drone clip from earlier in the season that showed a panga stuffed with totoaba motoring along in broad daylight.

Such lawlessness, alarming to me, had become routine for Thomas. "Poachers don't care about drones anymore," he told me blandly. The Mexican Navy deploys drones, too. Authorities see the footage, but nothing comes of it. So, when the *Sam Simon* reports an illegal panga, most *bucheros* just continue to work. That said, they somehow manage to disperse right before the Navy arrives.

"At first we thought it was a coincidence. But it is happening always." Thomas eyed me. "As if they've been notified."

~

On June 7, 2017, Enrique Peña Nieto, Leonardo DiCaprio, and Carlos Slim convened for a meeting in Mexico City. The media made great fanfare of the occasion. Minister Rafael Pacchiano, Barb Taylor, and Lorenzo Rojas were among the impressive list of attendants. All eyes were watching.

DiCaprio is no newcomer to high-profile discussions about the environment. Since establishing the Leonardo DiCaprio Foundation in 1998 "with the mission of protecting the world's last wild places," the celebrity activist has met with many global leaders, including three US presidents. People may remember the paradigm-shifting image of him pulling up to the Oscars in a Prius, yet they might not be aware that, since 2010, his foundation has granted more than $80 million to conservation projects worldwide.

Slim is a business tycoon from Mexico who for several years surpassed Bill Gates as the wealthiest person in the world. He's also an admired philanthropist whose humanitarian organization, Fundación Carlos Slim, founded in 1986, has "benefited millions of people through high-impact programs focused on the most vulnerable population in Latin America." From economic development to health care and education to environment, he has not only served as a corporate magnate, but also as a voice of social responsibility.

As cameras flashed, the trio of men signed a memorandum of understanding, officially agreeing to a collaborative partnership intent on saving the vaquita and its habitat. The MOU stated that within thirty days, Mexico would establish and enforce several new laws to abolish poaching. President Peña Nieto soon announced a permanent gillnet ban, which this time he would legitimize in the *Diario Oficial de la Federación*.

The consequent laws, posted into Mexican doctrine at the end of June, now prohibit any night fishing in the Alto Golfo between 9:00 p.m. and 5:00 a.m. and insist that all permitted boats carry mandatory location-tracking devices and use designated docks, which (theoretically) act as checkpoints for ferreting out criminal activity. They also state that (translated) "fishing gear may not be transported in that marine area or by any other terrestrial or aerial means to, or between, the cities, towns, *ejidos*, communities and/or fishing grounds adjacent thereto."

The bad news is that gillnets are still perfectly legal to own, to make, and to sell.

The better news is that poaching is now a felony in Mexico on the level of organized crime. So, instead of watching criminals picking off vaquitas one by one, authorities can finally begin picking off criminals one by one and locking them away.

After the MOU meeting in Mexico City, a pleased DiCaprio tweeted:

@LeoDiCaprio: "Honored to work w/ President Nieto (@EPN) & Carlos Slim to ensure the future viability of marine life in the Gulf. https://www.apnews.com . . . " 4:13 PM - 7 Jun 2017

~

As anyone might have expected, corvina is exempt from the permanent gillnet ban.

I am told it is because corvina fishing is an active process, so nets are never left unattended. In addition, corvina are gutted and cleaned in private homes, so the fishery supports some three thousand families in the Upper Gulf, making it an important source of revenue. Still, with so much documented abuse, how could permits be justified?

Looking for insight, I turned to Rafael Ortiz at the Environmental Defense Fund. As senior manager for the Gulf of California Fisheries, Rafa is helping fishermen implement rights-based management in which each corvina fisherman is given secure rights to a percentage of an established total catch limit. With a stake in the fishery, fishermen are more likely to plan and conserve the resource.

The program, launched in 2012, has apparently made progress. "The catch limit is science-based, and it's published every year," Rafa told me. "We have already cut the historic maximum catch in half."

Rafa supports corvina as a legal and potentially sustainable fishery. "There is no evidence that vaquitas are entangled in corvina nets. So, we are trying to keep that fishery working. But only if it can show unequivocally that, number one, it continues to demonstrate that it does not kill vaquita, and two, that it provides no cover to the poaching."

The latter, I suggested, seems an impossible hurdle.

"Yeah," Rafa admitted, "the problems are very systemic. There is lots of corruption, and the culture around the Upper Gulf is very hard to overcome. It's sad for me as a Mexican that this has not been solved. But we do have hope. We are working with fishermen and experts to make sure zero interactions with vaquita are the norm."

Despite my skepticism that corvina permits could ever escape exploitation, while talking with this levelheaded optimist I was reminded that local fishermen, given proper support, have historically tried to be compliant with certain regulations.

∼

In 2008, my girlfriend Donna and I took a weekend trip to Puerto Peñasco. Although Rocky Point is a fairly common destination for Arizonans, I'd never been before, and poking along back roads flanking the Vermilion Sea, I was delighted to find a research station marked by a fifty-five-foot fin-whale skeleton. Entering the Intercultural Center for the Study of Deserts and Oceans, or CEDO, proved momentous, for it is where I first heard the word *vaquita*.

I would later meet CEDO's executive director, Peggy Turk Boyer, and ask her about the history of *Phocoena sinus* along that side of the gulf. She told me that right after they opened their doors in 1980, they found a dead porpoise on the beach. More corpses followed. "Maybe eight over a fifteen-year period," said Peggy. "But that's been a long time ago. We don't really see them here anymore."

Although CEDO is credited with generating early attention concerning the decline of vaquita, the organization's primary focus has been fisheries, especially as they relate to conservation. Early on, Peggy conducted interviews with fishermen regarding the Biosphere Reserve. She also coauthored a 1998 book, *Pescando Entre Mareas* (Fishing Between Tides), that exposed the boom-or-bust history of the region. Since then, she has been helping fishermen move toward more sustainable practices.

In a recent attempt to abide by the regulations, fishermen from all three Alto Golfo communities hired CEDO to help develop and implement an environmental impact study—called a MIA—for all their fisheries. By law in Mexico, a MIA must be produced for any economic activity taking place in a protected area or where an endangered species is involved. The study must propose mitigation actions, and collected data must verify that those actions are being met.

Because the government has not been consistent in applying the law, the undertaking of a MIA on the part of the fishermen showed unprecedented initiative. "It included the most comprehensive education program," Peggy said. Her voice was tinged with both pride and sadness.

"We were training them on the rules and regulations. Our goal was to build a culture of compliance. And not just the leaders of the cooperatives, but the fishermen themselves were actually participating."

The MIA, in effect from 2010 to 2014, was structured to provide social and economic benefits to those who partook. "But the government made a farce of it," Peggy said. That's because the dutiful fishermen earned no advantage; they were treated the same as those who did nothing. "It's disrespectful to fishermen when the government comes in and sets laws and then nobody follows up on them. It gives them no hope and nothing they can count on."

When the MIA expired, the fishermen—who had previously paid and participated and who had been readily complying with the law—did not renew. I could understand their feelings. Why put forth the work for a MIA only to have it regarded as meaningless?

"So basically," Peggy said, "for all of 2015, they had no authorization to fish in the reserve. But nobody cared or did anything about it." (The fallout came in 2016 when SEMARNAT pulled the MIA card to prevent commencement of the corvina season.)

Peggy knows that there's corruption, but she said that a big part of the fisheries problem is just plain negligence on the part of authorities. And their mismanagement is now causing conflict between communities.

Boats from El Golfo de Santa Clara are motoring down into Puerto Peñasco's fishing zones. "Since they can't fish up there, those guys are just pouring into the area and taking everything here—while they are being paid not to fish," Peggy said as she raised an eyebrow. The fishermen in Puerto Peñasco, who are already upset about being excluded from the compensation program, are now losing fish stocks to government beneficiaries. "It's complete chaos."

As for little porpoises trying to survive in the fray, Peggy sighed and said, "Their chances are not very good." She showed me CEDO's vaquita skeleton, the only fully assembled one in the world. Looking at the delicate artifact, I was taken by the animal's petite body size, its little skull, and its tiny shovel-shaped teeth.

I asked Peggy if she had ever seen living vaquitas. Yes, she said. She saw them in the wild in 1984. Then there was the orphaned newborn who washed up on the shores of Puerto Peñasco in 1994, listless but alive. The tiny calf was rescued from the surging tide and rushed to CEDO's field station. But what could anyone do?

A video that has broken the hearts of more than fifty thousand viewers on YouTube shows the baby in a chest of seawater, so tiny and so innocent.

It died within two hours.

A gillnet was likely to blame for its mother's disappearance. An early CIRVA report even "pointed out that lactating females may be more at risk of entanglement" while attending their calves. However, it's important to remember that the main threat to vaquitas in 1994 was not totoaba poaching. It was legal fishing for finfish and shrimp. And who was eating all those savory crustaceans?

Americans.

∼

Sarah Mesnick is an ecologist at NOAA's Southwest Fisheries Science Center (where Barb also works). Originally a researcher of sperm-whale behavior, Sarah is now dedicated to human behavior, namely as it relates to food choices.

"I call what I do 'culinary conservation,'" she told me as we sat in her California office. "Most people have no idea where their food comes from. So, a lot of what I do is connecting people to their food source. For vaquita, that's critical."

Sarah believes that one way to get gillnets out of the Upper Gulf is to replace their earning potential through a viable market for seafood caught with vaquita-friendly gear. To that end, she and her American and Mexican colleagues have connected the alt-gear shrimp fishermen with US buyers interested in sustainable seafood.

"The reason we focus on shrimp," Sarah explained, "is that 90 percent of it comes into the United States. What that means is that up until fairly recently, when totoaba once again became the biggest issue, Americans were eating vaquita extinct. And they didn't know it."

There's another reason for the focus on shrimp: it's a high-value product. Sarah showed me a chart of shrimp values from around the world. Pointing to the top of the page, she said, "Mexican wild-caught shrimp is the most valuable wild-caught shrimp in the world. Here in La Jolla, it sells for around $29 a pound."

Jumbo shrimp—a luxury item for American diners with discretionary funds, a cultural delicacy perhaps not so different from fish maw soup in China.

"You have this really valuable product. And there's not much of it. So we essentially created a new value chain," Sarah said. "Once we build in traceability, we can prove the shrimp came from vaquita-friendly gear."

Contemporary trends in American culture promote healthy oceans, and Sarah is excited by the idea of selling shrimp that supports fishermen who are doing the right thing. She knows consumers will pay more for seafood with a legitimate eco-label. And that's good news because even if alternative gear doesn't produce as much shrimp as *chinchorros*, fishermen can still earn a living. "This would be the best possible outcome—economics and conservation working together to save vaquita and support communities."

Her enthusiasm showed as she continued. "We have experienced buyers who have been buying shrimp out of the Upper Gulf forever," she said. "We have award-winning chefs who understand and support sustainable seafood. And we have restaurants and communities that care. So the market is ready. Here's the problem."

She handed me a beautifully printed box labeled San Felipe Mexican

Shrimp; a prominent stamp in the upper right corner read VAQUITA FRIENDLY. I turned it over in my hands.

It was empty.

"There's nothing in the box," Sarah said. "That's the problem. There's no product."

She explained, "The fishermen could sell every single shrimp caught with vaquita-friendly gear, but we haven't been able to help make that happen because they need their alternative gear permitted by the Mexican government."

I thought back on all I had learned about Pesca and its frustrating resistance to alternative gear. Would willing fishermen ever obtain working permits for vaquita-friendly equipment? Could traditional fishermen ever be convinced to make the switch?

When it comes to shrimp fishing, there are two important benefits of gillnets. First, they capture the largest, most valuable shrimp—blue shrimp. Second, fishermen pick those shrimp out of the net one by one so that they arrive at market "in really good shape." Because it's essential that alternative gear meet the same criteria, at least to a reasonable degree, INAPESCA really needs to run transparent gear trials to establish what kind and how much shrimp can be harvested without ecological damage.

The *chango* I saw at Javier's isn't the only option. Other types of equipment may prove even better. One that holds promise is the suripera. Jose Angel Trigueros Salmeron reported positively on its use farther south, off Mazatlán. In a 2012 presentation, Trigueros Salmeron wrote that the suripera's skirt-shaped, mesh-funnel design is (translated) "ecologically very good" and "mostly captures target species"—about 95 percent shrimp, of which nearly 70 percent were blue—with "low cost in its operation."

In 2015, a commercial company called Del Pacifico began selling that Sinaloan suripera-caught shrimp, marketing it as "the only shrimp fishery certified by Fair Trade in the world." The company even has a web page where consumers can track their purchase back to the shrimper who caught it, boasting traceability from sea to plate.

So wait. Sustainability and traceability are already available in Mexico?

Yes. In fact, both INAPESCA and CONAPESCA are stakeholders in Del Pacifico's sustainable market. Yet for all the years of struggle and strain, of wasted money and mounds of dead marine life, large-scale trials for suriperas have yet to be conducted in the Upper Gulf. What's more, even though a few early tests in the region showed promise, local fishermen are already denouncing the suripera's efficacy, forming a block wall against change.

On the other side of the aisle, a respected alternative-gear designer named Antonio "Tonicho" García has been experimenting with prototypal fish traps for quarry other than shrimp. *Trampas*, as they're called, could theoretically replace small- to midsized-mesh gillnets for catching finfish. Last year I saw a few sample *trampas* at Tonicho's house in San Felipe. I remember thinking that something constructive is bound to come of so much hard work. But in August 2016, INAPESCA tested six types of *alternativa* for potential use in Alto Golfo, including various forms of *changos* and *trampas*. None were sanctioned.

The gillnet ban was originated in 2015, and there are still no occupational options for honest men. The Mexican government has paid community residents almost $70 million not to fish. Why weren't those conservation dollars spent on developing and testing equipment that would allow workers to earn income while simultaneously protecting vaquita? How long can legal fisheries remain closed?

As Alex Olivera from the Center for Biological Diversity wrote (translated), "Fisheries policies should be aimed at conversion to vaquita-friendly fishing gear, fishing regulations and conservation instruments that benefit fishing. The majority of resources go to subsidies that only encourage corruption, overexploitation of fishery resources and poor fishing practices that harm species at risk of disappearing."

Sarah offered a complimentary point. "When you shut down fisheries, you take away the people who care most about the resource. You disempower them," she said. "And what we see is that illegal fishing is now rampant. So we need to look at ways to put people in care of their communities and support that with our buying power."

She pointed out that Mexico has an opportunity to be a leader in innovations for sustainable fishing gear and product traceability and that American shoppers and diners have a responsibility to make market choices that protect marine life. "Consumers have a lot of power. And we abdicate that power," she said.

Until fairly recently, most Americans didn't even know vaquita existed. They certainly didn't know about the deleterious production chain of traditionally caught shrimp from the Gulf of California. With knowledge gained, will we make better choices?

Sarah rotated her chair and glanced out her office window at the gray afternoon sky. "People who love the ocean often ask me what they can do to save it," she said.

"And what do you tell them?"

She swiveled to face me. "Eat sustainably caught seafood. Ask where your seafood comes from and support people who are doing the right thing. And you will bite by bite change the world."

~

It all comes down to the power of the people.

Time and again we have come together to alter the course of history.

If only vaquita could rally our masses to speak—to act—on her behalf. Imagine three hundred twenty-three million Americans calling for protection and one hundred twenty-seven million Mexicans responding in kind. A movement—yes, a movement—could save vaquita.

In this spirit, three powerful organizations are helping US citizens take action. Specifically, they are pushing for enforcement of US national importation laws and asking people to refuse the purchase of seafood that implicitly kills porpoises.

The US Marine Mammal Protection Act already "requires that all imported fish or fish products be accompanied by proof that the technology used to land the catch does not kill or seriously injure whales, dolphins, and other marine mammals in excess of U.S. standards." As expected, MMPA standards do not allow for incidental capture of critically endangered species, yet it's happening with gillnets all around the world.

"Few realize it, but nearly every foreign fish product sold in the United States enters the U.S. market in violation of federal law," states a Natural Resources Defense Council report titled *Net Loss*. "Americans unwittingly consume foreign fish or fish products caught using techniques that needlessly kill a multitude of marine mammals each year. . . . The numbers are staggering: Scientists estimate that more than 650,000 marine mammals are killed or seriously injured every year in foreign fisheries." (A separate but related statistic indicates that 640,000 tons of ghost nets are skulking around oceans worldwide.)

Now, Natural Resources Defense Council, the Center for Biological Diversity, and Animal Welfare Institute are seeking action under the MMPA. When I spoke with Zak Smith, a senior attorney for NRDC, he told me, "Our National Marine Fisheries Service has a duty under the law to bar the imports of all seafood into the United States from Mexico that is harming the vaquita in violation of the US standards."

Simply put, all imported shrimp and fish are, by law, supposed to be vaquita-friendly, just like tuna imports must be dolphin-safe—a requirement that stemmed from a 1990 embargo on Mexican tuna due to excessive dolphin bycatch. Clearly, the United States has not been abiding by its 1972 Marine Mammal Protection Act any better than Mexico has been abiding by its 1992 ban on totoaba-sized gillnets. Maybe it's time for Americans to stand up and demand enforcement.

"The law is very explicit," Zak insisted. "It says, 'The United States shall bar the importation.'"

Once the National Marine Fisheries Service received the organizations' petition for emergency rulemaking pursuant to the MMPA, it called for public comment. Responding to that call, I found myself in the US Federal e-Rulemaking Portal. Admittedly, it felt a bit strange to be writing my opinion on a government website, but I reminded myself that it's the equivalent of voting, a way to have my voice heard. If I personally want to help stop bycatch—and I do—I need to help solve the food part of the problem. And establishing a new precedent under the MMPA could eventually lead to the protection of other marine mammals being annihilated by entanglement fisheries worldwide.

In addition to the MMPA petition, the Center for Biological Diversity has also submitted a petition to the Trump administration under the Pelly Amendment. It asks the United States to certify Mexico for undermining international wildlife laws by failing to crack down on the illegal totoaba trade. The Obama administration ignored the previous petition, so it has since been reissued to Trump. Once Mexico is certified, embargoes on wildlife products can then be authorized. Both the MMPA and the Pelly Amendment impose economic pressure through the enforcement of federal law.

Governmental policy is also being pursued on a state level.

In February 2017, California Assembly member Todd Gloria introduced Assembly Bill 1151, known as the Vaquita Protection Act. Because California is a major consumer of products derived from the Gulf of California, the bill seeks to make legislative changes to that state's Fish and Game Code regarding imports. If passed, it will become "unlawful for any person to sell, offer for sale, trade, or distribute fish and fish products that are not vaquita-friendly."

But there's a big problem. It's to be effective January 2019.

It is exasperating that legislative avenues can take years to reach enactment. Fortunately for vaquita and totoaba, there is another equally powerful and much more immediate strategy in play: an American boycott of Mexican shrimp.

NRDC, the Center for Biological Diversity, and Animal Welfare Institute have been joined by four dozen other organizations, including VIVA Vaquita, Environmental Investigation Agency, and Defenders of Wildlife. This immense coalition is encouraging American diners to read labels and stop buying Mexican shrimp until that country makes an operational transition to alternative fishing gear.

In 2016 alone, US consumers bought more than $274 million worth of shrimp from their southern neighbor. Presumably, Mexico does not want to lose that income. Indeed, embargoes and boycotts are said to be Pesca's greatest fear. CONAPESCA has a mandate to increase earnings from the marine environment, which it cannot do if there is no market—so an American boycott definitely has power to force its hand.

It is also a chance for each of us, as consumers, to decide where we stand on the gillnet issue. Alternative gear must remain a fundamental goal. The hard fact is that any hope of long-term survival for *Phocoena sinus* requires Americans to insist on eating gillnet-free seafood.

Before I hung up with NRDC's Zak Smith, I asked what drives his commitment to vaquita. He replied, "I want to be able to tell my children that I did what I could."

CHAPTER 13

Meet the Totoaba

A CURTAIN OF BLACK FABRIC rested heavy against my back as I peered through the small square window into a dim turquoise world. At first the space appeared empty, distant and dream-like. Then an enormous figure slipped past the window, momentarily eclipsing the depths of teal. Another appeared, farther from the glass, resolving into the unmistakable shape of a fish.

More and more came. With tails fanning side to side in lazy, slow motion, a whole clan of totoaba drifted by like giant aquatic dinosaurs. To see this endangered fish in the flesh brought an unexpected thrill, visceral and stirring.

One decidedly curious individual approached the window, its plated eye shimmering as it tilted toward my face. Its downturned lips formed a prophetic frown, as though I might be held accountable for its current predicament. It was nearly my size, vaquita size, and quite magnificent, with its copper-gold chromatophores sparkling like the finest crystal organza.

I was struck again by the idea of totoaba and vaquita as strange fraternal twins, taxonomically divided yet fatefully bound. Because any effort to protect one will surely aid the other, I wanted to ascertain whether totoaba has a real chance for recovery. If yes, perhaps vaquita does too. Thanks to Paco, who connected me with his nephew Alán Alexis Valverde, I was now on campus touring the Autonomous University of Baja California totoaba hatchery in Ensenada with program director Conal David True.

Conal is a biologist. He's been working with *Totoaba macdonaldi* for the same amount of time that Lorenzo and Barb have been working with vaquita. Conal's hatchery and all its activities fall under SEMARNAT, in a division that's the equivalent of US Fish and Wildlife. As with its endemic vaquita, the Mexican government has been spending millions of dollars to support its endemic totoaba. The hatchery is now, by all intents and purposes, a shining success, although the road hasn't been easy and there are still serious challenges ahead.

Conal has some logical, if provocative, ideas about how to avoid extinction with totoaba, and I had come to discuss those ideas with him. First, though, I wanted see his program's facilities and learn about the process of raising totoaba in captivity. I was currently seated at the viewing window of a broodstock tank, an enclosed cylindrical structure that looks something like a massive, squat propane gas tank. As I continued to peer in at the watery scene, my heart was reeled in by the grace and inquisitiveness of the animals inside.

"The fish you're looking at are broodstock," Conal announced. His voice, dampened by the light-blocking curtain I was huddled beneath, sounded like the unseen narrator of a wildlife documentary. "Right now we have fourteen wild-caught breeders, plus forty F1-generation fish, which are captive-raised offspring of the wild ones we caught early on. They have grown into adults and are now breeders themselves."

Conal says it helps to raise breeders in-house when possible because removing animals from the wild takes a toll on a limited population.

Moreover, many wild-caught drum fish die from capture-induced baro-trauma, a form of decompression sickness. Conal scientifically described the condition in totoaba in 1997 after a broodstock-collecting trip.

"Totoaba have a 'closed swim bladder,'" he explained, "so when a fish is brought up to the surface, the change in pressure makes the bladder blow up out of proportion. They have no way of controlling the over-inflation. Once the fish has decompression sickness, it will not recover without treatment." He explained the treatment as puncturing the swim bladder with a large hypodermic needle and suctioning out the excess air with a syringe. Even with this rudimentary care, Conal said, most fish don't make it. Published statistics report 60 percent survivorship, but he admitted, "Sometimes you pull up ten and three survive."

He and his team have made four trips to collect wild broodstock from the Sea of Cortez. Only the fourth group is still alive. The fish are generally brought in at about three feet in length and "grown out" at the hatchery, where care is taken to protect them from parasites and bacterial infections, both of which commonly sneak into the collection. Although free-living totoaba have an estimated life span of fifty years, most don't make twenty years in captivity and, with limited space and time, never reach their full size potential. As the world's largest sciaenid, wild totoaba are capable of growing to three hundred pounds. The old-est and largest captive individual was around half that weight.

Because it's impossible to visually distinguish males from females or one fish from the others, blood tests are performed on captured fish to determine gender, and microchips are embedded for individual identi-fication. By age seven years, when totoaba weigh in at twenty to thirty pounds, they are sexually mature. Adults are held in broodstock tanks. The containers, as I am witnessing, are fully enclosed, allowing for the control of environmental conditions that trigger reproductive readiness.

Natural spawning takes place in late spring. At that time of year, though, students are too busy with classes to assist at the hatchery, so

Conal has cleverly shifted reproduction to overlap the midyear break. By manipulating the light (length of day) and water temperature (season), he fools the totoaba into thinking that summer is spring. Luck had scheduled my arrival at the university in July with spawning season in full swing, so I was able to observe the process.

Exactly how does a human team manage to breed and raise critically endangered fish in the confines of captivity? It's quite a feat.

~

The hatchery's main room is capacious and moistened with that brackish humidity known to all marine facilities. Ducking under an elevated platform, I waved up at Alán Alexis, who was working overhead on one of the massive tanks. When Alán was just a baby, his grandfather, Javier, helped Conal capture the first eleven totoaba that were brought to the university as broodstock. Now a fresh-faced college student and hatchery assistant, Alán seemed to be following in the Valverde family footsteps, doing his part to serve conservation.

Approaching a ten-foot pool that at first glance reminded me of a backyard aboveground swimming pool, Conal introduced me to one of that day's spawning groups. Two males and one female paddled placidly around the pool's circumference. By evening, they would be making babies.

Like all endangered species breeding programs, mating pairs—or, in the case of totoaba, mating triplets—are carefully arranged to ensure as much genetic diversity in the offspring as possible. Cetaceans conduct fertilization through intercourse, and the female carries a single infant to term as an internal pregnancy. In fish, on the other hand, the female lays a mass of gelatinous eggs, and one or more males release sperm to fertilize those eggs.

Female totoaba will spawn for several consecutive days, associating with a different group of males each time and creating genetic diversification in her offspring. After seven to nine days, she is done; that female will not spawn again until the following year. Not all totoaba females spawn at the same time. Over the course of a multimonth breeding season, different females become ready, allowing males to focus on a limited number of potential mates at a time.

In captivity, Conal determines the exact stage of each female's readiness through a minor surgical procedure, done in the water at the start of each breeding season. Anesthesia is given to sedate the fish so that it can be rolled onto its side, and then a minute tissue sample is excised from the ovaries and examined under a microscope. Establishing a time line for which females will be early-, mid-, or late-season spawners—and implanting time-release hormones—ensures the greatest possible productivity.

When a female is ready to spawn, she is put together with a couple of males. The next day, those males are moved to another spawning female, and two new males are brought in. This move, like a game of musical chairs, is repeated daily. As females finish spawning, they are sent back to the broodstock tanks, and newly ready females are brought out. These daily rotations mimic the fishes' natural mix-and-match reproductive style and produce a variety of genetic combinations called families.

"We know the genome for every one of our breeding adults," said Conal with an emphatic tone that made clear that this piece of the puzzle is essential. Every living organism has a unique group of genetic markers that will be passed on to its offspring, then from that offspring to their offspring, and so on. Generation after generation, a family's distinctive chain of microsatellites—its genotype—can always be recognized. One geneticist has zoomed in on a series of microsatellites that are perfect identifiers for totoaba.

Totoaba 324 is nicknamed Jenny. Taken from the wild, Jenny has been in the captive breeding program for eight years and is always reliable for consecutive spawns. She has been paired with dozens of males and has produced a multitude of families. At twenty-four years old, she is the largest and strongest female in the hatchery, weighing in at one hundred thirty pounds.

"It takes four of us to handle her," Conal told me.

How do they move such mammoth fish from pool to pool? They lift them by hand, using fine-mesh nets or slings made of tarp. It's a strenuous affair. While moving the males, Conal says they can sometimes feel them croaking, flexing, and snapping the muscle that lines their swim bladder like a gigantic sciaenid drum. *Rrrruuuut, rrruuuut. Rrrruuuut, rrruuuut.* Apparently, only the males croak—and only during reproduction.

"They can make a sound like a firecracker. *Pow!* Or they make a drumrolling sound. Or they can *purrrr*, like a cat," said Conal. He added that they really get going during courtship.

This single biological trait has brought such misfortune to totoaba. The drumming—powerful reverberations perceived as echoes of virility—led early Chinese to believe that swim bladders bestow youthful skin and strong circulation to those who eat them. Naturally, we cannot absorb an animal's transcendent power any more than a photo can steal a soul. But altering cultural convictions is exceptionally difficult. Even with time and education the endeavor may prove futile.

Despite all the shuffling around, the fish in the spawning pool didn't seem at all stressed. I listened for any hint of croaking but the boys just swam slow loops, awaiting the bliss of sunset. Later in the evening, after the big event, the female's fertilized eggs would be mechanically siphoned from the pool. Conal pointed to a nearby filter basket from which the eggs, like miniature tapioca balls, would be manually scooped up for delivery to the nursery.

Thus, navigating across the room—an industrial jumble of pools, pipelines, water tanks, bins, and control boxes—we slipped between a pair of heavy drapes into a narrow, curtained room.

~

In the dim quarters of the nursery, cone-shaped sunlamps hovered over large aerated barrels, each tending a different phase of development. I peered into the first barrel. Under the full-spectrum light, totoaba eggs floated like tiny opalescent pearls. It takes about twenty-four hours for eggs to hatch. After that, the delicate embryotic hatchlings, like those I studied in an adjacent barrel, spend another seventy-two hours absorbing their external yolk sac, growing mouth parts, and developing functional eyes and fins.

For the first twelve to thirteen days of life, captive totoaba larvae are fed a nearly microscopic form of zooplankton called rotifers. They are then switched to a minuscule brine shrimp, *Artemia salina*, known to my generation as sea monkeys. Both feeder species are cultivated in floor-to-ceiling Plexiglas-like tubes at the back of the hatchery.

From the nursery, I followed Conal up a flight of wood plank stairs to an enclosed space just above. In the larval rearing area, more barrels harbored infantile fish. Hanging over a circle of rippling water, I adjusted my glasses and strained to make out the swimming specks of yellow. Most blended into the water like cloaked Klingon warships. However, I noticed some were strangely formed, floating at the surface, pasty white and engorged.

"Overinflated swim bladders," Conal told me. "It's a problem we face in captive rearing."

I studied the babies that appeared afflicted. Some still wiggled despite their swollen midsections. Do they ever survive the problem?

"No," he said. "The dead ones will be netted out later."

I sighed. It sure seems like swim bladders are the bane of this poor species' existence.

At around five weeks of age, the young totoaba are weaned onto a diet of dry commercially produced fish pellets that come in various sizes to meet the nutritional needs of growing stock. The initial pellets look exactly like mouse droppings, but larger fish eat larger pellets—or one another. Cannibalism is common at that stage.

I couldn't help imagining what it must be like for Alán and his classmates to be responsible for netting and relocating so many fish—switching them from tank to tank all around the building, with new broods constantly hatching and growing. It's no wonder that student availability plays such an important role in the program.

Our last stop was the outside pavilion, where four raised concrete pools housed juvenile fish called fingerlings. I was mesmerized by the shoals of three-inch-long totoaba. Thousands of gold-green darts flashed in the light, swirling about, this way and that, like the glorious murmurations of starlings. Even after years of working with wildlife, I couldn't help bending over and cooing at the little cuties—they were absolutely captivating. With a bit more time to gain size and strength, this batch would soon be swimming in Alto Golfo.

Hatchery totoaba are released into the waters off Puertecitos, south of San Felipe. They are set free at a mere four to five inches in length, which may seem small, but it's logistically impractical to retain thousands of bigger fish in a captive setting. Like the adolescents of all species, the slender fingerlings appeared bright-eyed and energetic, ready to face the world, yet even with spots for camouflage, most would become quick casualties of the food chain. Of those that survive a year, how many will end up being bycatch statistics of industrial trawling? And of those that reach adulthood, how many will die in a *buchero*'s gillnet?

As one hopes for any youngster starting down the path of life, I wanted each fingerling to reach his or her potential. Reaching potential is particularly important for endangered species. If individuals can make it to sexual maturity, their value is twofold. First, they contribute their DNA to the population and that diversity strengthens the gene pool, and second, the babies they produce are the promise of tomorrow. It's a numbers game. Increasing the count of wild totoaba is the only way to irrefutably pull the species back from the edge of extinction and create population stability, so adding fingerlings to the habitat is where Conal says the hatchery makes its greatest contribution.

Based on the fecundity of totoaba, he explained, broodstock can easily generate more than forty million fertile eggs per year, but the team only raises a fraction of that number because of mortality and limited capacity. In the first year of releases, Conal and his team put out a few hundred fish. In the decade that followed, they managed from one thousand to two thousand releases per year. Then came some down years with no production due to various problems; a lot of things had to be rebuilt and redesigned before they got going again. More recently, release numbers have escalated from twenty thousand to forty thousand to eighty thousand fish.

Conal wanted to show me something exciting. Walking a short distance along the university's waterfront path, we came to a tremendous construction zone for a new hatchery. He said that the state-of-the-art facility would dramatically increase capacity for holding and growing out fish. His team will be able to raise up to a million fingerlings per year. And, instead of the twelve families he is currently producing each season, he will make forty to sixty families.

Even with Mexico's whopping investment in the production of totoaba, the hatchery remains exceedingly controversial. Many people contend that the raise-and-release program is fueling the Chinese black market, merely restocking the Gulf of California so that poachers can poach. They say that the government is spending money to breed endangered fish only to have them carved open and heedlessly dumped, their bladders smuggled out of the country for huge criminal profits. They ask, who benefits from that?

~

The wind tousled Conal's strawberry-blond hair as we sat at a seaside picnic table and talked about the future of *Totoaba macdonaldi*. He probably knows more about the species than anyone else alive. Conal considers himself Mexican, although he was born in the United States and has a ruddy complexion that makes him appear of Celtic decent. He grew up in the central mountains of Guanajuato and, moving west, received all his degrees from Autonomous University of Baja California, including a doctorate in fish production. Mexico is the only homeland Conal has ever known, and his patriotism was evident as he shared his hopes for the people of his country. His goals for totoaba are somewhat polemical, however.

It turns out that the hatchery was not designed solely for the purpose of repopulating the Sea of Cortez. Conal would like to see some of the stock raised for a legalized meat industry. A totoaba aquaculture practice could prove reasonably sustainable, he said, because farmed fish reach about six and a half pounds and are ready for harvest within eighteen to twenty-two months. Filets would be genotyped, identifiable, and sold in a controlled and traceable market.

He envisions fingerlings being sent to farm sites—sea pens stationed along the coast from San Felipe south to Bahía de Los Angeles. Local fishermen would manage day-to-day care. It's important to Conal that they participate in the benefits of aquaculture as a way to replace revenue lost to the gillnet ban. Fingerlings would be fed in the sea pens for four to six months, at which point a sizable percentage of juvenile stock would be released to bolster the wild population. The remainder would be kept another twelve to eighteen months until ready for market. As needed, larger fish could be transferred back to Ensenada and grown out for broodstock. The hatchery would continue to provision the farmers, and dividends earned would help fund the program.

"I think it could work because totoaba is really valued and there's a lot of interest in the species," Conal said, his shoulders framed against the distant horizon. "But there are also a lot of questions around conservation. What does a legal trade of an endangered species look like? What do people think about it? Some people will understand it, but there are a lot of people who won't understand it."

In additional to the ethical dilemma of eating filets from an endangered species, there is the even-trickier *buche* market to consider. Because it takes ten years for a captive fish to grow a valuably sized swim bladder, aquaculture cannot produce enough product to stop the black market. But as the hatchery adds more and more fish into the habitat, Conal recommends implementing legislation that would allow a certain amount of wild totoaba to be taken through quota-based hook-and-line sportfishing. The swim bladders, he suggests, could be sold to China, legally and at exorbitant prices.

A quota system for elephants was imposed in the 1980s. It allowed a certain number of socially intelligent pachyderms to be killed for the ivory trade, with the goal of balancing conservation and commerce. The plan proved reckless. It merely blurred the line between authorized ivory and criminal ivory. With a legitimate loophole to exploit, elephant poaching exploded. Today, years later, those noble animals are still suffering greatly.

Even though there is a certain logic to permitting fishermen to return to the hooks of the 1920s, one must ask, could a white market, in all practicality, work? To date, every attempt to control Alto Golfo fisheries has been met with collusion. Wouldn't legalizing a fishery for a highly prized species simply create a new cover for illicit trade? After all, Pesca would be at the regulatory helm, and its track record is somewhat questionable.

Lorenzo once told me, "The goal of aquaculture should be the meat, not the swim bladders. They cannot solve the issue of the swim bladders in China. And restrictions of CITES would not allow a market." The Convention on International Trade in Endangered Species would have to downlist totoaba to Appendix II. That's no small thing.

Conal believes that it is still worth pursuing. "I don't see that the totoaba black market is going to disappear," he said. "There is only one way this is going to get better. That's finding a way to develop a very small and very well-policed legal fishery that will make the illegal market less worthy. If we can build the aquaculture program and keep restocking, and the government goes back to hook-and-line fishing for wild totoaba, I think the fishery would do fine. I think that's the way they should go. I have been over and over the possible solutions, and nothing else seems viable."

As an outsider, my sense is that if China were out of the equation, it might be possible for totoaba to recover enough for a quota to be allowed for (non-*buche*) sportfishing. A good business model might arguably resuscitate communities. But with China hemorrhaging money and with Mexican cartels in the driver's seat, I just can't imagine that there is a chance for sustainability. Like elephant tusks, the fewer that remain, the greater the value. There is so much cash to be made—the Upper Gulf will almost assuredly be fished out before the black market rests.

Conal is committed to his platform. Legal or illegal, totoaba has been an active fishery for the better part of a century, served on dinner plates and slurped as fish maw in the United States, China, and Mexico, among other countries. "If we can provide the *buches* and the meat and everything, there will be no reason to have large nets in the water," asserted Conal.

Traceability, he said. That's the key.

~

Standard NOM-059—the Endangered Species Act of Mexico—states that any restricted specimen must be traceable for transport. Meeting that requirement is a big part of Conal's proposal. Because a simple DNA sample can now link a hatchery-released fish to its genetic family, the swim bladders of individuals later caught in the wild are indeed traceable. Geneticist Luis Enríquez has already identified two poached totoaba, both released from the hatchery a decade before their capture. The match-type DNA came from confiscated *buches*—one from US Fish and Wildlife and the other from Mexico's environmental police.

Even more tantalizing is Conal's plan to establish a totoaba population estimate through genotyping. Instead of catching and counting fish as with a traditional survey—risking barotrauma in several hundred animals—the first-ever abundance assessment might be done in a lab. He explained, "Using genomic studies, you can establish all the families that reside in the gulf. You just need DNA samples. And there are lots of DNA samples already available."

Every time the newspaper reports another swim bladder seizure, he and Enríquez try to gain access to samples. "It's not easy because it's evidence being held for prosecution," Conal said, "but we continue to pursue this course." In four to five years, they have obtained a couple thousand samples, with which Enríquez has begun building a data set of wild totoaba families.

I was fascinated by the simplicity of the science. By measuring the confiscated *buches*, they've created a model that correlates size to age. A *buche* of a certain size means a fish of a certain age. In addition, measuring the thickness of the bladder wall tells them whether the animal was male (thin wall) or female (thick wall). Using those data, they can determine the number of males versus females and average ages. Deductions can then be drawn. If a female is twelve years old, for example, she has been spawning for five years, and the number of her offspring can be estimated.

By employing those statistics, along with everything known about fecundity, survivorship, growth, and life span, Enríquez is developing mathematical models that can predict the size of the population. It will take years of data to fully refine such a model, but information about the species is starting to emerge. One happy discovery is that genetic variance appears higher than expected, which means that totoaba were not genetically decimated by the mid-twentieth-century population bottleneck. The species could theoretically recover.

Many of today's fishermen maintain that totoaba has already recovered. They argue for the fishery to be reopened. With thousands of fish being illegally harvested every year, totoaba is obviously not as endangered as vaquita. Claiming recovery is still tricky business, however, because nobody knows the original size of the population. Just because there are more now than there were in 1975 when the fishery was closed does not mean that the population has recovered.

Remember that eighty years ago, you could, at a glance, observe the backs of hundreds of totoaba gliding along the coast. If that's the baseline, recovery is still a distant dream.

~

What about vaquitas? How do they fit into Conal's vision?

Conal subscribes to the evolutionary-extinction theory, but he seemed legitimately disturbed that fishermen's gillnets have artificially sped up the process. "Just because I work with totoaba doesn't mean I don't care about vaquita," he said. "They should definitely be given a chance. Every species should remain as long as they can in nature. SEMARNAT and Pesca have to get together on this.

"But," he asked, his voice tinged with justified resentment, "as conservation commodities, why are people so much more interested in vaquita than totoaba?"

It was a good question.

We both knew the answer: humans love mammals. This one simple fact relegates the majority of imperiled animals—including frogs, insects, birds, and fish—to struggle for their survival outside the hearts of those in power.

Conservation castes do exist. They influence the direction of public funds and attention, and they create professional competition. After all, it is hard for an egg-laying fish to contend with a baby-birthing porpoise, just as it is hard for a shy porpoise to contend with a gregarious dolphin or for a sea-dwelling dolphin to contend with a cuddly home-raised dog. As George Orwell surmised, "All animals are equal, but some animals are more equal than others."

Still, just because a totoaba isn't furry or doesn't smile, should it deserve less from us?

"Do fish have personalities?" I asked Conal.

Without hesitation, he answered, "Oh yeah! Totoaba are smart in their own way, but they are not overly expressive. Still, some of them are pushy, always eating first and imposing on the other fish. Others are more held back. Some are very, very, very curious and will immediately come up to the window—always the same ones. So they're all different."

In the manner common of population biologists, Conal claims more attachment to his program—to the big-picture goal of sustaining the species—than to his individual fish. But when I mentioned Jenny, totoaba number 324, whom he has known for almost a decade, his cheek hitched up in a small smile that exposed a more tender side to his scientific stance.

～

Driving away from the hatchery, my mind swirled with troubled thoughts. It wasn't Conal's totoaba that caused my fret. It was the last few vaquitas, living on borrowed time.

Pushed to extremes and cornered by circumstances, scientists were gearing up for an attempt at ex situ conservation. Ex situ means "off site." The idea of catching vaquitas and securing them in sea pens had only recently surfaced as a legitimate consideration, and it scared me beyond words. No vaquita has ever been held in captivity. Furthermore, captive programs, no matter the species, are fraught with life-threatening trials for the animals involved.

Fish hatcheries have been operated since the 1800s, and Conal is quick to say that his successes came on the heels of many historical failures—lessons learned and systems improved over two arduous centuries. He himself started with a well-studied and technologically advanced fishery protocol, and by further fine-tuning it over twenty years to meet the specific needs of totoaba, he has finally found a method that works.

His program appears successful. Adult totoaba are effectively kept and mated. Healthy offspring are released back into the wild. Yet there is still an incredibly high mortality rate. Loads of dead fish. Dead from capture. Dead from infection. Dead from weird side effects of captive care (at one time, overinflated swim bladders in hatchlings killed more than 95 percent of the stock). In fact, the hatchery only works because there are enough wild fish in the gulf to keep taking broodstock, and those breeders produce millions of fertile eggs to work with.

With fish, even a modicum of offspring survival equates to thousands of babies. That's not the case with marine mammals. A female totoaba may lay trillions of eggs in her lifetime, whereas a vaquita, if successful in her reproductive life, might produce seven offspring, each of which is parentally cared for. Despite my notion of totoaba and vaquita as twins, they are not the least bit biologically similar, not at all.

I thought of those giant totoaba in their tanks, suspended in their temperature- and light-controlled realm. Could vaquitas ever thrive in a fabricated habitat?

Could they even survive capture?

CHAPTER 14

Last-Ditch Effort

THE PORPOISE I SEE APPEARS PLUMP and healthy; its smooth, dark skin shines in the sunlit depths. As it twists playfully, rushing forward in the green-gray water, I can hear its sonar targeting an unseen object. Suddenly, a fish pops into view, but something's strange about it. Oddly bent at the waist, it begins to sink. The porpoise, perpetually smiling, zooms close, pummels the fish with rapid-fire clicks, and snatches it up before turning tail and fluking off into the foggy void.

That was my first look at a captive porpoise. On YouTube.

As with my first look at captive totoaba, I saw it through a window, but this time it was my computer screen. The animal was filmed halfway around the world, eating dead fish in a Denmark aquarium, its high-frequency sonar recorded for playback. The Fjord & Bælt Center currently has two porpoises. Freja and Sif were rescued from fishing nets at one to two years old and brought to the aquarium for rehabilitation. After recovering, they simply stayed on. They have now lived in captivity as research subjects for between thirteen and twenty years.

SOS Dolfijn at Harderwijk in the Netherlands is also successfully rescuing and rehabilitating sick, entrapped, or stranded porpoises. It reports that "over 90% of the total number of animals rehabilitated consist of harbor porpoises," with success rates above 50 percent. Although certain recovered individuals are deemed nonreleasable, they express pride that more than forty of the rehabbed porpoises have been safely returned to their natural ocean home.

Once, in early 2016, when I first asked Barb about putting vaquitas in captivity, she said, "Doing something like that would be outrageously difficult and expensive. Because where would you keep them? And how would you feed them? Even finding them and capturing them without killing them is an enormous hurdle."

With the exception of the short-lived orphan at CEDO, no vaquita has ever been in captivity. So very little is known about the natural life cycle of the species that the undertaking would be entirely experimental.

Nevertheless, a couple months after that conversation, Barb and her CIRVA colleagues officially announced that they were considering ex situ conservation—a captive recovery program. With the vaquita population estimated at that time to be fewer than sixty individuals and with totoaba nets still stalking the waters of Alto Golfo, the committee's spring 2016 report claimed that "it would be irresponsible of CIRVA not to evaluate *ex situ* options as potential conservation tools despite the difficulties."

Although "members stressed that captivity is not a permanent solution to the conservation of the vaquita" and unanimously agreed that capturing all remaining vaquitas would not be a viable strategy, they conceded that an ex situ initiative, if successful, could buy time for Mexico to get a handle on the *buche* crisis.

I knew from personal discussions with Lorenzo that he, like Barb, prayed that the Mexican government would solve the gillnet problem through legislation and enforcement before they ever had to take any real steps toward ex situ management. Lorenzo actually began his career as a dolphin trainer in a Mexican aquarium, but after going out to assist the capture of wild dolphins, he quit that job. He went back to school and became a scientist. Catching a wild cetacean is a harrowing event for everyone involved, and the experience deeply shaped Lorenzo's feelings about captivity and the explicit cost of yanking animals from their natural lives.

Knowing his background, it's no surprise that Lorenzo was decisively opposed to catching vaquitas—especially when it was first suggested by Pesca as a way to rid fishermen of the nuisance. He gave no further credence when ex situ conservation was broached at subsequent CIRVA meetings. By 2016, however, Lorenzo felt his steadfast resistance slipping.

When I spoke with Barb in 2017, she said, "You have to recognize when what you have been doing—even though it seems like the right thing—is not accomplishing its goal. Vaquita and gillnets are incompatible, and so you have to come up with alternative gear and alternative livelihoods in those villages in order to save vaquita. That's still true. That's plan A. But plan A saw vaquitas go from five hundred and fifty to now well less than thirty. So plan A isn't working. We're not giving up on it, but we have to try something else. Plan B."

Plan B: VaquitaCPR, short for the Consortium for Vaquita Conservation, Protection, and Recovery, has a team of experts preparing to capture up to ten porpoises in October. The goal will be to hold animals in protective custody until Alto Golfo can be rendered 100 percent gillnet-free. Reintroduction is critical, Barb explained, and captives are expected to eventually return to their natural habitat and, it is hoped, rejoin any individuals who may have miraculously survived in the wild.

The $5 million binational effort is sanctioned and significantly funded by the Mexican government, under advisement of CIRVA, and logistically supervised by the US National Marine Mammal Foundation. Cynthia Smith is a veterinarian and the executive director of NMMF;

Brief Timeline of Vaquita (and Totoaba) in the Upper Gulf of California

1920s   Fishermen from Guaymas follow totoaba to the Upper Gulf and begin harvesting with hook-and-line techniques; small communities ensue

1940s   Gillnets become the backbone of most fisheries in the Upper Gulf; vaquitas first seen by fishermen as bycatch

1950   Bleached skull of unrecognized cetacean species found near San Felipe

1958   Norris and McFarland first describe *Phocoena sinus* (from three skulls only); totoaba is commonly served on American dinner plates

1975   Mexico closes and illegalizes totoaba fishery

1976   CITES adds totoaba to its list of protected species

1978   IUCN Red List lists vaquita as vulnerable

1979   CITES adds vaquita to its list of protected species; US Endangered Species Act lists totoaba as endangered

1982   Brownell describes basic anatomy of *Phocoena sinus* and reports substantial exploitation of the species

1985   US Endangered Species Act lists vaquita as endangered

1986   IUCN Red List lists totoaba as endangered

1990   IUCN Red List lists vaquita as endangered

1992   Totoaba-sized gillnets banned in the Gulf of California; Mexico mints a commemorative 100-peso vaquita coin

1993   Mexico establishes Upper Gulf of California and Colorado River Delta Biosphere Reserve

1994   Mexican Standard NOM-059-ECOL lists vaquita "in danger of extinction"

1996   IUCN Red List lists both vaquita and totoaba as critically endangered

1997   CIRVA convenes for the first time; large-scale visual survey estimates vaquita population at 567; acoustic monitoring program launched

1999   2nd meeting of CIRVA

2003   La Vaquita Marina Restaurant opens in San Felipe

2004   3rd meeting of CIRVA

2005   Mexico establishes Vaquita Refuge, all gillnets banned within its borders (no enforcement); Islands and Protected Areas of the Gulf of California listed as a World Heritage Site

2006   Baiji (China's Yangtze river dolphin) announced extinct after large-scale visual survey fails to locate a single individual

2008   INECC acoustic research team begins testing PAM devices; large-scale visual survey estimates vaquita population at 245; Mexico launches PACE-Vaquita and begins alternative fishing gear development

2011   INECC begins annual deployment of c-pods inside Vaquita Refuge; totoaba poaching quietly begins to surge

2012   Mexico elects Enrique Peña Nieto as president; 4th meeting of CIRVA; totoaba swim bladders increasingly smuggled to China and United States

2013   Mexican NOM-002 mandates 3-year switchover from gillnets to small shrimp trawls; US Customs agents confiscate 214 totoaba swim bladders with street value of $3.6 million

2014   5th meeting of CIRVA, called CIRVA-5; catastrophic decline of vaquitas shown by acoustic monitoring reported to Mexico's Presidential Vaquita Commission

2015   Sea Shepherd arrives in the Upper Gulf for vaquita campaign, Operation Milagro (January); Mexico announces 2-year emergency gillnet ban in the Upper Gulf (April); CIRVA-6 calls for a permanent gillnet ban (May); Expedition 2015 conducts large-scale sighting/acoustic survey (October–December)

2016   Three vaquita corpses recovered for necropsy, including Ps2 (March); CIRVA-7 announces population estimate of 60 (April); Sea Shepherd announces totoaba campaign, Operation Angel de la Guarda (May); Center for Biological Diversity asks US to certify Mexico for failure to control totoaba trade (June); UNESCO threatens World Heritage Site status for Sea of Cortez (July); Presidents Peña Nieto and Barack Obama agree to a permanent gillnet ban in the Upper Gulf (July); ghost net recovery project commences (October); CIRVA-8 (November) announces population estimate of 30; China sponsors first Totoaba Enforcement Workshop (December)

2017   Four vaquita corpses recovered for necropsy (March–April); CIRVA-9 (April); San Felipe fishermen burn boat in protest of vaquita conservation (April); American actor Leonard DiCaprio and Mexican magnate Carlos Slim sign foundational Memorandum of Understanding with President Peña Nieto (June); permanent gillnet ban finally goes into Mexican law (June); VaquitaCPR attempts captive care (October/November)

she and Lorenzo are the coleaders for VaquitaCPR. Several organizations are supporting the cause, including the Marine Mammal Center in Sausalito, California, which is busy cultivating private-donor dollars, and the Association of Zoos and Aquariums, which raised $1 million for the *Phocoena sinus* "rescue operation" through its international SAFE program, Saving Animals From Extinction.

When I visited Cynthia in California, she described four key elements of the VaquitaCPR program: capture, housing, long-term care, and eventual release. "It's a phased approach with many go/no-go points along the way," she said. She was quick to add, "We have the world's experts. And those experts are leveraging all available knowledge about the safest—not the easiest or the cheapest but the safest—methods and materials to use."

The catch project manager is renowned cetacean specialist Randy Wells, who has extensive experience capturing and releasing bottlenose dolphins as the director of the Sarasota Dolphin Research Program. The capture plan is centered on the technique Harderwijk employs for harbor porpoises in the Netherlands. Essentially, a modified salmon net will be used to encircle the vaquitas. When a porpoise hits that kind of net, it apparently does not get entangled and rises straight up to breathe, which theoretically means that all handling can be done at the surface. Cynthia explained that visibility is critical. "It's very murky in the Sea of Cortez," she said, "and we want to be able to see as best as possible to ensure the animals are safe during the capture process."

Needless to say, before any porpoises can be caught, they must first be found. Herein lies one of the most astounding elements of the plan. Large search vessels will comb the area with skilled observers on the lookout. But because it's exceeding difficult for humans to spot vaquitas, even using Big Eyes, a group of cetaceans is being called upon for help: US Navy–trained dolphins.

Four female bottlenose dolphins named Katrina, Fathom, Andrea, and Splash have been training off California and will soon be transported to the Upper Gulf. There they will apply their natural sonar to help find any remaining vaquitas and signal their handlers on the capture team. The dolphins will also track porpoise groups visually detected by human observers.

"I love that part," offered Cynthia. "I love that we're having an animal help save another animal."

～

Despite every detail being meticulously plotted out by the most prestigious of participants, the announcement of VaquitaCPR generated immediate opposition. Placing wild animals into captivity is a complex, emotionally charged, and philosophically polarizing subject. And with some of the largest animal-welfare organizations disapproving of the plan, including Sea Shepherd, the undersized vaquita conservation community is now sorely divided.

I am told that Omar Vidal—a well-known scientist, frequent attendee of past CIRVA meetings, and long-standing director of World Wildlife Fund Mexico, who was relieved of his post in 2017 in the middle of this crisis—remains adamantly opposed to the idea of catching vaquitas. He has consistently held that the risks are too high and that any further loss of reproductive females could mark the end of the species. It's a reasonable concern. An overzealous capture plan could swiftly imperil the last vaquitas.

It's worth noting that porpoises in gillnets die fairly quickly. One might presume that a cetacean that can hold its breath for several minutes would take time to drown, but I'm told that that's not the case. Fear and stress cause the animal to expire quickly. Some porpoises caught by humans have panicked and died in hand.

And even if vaquitas survive capture, it would not in any way guarantee that they would survive captivity. Trauma, disease, chronic stress, and anxiety are but a few of the long-term concerns.

Different species respond differently to being enclosed. The Fjord & Bælt residents as well as those cared for by SOS Dolfijn at Harderwijk and other European facilities are harbor porpoises. Native to the cool waters of the northern Atlantic and Pacific Oceans, *Phocoena phocoena* is one of only two porpoise species successfully kept and bred in captivity. The other is the finless porpoise, *Neophocaena phocaenoides*, found in warm, coastal areas of the Indo-Pacific and held in several Asian aquariums.

Attempts to wrangle other species into captivity have proven less successful. In November 1956, a 225-pound male Dall's porpoise, *Phocoenoides dalli*, was captured off Catalina Island and transported to a California dolphinarium. Despite efforts to calm and protect him, the disoriented cetacean relentlessly battered his head against the walls of his pool. After sinking to the bottom and nearly drowning, he was hung in a sling at the water surface. He was dead in less than twenty-four hours.

In the years between 1964 and 1966, four other adult Dall's porpoises were taken into captivity. One started failing the morning after capture and quickly died from trauma and internal bleeding. Two others perished in just less a month, after falling sick with symptoms that ranged from sloughing skin to weight loss to vomiting blood and suffering treatments that involved lots of hypodermic needles and a stomach pump.

The last and longest-lived Dall's porpoise survived a mere twenty-one months. Marty, as he was called, appeared to tolerate captive care and worked amicably with his trainer before succumbing to lung abscesses and stomach ulcers.

Of all the captured Dall's porpoises, two were female, and upon necropsy, both were found to be carrying near-term fetuses. Thus, seven animals met a tragic fate. At that point, keepers decided that Dall's are not properly tempered for captivity.

Nobody knows yet if vaquitas are properly tempered.

Once, a rarely seen Burmeister's porpoise—the species genetically closest to vaquita—was taken into captivity. Eight days later, it died of bronchial pneumonia. In all fairness, though, that animal had stranded itself on an Argentinian beach, so it's possible it was already stressed or ill.

Cynthia insisted that VaquitaCPR is designed to mitigate as much risk as possible. "If they're like a harbor porpoise, then we're probably okay," she said. She exhaled before she conceded, "If they're like a Dall's porpoise, then we're all going to have to accept the fact that it's not going to work."

She thinks they will know right away if vaquitas are like Dall's porpoises, and the veterinarians will be poised to execute an immediate release. "We have strict criteria for evidence of external stress. And if we're hitting those, we're releasing them. That would be hard but"—she recited the core message of her veterinary oath—"'above all, do no harm.'"

In this high-stakes pursuit, there is a real chance for failure. Indeed, the whole procedure could be aborted at stage one. But supposing vaquitas tolerate human handling, I asked, what is the plan for housing?

Cynthia told me that a sea-pen aquarium called *Oceanico*, which normally holds tuna off Ensenada, is being towed around the Baja peninsula. It will be anchored near San Felipe. Detained vaquitas will temporarily be placed in a floating sea pen that's twenty feet across and four feet deep, shallow enough to permit continuous observation during initial evaluation. Caretakers will introduce live fish. Once the animals are eating, they'll move into a slightly larger pen, thirty feet across and ten feet deep.

The aquarium structure includes a floating barge for chief staff and security. There will be round-the-clock guards, and additional staff will be stationed in San Felipe on the shores of Machorro Cove. A military-style land-based facility, called the Vaquita Care Center, is being built to hold a small veterinary lab and a fish house for stocking food. Its aboveground pools will provide backup housing if the sea pens fail or safe haven should extreme weather strike. People and equipment (and, if need be, vaquitas) will be ferried between posts.

A veterinarian will be with each vaquita from the moment of capture, Cynthia explained, monitoring vital signs, looking for signs of stress, and making critical decisions about whether or how to proceed. Not surprisingly, some of the most elite cetacean doctors in the veterinary community have agreed to serve with her and Frances Gulland on the VaquitaCPR medical team.

"We'll be doing full evaluations. Looking at cortisol blood levels and doing full-body ultrasounds," said the coleader. If the porpoises do well in the smaller sea pens, they will be moved to one that's sixty-five feet across and thirteen feet deep. Then, should further observations show them settling in, a full sanctuary will be built in Machorro Cove, "one that's big enough for them to thrive and breed until they go back into the wild."

～

There is a new attraction near where I live in Arizona. The OdySea complex with Dolphinaris touts a swim with the dolphins package. Months before it opened, a Whale and Dolphin Conservation representative commented, "I think it's going to be a nightmare for the dolphins."

Others thought so, too. For almost a year during and after construction, local residents protested in peaceful but passionate rallies. Weekends could find up to two hundred picketers lining Scottsdale's city blocks with signs like "Dolphins DON'T Belong in the DESERT," "Captivity Kills," "Thanks but NO TANKS!" and "We like dolphins . . . in the ocean."

P. T. Barnum, of circus notoriety, was the first person to put a cetacean in captivity. In the century that followed, thousands of them were wrangled into commercial venues. Even in modern times, wild hunts were (and at times still are) how aquariums secured the stock they needed to fill their viewing pools. Any animals that survived the ordeal were trained to perform for the public in sensationally marketed whale and dolphin shows that promised oodles of derring-do. Because most captives died early, they were simply replaced.

Think of Shamu.

Through the 1960s, 1970s, and 1980s, America fell in love with Shamu, the famous SeaWorld orca. As we now know, Shamu was "played" by different animals through the years—a promotional scheme that took advantage of visitors' inability to distinguish one killer whale from another. Most patrons had a complete lack of knowledge about the park's catch-and-cage system.

Today, in the wake of the documentary film *Blackfish*, which showed the haunting effects of captivity on the intelligent minds of cetaceans, places like SeaWorld are plunging in popularity. With awareness on the rise, we are seeing a dramatic shift in public opinion. People are increasingly sensitive to cetaceans held in small enclosures or exploited for human entertainment.

Of course, bringing vaquitas into captivity for the recovery of the species is pointedly different than the exploitive agendas of dolphinariums. Although ex situ conservation is not ideal—nobody denies that there are health and well-being concerns for the animals, namely related to stress—captive recovery programs are founded on the premise of preserving and increasing at-risk populations. The truth is that without them, many cherished species—including the panda, red wolf, California condor, Sumatran rhino, whooping crane, Bactrian camel, black-footed ferret, and Iberian lynx—might already be extinct.

Accredited zoos and aquariums can connect remote habitats and endangered species to the mainstream world. They can raise both funding and awareness. So, the most substantial procaptivity stance has to do with educating the public. Seeing animals up close makes us want to help them in the wild. Captive individuals are often called ambassadors and are liaisons between wild populations and the human heart. The movie *Blackfish* was so profoundly disturbing because we all love killer whales—thanks, ahem, to Shamu.

The irony should not be lost here.

Would your average landlocked American even care about dolphins if not for the 1960s television series *Flipper*? As a little girl, I loved that show. Flipper was my first exposure to the intelligence and beauty of dolphins. And who among us, adjusting the rabbit-ear antennas atop our television sets, did not delight to the sound of Flipper's clever chirps and whistles?

But like Shamu, Flipper was not played by one dolphin, and despite being depicted as a boy, the role was filled by females. A sea-park dolphin trainer named Ric O'Barry successfully captured five wild bottlenose dolphins and trained them to perform on camera. After one of his "stars" died in his arms from stress, O'Barry became obsessed with exposing the mental anguish imposed by captive conditions. He has served as an anti-captivity advocate ever since, earning mixed accolades for his radical tactics.

O'Barry, though, would never know what he knows without having worked on *Flipper*, and more importantly, he would never have obtained public support for his cause if so many of us hadn't watched the show and fallen in love with dolphins. We adore animals because we feel connected with them. Compassion is the love child of connection. Ideally, that connection comes from an eco-friendly trip into native habitat where species are benignly observed. For most of us, however, it still comes from a childhood trip to the zoo or aquarium.

Barb, who hates the idea of pen-bound vaquitas as much as anyone, admits that captive animals just might bring some desperately needed awareness to the species. "I have to say—and I would not be popular for holding this idea," she told me, "but if you even just took two vaquitas and you put them on a camera where people could see them every day—like panda-cam, you know—it might be enough to get the public and political will to do what it takes to save them in the wild."

Will captive vaquitas ever be on display? Challengers of VaquitaCPR, who worry that there is an economic incentive to the enterprise, cite a passage from the CIRVA-8 report that states that the "shore-based sea-pen sanctuary" will have "potential for observation by the public for the purpose of conservation education and outreach, as deemed appropriate by the Mexican government." So, if vaquitas are successfully captured, visitors may someday be allowed to see them.

Even Fjord & Bælt, a research center reportedly focused on gaining conservation-driven data from its porpoises, takes advantage of public passion by charging entrance fees to its aquarium and offering daily training shows with Freja and Sif.

Institutions want revenue. People want a personal experience. Despite everything now known, we too often allow ourselves the comfort of denial. Fighting for our own freedom, we manage to overlook the injustice and emotional cost of captivity to so many living beings we profess to love. We are charmed to see animals, even if they are locked in cages.

Against fervent protests to the attraction near my house, including an online petition begging Americans to stop the circus-style entertainment of forcing confined dolphins to interact with paying humans for a dole-out of fish, exploiting the animals' base need for food—a petition that garnered more than 170,000 signatures—OdySea and Dolphinaris opened their doors in 2016.

Their parking lot has been full every day since.

~

If it turns out that vaquitas can be kept alive and in good health, would they, could they, ever reproduce? Captive breeding is an extremely challenging and often drawn-out proposition—if it ever works at all.

Porpoises have been successfully bred in captivity, but the cases are rare. Both Fjord & Bælt females were mated with their (now deceased) male, Eigil, and at least three resulting pregnancies went full term. Still, no offspring have survived. Even though the porpoises appear contented in captivity and medical monitoring offered no sign of trouble during each one-year gestation period, something has gone awry after every birth. When Freja delivered her calf in 2006, it died within a few hours. Sif had a calf in 2013 that was deceased within a matter of days, and her 2014 calf perished two days postpartum.

Because miscarriages, stillborn births, and short-lived calves are common among confined cetaceans, saving vaquita through captive breeding is pure gamble.

And then there's still the final hurdle: reintroduction.

It has been empirically shown that some whales and dolphins can be successfully returned to the sea after periods of captivity. It has been speculatively proposed that cetaceans born in captivity, taught to hunt and released in social groups, might also survive. The latter is encouraging because a victorious species-recovery program requires more than getting animals to make babies in man-made enclosures; at least some must be reintroduced to suitable habitat and lead the way back to healthy wild populations.

Unfortunately, unless Mexico removes gillnets from Alto Golfo virtually immediately, vaquita recovery could require decades of captive care. What happens if those original porpoises pass away and their offspring are left with no prior knowledge of the habitat and no leaders to demonstrate key points of navigation and foraging in their native world? It's hard to say. Every successful save-a-species program began with a terrestrial species. Releasing captive-bred cetaceans to re-create a wild population has never been endeavored.

For some hint at what vaquita biologists might be facing, people often refer to the California condor recovery effort. *Gymnogyps californianus* is a giant prehistoric bird native to the United States and Mexico. With a life span of up to seventy years and few natural predators, this iconic scavenger, like vaquita, probably survived quite well until humans arrived on the scene.

For at least two centuries, condors were indiscriminately shot from the skies, inadvertently killed by poisoning campaigns against nuisance animals, reproductively restrained by egg collectors, and—most importantly, as it still occurs today—poisoned by lead shot left in rotting carcasses by sport hunters. By 1984, only fifteen wild California condors remained. When seven of those disappeared, a full-fledged captive recovery program was spurred into existence, with the last free-ranging bird trapped in Southern California on April 19, 1987.

Captured birds were placed in well-equipped facilities at the Los Angeles Zoo and San Diego Zoo's Wild Animal Park, where qualified teams were prepared for the task of eliciting reproduction. Birds, like fish, have been bred in captivity for hundreds of years, so there was a knowledge base to work from. By 1992, the program had successfully hatched enough offspring to reintroduce twelve juveniles back to the wild.

Serious challenges ensued. Not having experienced members in the social hierarchy from which to learn, the hand-raised juveniles began playing on power lines. After four were electrocuted, the rest were caught and put back in cages. Thereafter, power line aversion training was implemented at the condor care facilities.

The next set of released birds fared better. They knew not to play on power lines, and some even started pairing up and producing chicks. But the wild-born babies then began dying. On necropsy, the infants' digestive tracts were found to be stuffed with glass shards, bottle caps, screws, coins, plastic, and other bits and pieces of human debris. Biologists deduced that condors of yesteryear delivered calcium-rich bone chips to their nest-bound youngsters. Somehow that behavior got misdirected, and the unindoctrinated parents were feeding microtrash instead. It was yet another glitch of captive rearing. To counter the problem, bone chips are now placed in and around nests.

On top of all that, released condors were soon dying from tainted meat. In fact, the number one cause of mortality in today's wild populations is lead poisoning. When scavengers eat toxic carcasses or meat left by hunters, they endure paralysis of the digestive tract followed by the agony of starvation and death.

With the enormous cost of the California condor program, with almost fifty years' evidence that lead kills condors (and other species, too, such as golden eagles, let alone the risks it poses to human health), and with the availability of high-performance copper bullets that have been shown to perform better, one might assume that lead ammunition is being eliminated from use. But it's still legal across most of the United States. In 2017, President Donald Trump's interior secretary even went so far as to reverse the ban on lead ammunition in national wildlife refuges.

If the United States can't get lead out of the hands of its sport hunters, how is Mexico expected to get gillnets out of the hands of its professional fishermen?

And, as it relates to VaquitaCPR, if Mexico can't eradicate gillnets to save the most endangered cetacean with $100 million and the whole world watching, how will it manage with vaquitas in sanctuary?

~

During his tenure as general director of WWF-Mexico, Omar Vidal repeatedly asserted that removing vaquitas from their habitat would lead to more illegal fishing, not less. Period. And, by eliminating the most pressing incentive for alternative gear, plans for developing sustainable methods will be undermined, he added. Captivity should not be the solution to a conservation crisis. It's too easy to push a few animals into cages and call it success. Letting governments and industry off the hook while integrated biomes collapse does not serve anyone's future, he claimed.

On the subject of ex situ management, the executive director of Greenpeace Mexico, Gustavo Ampugnani, said, "This drastic measure will do very little if the underlying problem of totoaba fishing and the use of gillnets has not been solved."

What if he's right? What if the underlying problem is never solved and Alto Golfo is never rendered gillnet-free? What if vaquitas can never be released back to their natural habitat? What will become of them? Will the world's tiniest porpoise be reduced to a pitiable cluster of captive-bound relics, refugees destined to live in a foreign camp?

These kinds of questions strangle enthusiasm for VaquitaCPR.

Nobody likes the idea of a species without a home. For China's baiji, one of the main arguments that pushed off plans for captive care was that reintroduction was not an option in the foreseeable future. Because the Yangtze River is no longer suitable for river dolphins, conservation organizations balked and decision makers stalled until the baiji went extinct. Should they have done things differently?

Whenever a species is walking the tightrope between life and death and ex situ conservation is proposed, there are always voices of dissent. Sophie A. H. Osborn wrote that the California condor captive breeding program was initiated "amidst dire prognostications from many environmental groups (including the Sierra Club, Friends of the Earth, and several local chapters of the Audubon Society) that insisted the condor be allowed to 'die with dignity,' free of radio transmitters and harassment by scientists."

People have said the same about vaquita. But that idea—the idea that someone would rather see the species go extinct than consider captivity—is beyond Cynthia's realm of thinking. "I've heard the term 'extinction with dignity,' but that doesn't seem acceptable. When the main cause for extinction is at the hands of humans, why shouldn't the hands of humans be there to make it right? Isn't it our moral obligation to try?"

In Lorenzo's words, "You die with dignity when you have cancer and you want to die. But there is no dignity with extinction. Extinction is never with dignity."

As a reminder to naysayers, there are now almost three hundred free-flying California condors. The species is alive and well—although even after all the years of support, wild populations are still not self-sustaining. In Mexico, more than thirty captive-raised birds have been released from the highest peaks of Baja's Sierra San Pedro Martir range. Soaring on thermals near Alto Golfo, those sharp-eyed scavengers can almost certainly see vaquitas, especially ones dead on the beach.

What if everyone had stepped aside and let the California condor go? Would that have been better?

"I see the extinction of a species as an assault against the evolutionary history of this planet," Tom Jefferson of VIVA Vaquita once told me. "For a species that has been evolving for millions of years to be snuffed out by our stupidity and greed, to me that is like the worst crime that can be committed."

But the actions required to change a species' trajectory have risks of their own. Even if the porpoises prove to be tolerant of captivity, losses are to be expected. As with totoaba, condors, and baijis, some vaquitas will likely die in the process of us learning how to properly care for them. That is a grim truth.

Oona, who would do anything to protect *la vaquita marina*, once said, "You'll never convince me that catching the last vaquitas and sticking them in captivity is a good thing." She empathically pointed to the fear and stress the animals would experience. She recoiled at the idea of physical injury or the potential psychological damage from living in an enclosed pen. And that's if they survive. "Can you imagine a vaquita dying in a biologist's hands?" she had asked, a horrified expression on her face.

The thought is indeed unbearable. Vaquitas are intelligent, thinking, emotional beings. They have already suffered dearly. Must they now endure this added penalty? Imagining myself in a locked space propels my mind to chaos. Imprisoning someone who has committed no crime is not only unjust, it's unconscionable. I completely understand how Oona feels, and I told her as much.

But reading Sam Turvey's *Witness to Extinction* remodeled my view. Even though I knew that the baiji had gone extinct before I cracked the book's cover, I found myself shocked when, in the final pages, it actually came to pass. Suddenly extinction was no longer a conceptual notion to discuss at the dinner table. No longer was it a pendant loss or some kind of abstract moral conundrum. Baiji was—is—gone. Truly, utterly, despairingly gone.

The weight and finality broke something in me. Captivity is unthinkable, but if it's not attempted or is delayed for any reason, *Phocoena sinus* will almost certainly disappear—forever. In this emotionally charged dilemma, how can we unite a divided conservation community?

On the simplest level, the debate boils down to individuals versus species. From the individual perspective, no animal should be allowed to suffer, even if the species goes extinct. From the species perspective, the survival of the genetic line is fundamental, and one animal's suffering is a terrible price worth paying. Eric Dinerstein insightfully wrote, "The challenge ahead for us in preserving rarities is to link the science-based approach that focuses on populations rather than individuals and the animal-welfare philosophy that gives ethical value to individuals and their well-being."

If such a resolution is possible, it's hard to imagine a better team of people to attain it. I think of Lorenzo, Armando, and Barb, of Oona, of Gustavo, of Javier and Paco, of Cynthia and so many others. These people are committed and kind, smart and experienced, and they are all suffering unimaginable misery to have arrived at this dreadful decision. Pressed to the rail, provisional captivity appears to be the short but only straw. Gillnet bans and active patrols, scientific data shared by a vocal media, pressure for boycotts and alternative gear—those strategies were not enough. The population has gone from sixty to thirty to maybe fifteen.

Soon there will be seven.

Then three.

Then zero.

"If you asked me about ex situ a year ago, I would have said I don't support it and I don't think it's a good idea—we need to preserve the animals in nature—but I've changed my view on that recently. And the reason is because the situation is so absolutely desperate now," Tom Jefferson told me in May 2017. His voice was steady as he continued, "The fact of the matter is that vaquita is heading very rapidly toward extinction, and there's a real chance this species might not be around on New Year's Day 2018."

In this do-or-die moment, we are called to reflection and are challenged to consider the broader ecological crisis. When I last spoke with Barb, she shared a weighty idea that still lingers in my mind. "This is a very destructive period in the story of *Homo sapiens*," she said, "and with the environmental devastation ahead, we're going to have to take some pretty extreme measures."

She paused briefly and then wrapped ex situ management into proverbial context. "If we want anything left," she said, "we're going to have to put some animals in the ark and ride out the flood."

CHAPTER 15

Hope Is a Life Raft (with a Persistent Leak)

In 2017, the *New York Times* published an alarming sentence: "Some of the scientists involved think the surviving vaquitas now number as few as two or three, and the latest two vaquitas found dead could even be the last ones—though it could take years to confirm that."

Was it possible that the protection effort had failed? All in such short order?

I reread the sentence, and then I cried. And once I started crying, like a ruptured floodgate, I couldn't seem to stop. I cried for that beautiful young girl, Ps2, who first grabbed my heart and whose memory carried me forward whenever courage faltered. I cried for that sweet premie, Ps5, who never even got a chance at life before landing on a necropsy table.

Tears ran for all the vaquitas slain in Alto Golfo since 1940, dead from entanglement in gillnets, for every body cut free and counted, and for the hundreds—no, the thousands—lost to history without as much as a footnote. I cried for all those precious souls, mothers and fathers, sisters, brothers, sons and daughters of a disappearing kingdom.

I cried for the totoaba, brutally gutted and thrown away, and for our shameless bycatch of rays and sea turtles, sharks, and whales. And as my grief expanded like ripples from a fallen stone, I was soon crying for all the at-risk species that once made this planet so wild, so breathtaking. The murdered elephants. The poor starving polar bears. Tigers. Penguins. Wolves. We are enduring such a tragic loss of biodiversity. Even the honeybees—who we personally depend on to pollinate our life-sustaining crops—are being decimated.

Biologist Stuart Pimm "calculated that the current rate of species extinctions was as much as 1,000 times the normal background extinction rate." That was 1995. In the years since, most of us have continued to sleep like babes under the cozy blanket of ignorance (or, perhaps, the ragged quilt of denial?).

More recently, a comprehensive study of data called the Living Planet Index revealed that Earth's vertebrate populations—mammals, birds, reptiles, amphibians, and fish—dropped more than 58 percent between 1970 and 2012. In other words, more than half of the iconic wildlife created to exist in this geological age vanished in just forty years, a statistic that leaves me raw. Moreover, the wheel of extinction is picking up speed. Should trends continue as they have, the loss will reach 67 percent by 2020.

There is talk of a "frozen zoo"—preserving cell lines in cryogenic hibernation to be reconstituted in some distant future. Think test-tube vaquitas. It's science fiction, really, a mental escape hatch for modern consumers who don't want the responsibility of caring for living gifts of creation. Even if such a thing were ever possible, it's not a viable conservation strategy. Animals don't exist in isolation; rather, they are part of an intricate biological and behavioral system, dependent on particular interactions with their native environment and one another.

"Saving only one population of each rare species simply as a token gesture would be of little ecological value, especially where those species play a role in maintaining a given ecosystem's integrity," wrote Dinerstein. "So an essential goal is to conserve multiple populations of species and the genetic, ecological, and behavioral features that these building blocks contain."

Cetacean experts Hal Whitehead and Luke Rendell concur. They wrote that diversity "gives the ecological systems that we depend on stability, resilience, and productivity, as well as aesthetic value." Sufficiently damaged, Earth will no longer be inhabitable to our kind. Saving species in captivity is not enough. We need to save whole ecosystems.

Here towers the moral truth: animals have a right to be here. This living planet was crafted with meticulous balance for flora and fauna to not only exist but to thrive. Nature was born to be robust, and it prospers from a profound complexity that remains beyond human comprehension. If we wipe the slate—erase the master design—the blueprint will be gone. And, as George Schaller put it, "We cannot recover a lost world."

My troubled mind wandered back to Puerto Peñasco and Memuco's studio. In a space littered with colorful pieces of jetsam, paint cans, cardboard cuttings, and inspired objects, his paintings—standing amid the clutter like statues—are visually striking. Memuco paints all manner of animals, not just vaquitas. Antelopes, salamanders, whales, owls, and sharks all emerge from his creative maelstrom, often accompanied by a fantastical maiden of exotic beauty with a powder-white visage, rosy cheeks, and exquisite cornucopian horns.

Who is this compelling character that plays so prominently in the artist's work?

She is *La Silenciosa*, the Silent One. Her shadowed eyes, ever closed, bleed black-mascara tears, perpetually streaking her peaceful countenance. Memuco created the Silent One, originating her poignant backstory. She is the imagined daughter of *La Catrina*, the Lady of Death, and the Nagual of Aztec mythology who has the power to transform himself into any animal.

"She is part animal, so she has great empathy for all animals and the power to communicate with them," Memuco told me as we gazed upon an eight-foot panel of the Silent One. As a curious octopus perched forward from her shoulder, the maiden's outstretched finger reached to touch the smiling lips of a lone vaquita. Her compassion was truly palpable. The whole scene appeared to glow, as though infused with warm light, in a splendid trick of artistry.

But those black tears.

"Of course, she is also part death," Memuco explained. "So when she grows up, her mom, *La Catrina*, comes and tells her, 'Okay sweetie, it's time for you to go to work. Your job will be nothing less than to collect all the endangered animals that are left on the earth and put them to sleep.'" He let that sink in. Prickles scurried up my arms, leaving trails of vertical hair. "So she has to go around and take all these creatures that are about to go extinct. And this is really, really painful for her, which is why she is always crying."

Now I, too, was crying—crying for the Silent One so much like Mother Earth.

At last drained, I wiped my eyes and sent an email to several vaquita scientists expressing my condolences for what had been reported in the *New York Times*. My chest ached to think of their sorrow. Dedicated to vaquita for years and years, they have worked tirelessly to avert the exact circumstances in which they now find themselves. How agonizing it must be to care so much and control so little.

Minutes later, an email popped back from Lorenzo. He described what I'd read as a "harmful and imprecise article." Information from the CIRVA-9 report, he said, had been presented out of context. The spring data had detected only two vaquita encounters, but that low number was a factor of the limited acoustic devices (six) deployed over a short period (March to April).

I'd actually suspected the same thing. Several discrepancies in the article had already made me question its veracity, so I was not entirely surprised to have it debunked. The reporter was mistaken, but no matter. My grief was not about believing vaquita was gone. It was about succumbing to the harsh reality that it may too-soon be.

We are standing on the precipice here. We are so close, so very close to the cliff edge, that we are all looking down into the dark abyss. One glance away and extinction will swoop up like a shadow and steal vaquita forever.

People tell me the story of vaquita plays like a movie. There are villains: cartels, poachers, heartless distributors, and consumers of fish maw. And there are heroes: conservationists, scientists, alternative-gear fishermen, and supporters. In between is the cherished innocent: a voiceless porpoise with dark haunting eyes and a pleading smile. We have come to the final scene, fear and tension choking us in our seats just before our heroes pull the final winning card.

Living in a Hollywood era, we all expect the surprising heart-rush of an eleventh-hour save. But this is not a movie. In the real-life rescue of a disappearing species, there is no promise of a happy ending.

∼

Yangtze River, Eastern China, 2006

Barb stood at the bow of a large vessel, scanning the water for pale blue-gray dorsal fins. She had been sent to China as part of a forty-person survey team tasked with locating the last of the species *Lipotes vexillifer*. "The goddess of the Yangtze," as it's called, is an animal espoused in Chinese literature for thousands of years.

The researchers were prepared to transfer all remaining Yangtze river dolphins, also called baiji (meaning white dolphin), from their native riparian habitat into the relative safety of an oxbow lake. "Basically we were there to save them because it was clear that they weren't being effective at the conservation actions necessary to let them recover inside the Yangtze," Barb once told me of the experience.

Baiji, the sole remaining member of the cetacean family Lipotidae, was facing a host of threats from human activity. The most pressing was small-type fishing—just like vaquita—although in the Yangtze it's not just gillnets, but also rolling-hook longlines, electrocution, and dynamite. There are said to be more than 160 types of fishing in the Yangtze River. In addition, dams divide the aquatic corridor. And tens of thousands of ships journey the waters with powerful motors that interrupt cetacean sonar and cause disemboweling prop strikes. Furthermore, the habitat is degraded by untreated factory waste, an amalgamation of noxious chemicals and heavy metals endlessly pouring into the waterway.

"It was hideously polluted. And dredged everywhere," remembered Barb. "And it has the highest ship traffic, highest human density on the planet. It was just like, Yikes!"

Naturally, the Yangtze River wasn't always so disfigured. It historically supported extraordinary aquatic and terrestrial biodiversity. Wildlife, such as rhinos, elephants, gibbons, and Père David's deer foraged across the region, while the river itself, the longest in Asia, was home to at least 350 recorded fish species, 177 of those endemic. Even Earth's largest freshwater fish (the Chinese paddlefish) and largest freshwater turtle (the Yangtze giant softshell) once thrived in the river, yet both have joined the prodigious list of regional species now rare, extirpated, or extinct.

After the first baiji sighting survey, conducted in 1978, scientists announced a population estimate of about four hundred individuals. Obviously, the species was already in severe decline. Eight years later, the issue of baiji gained ground at an international conference held in Wuhan, China. By 1992, conservation programs were well under way with funding and plans to ban fishing, control pollution, regulate ship speeds, and provide public education.

Baiji reserves were established. Regrettably, they were naught more than "paper parks"—bureaucratic documents that never really protected the animals under their guardianship. Less than 10 percent of the laws created to protect the river dolphins were ever enforced. Sam Turvey, another biologist on the survey with Barb, wrote in his book *Witness to Extinction*, "Despite all the legislation, publicity, and baiji beer, everything was just lip service."

In the mid-1990s, a new estimate for baiji was publicized. One hundred dolphins. Still, legitimate acts of conservation, deadlocked in political elbowing and human debate, failed to proceed. It took another decade of conferences, meetings, and workshops (and a few botched captivity attempts) before those in power managed to coordinate a plan that might actually work: captive care in an oxbow sanctuary.

At last, in 2006, the rescue team was sent out. They searched and searched, up the river and back again, covering the species' range four times over. But there were no baijis left.

"The last baiji died while no one was looking," Barb said. Her words made me wobble.

An exquisitely unique life-form whose ancestors graced the watercourse for at least a hundred times longer than the entire history of humankind—a true living fossil, adapted for survival—had effectively been snuffed out by greed, futility, discord, and indolence. It was the first human-caused extinction of a cetacean species.

"This is a tragedy, but it is also more than that: it is a travesty," wrote Turvey. "It is simply not true that this extinction happened so quickly that it caught us unawares. For almost thirty years, scientists and conservationists have repeated time and again what needed to be done in order to save the baiji."

Baiji belonged to the earth. It was not ours to destroy. There is a steep price for safeguarding a species. But on the day of reckoning, I believe there will be a steeper one for failing to.

~

When I spoke with Sara Amozurrutia in August 2017, she sounded happy. The *Narval* had recently pulled fourteen totoaba nets out of the Vaquita Refuge. And the total number of gillnets removed from Alto Golfo since early 2016—including those hauled in by Sea Shepherd during its regular patrols—had surpassed 450.

Because summer was quiet, the team worked almost straight through. They were taking a short break but would soon resume, with plans to continue into December. Apparently, since Leonardo DiCaprio's visit to Mexico, the ghost net project has been deemed extremely critical. Even CONAPESCA has joined the effort, funding the fishermen contractors. "And we are adding plastic to the Parley donations," Sara offered cheerfully. "It's way for local restaurants to recycle."

Now, in late September, everyone is in high gear. Mauricio is wrapping up INECC's standard acoustic monitoring season. He managed eighty-seven c-pods through summer, exchanging them every two weeks—those data will provide a rate of change for the vaquita population between 2016 and 2017. Then, given the abundance estimate from 2015, an updated number of survivors may be obtained.

Meanwhile, Armando and Gustavo are getting ready for VaquitaCPR, the precarious rescue plan, which will commence in just three weeks. During the capture period, the acoustic team will maintain thirty-six strategically placed c-pods and will be swapping them daily—yes, daily! Their goal will be to guide the on-water search team by tracking areas of high acoustic activity. Lorenzo, Barb, Cynthia Smith, and their vaquita-rescue teammates will work shipboard, looking through the Big Eyes and following dolphins trained by the US Navy to locate and track the last living vaquitas.

Front row, left to right: Lorenzo Rojas, Barbara Taylor, and Minister Rafael Pacchiano hold up a life-sized vaquita model during the Expedition 2015 survey; several visitors stand behind them. (Courtesy of Todd Pusser)

Mexico's environmental minister, Rafael Pacchiano, will soon arrive in San Felipe, and he's planning to stay awhile. "I really like Pacchiano," Oona once told me. "I met him maybe five times, and I always felt that he really cared about the vaquita. He just invested so much in this project, and you can see he's frustrated when I say to him that things are not working well."

Barb says Pacchiano sees this effort as his legacy, and she believes he's going to hold out until the very end. Her assessment appears accurate, and I admire the man's fortitude—his resilience in the face of so much political obstructionism.

"What will happen to Pacchiano after the election?" I asked Gustavo when we spoke.

"I don't know."

As an executive cabinet member, the environmental minister is appointed by the president. With Mexico's upcoming presidential election—to be held July 1, 2018—the single, six-year term of Enrique Peña Nieto will come to a close. One can only hope the incoming minister of environment will carry a torch for vaquita against INAPESCA's inaction and ongoing proclamations that gillnets are not killing them.

As for the president-elect, he or she will inherit not only the looming extinction of Mexico's emblematic marine mammal, but also the scandalous burdens of the Upper Gulf. How will the new head of the nation stop criminal fishing when a pound of totoaba swim bladder can earn its poacher $4,000—versus $9 for a pound of legal shrimp?

And things are poised to get worse. The government compensation program ended in May 2017 at the conclusion of the original two-year gillnet ban, creating more incentive to poach. I've been told that a month-by-month subsidy is being dispensed to fishermen, but details of that allowance remain unclear. What's more, while alternative gear is still log-jammed, word on the street is that totoaba will soon be legalized. Pesca (with a surprising stamp of approval from Pacchiano) has promised to start issuing permits by early 2018. Elections are coming; perhaps this promise is some kind of political foreplay. But if it doesn't come through—and I cannot imagine how it could with no abundance data for the drum fish and the fiddly red tape of CITES and Mexican NOM-059—communities are doomed to disappointment yet again.

Even if regulatory hurdles could be overcome, what can possibly be the plan? A legal fishery is bound to smooth the rails for illegal pursuits. Fishermen are not interested in earning a few bucks helping sportfishing tourists catch a single totoaba. Nor are they interested in procuring filets for dinner. Fishermen are only interested in swim bladders. And with the prospect of having vaquita out of the picture, either extinct or in a sanctuary, and permits for money fish in hand, dollar signs are already flashing in their eyes.

As for the totoaba black market, we must follow its trail out of Mexico. US president Donald Trump is allowing contraband into and through the United States, a major trafficking route to China. In a recent data analysis report entitled *Hooked*, a US Fish and Wildlife Service officer was quoted as saying, "Many Chinese gangs operating in Mexico smuggle [totoaba bladders] north to California." Once stateside dealers and diners take their cut, some plunder ships from Los Angeles and San Francisco to the Far East. I always imagine straw-lined crates bound for China, but transport is rarely so obvious. Three lone bladders, for instance, were discovered in a cargo shipment marked as corn flakes.

Despite China's commitment to cut off its consumers, very few busts occur on that end of the distribution chain. Although street trade of fish maw appears to be moving underground, sales persist. There are also claims of collusion. The *Hooked* report states that Hong Kong officials who conducted "undercover investigations of the retailers and wholesalers . . . found no evidence of totoaba sales." In Guangdong, a few documented offenders suffered small fines, which is no deterrent in a country where the priciest bladder can garner $250,000.

Corruption is insidious and pervasive. Too often, well-connected men are untouchable. Remove vaquita from the equation, and the effort to abolish gillnets in the Upper Gulf is still valid—lest cartels continue to oppress and victimize communities. The *Hooked* report states that "organized criminal groups have solidified their hold on the totoaba trade in the Gulf, . . . frightening the local populations into silence."

"There is no hope because the mafias are everywhere," a Mexican national confessed to me. "I feel really frustrated. I feel shame of my country."

Even though poaching has become a felony under organized crime, not a single person has gone to prison. Criminals caught red-handed by Mexican officials and arrested are routinely released. Evidently, the new law requires a provable connection between apprehended poachers and a crime boss. No crime boss, no crime. Needless to say, if you could prove criminal connections, the whole poaching scheme would crumble. But corruption is said to ensure that enforcement agencies lack tools and protocols for collecting sufficient evidence.

"I just want those at blame to suffer some kind of punishment, so they will feel an impact for their actions," said a Baja resident. "The message right now is, 'Do illegal things. There are no real consequences. The government will even give you money.'"

Given the current amount of international attention and aid, will Mexico find a way to shut down the cartels so that threatened communities can reclaim their social freedoms?

Relevantly, the failure to enforce basic laws is what keeps tourists from feeling entirely safe in Mexico and infusing their tourist dollars. And with no money coming into the villages, fishermen break the law, knowing that enforcement is weak. But if leaders take this opportunity to improve social policy and foster safe eco-tourism, foreigners will surely arrive from all corners to enjoy the region's remarkable natural beauty. By broadening professional opportunities and diversifying community income, fishermen will then be free to work sustainably. They might even return to the sea as whale guides, taking visitors out to explore the watery world of the famous *la vaquita marina*.

That is, if their black-lipped beauty can be rescued from her current fate.

∽

With so many causes in the world, why is vaquita important? What would be the ramifications of her extinction?

On an ecological level, the loss of an apex predator triggers a trophic cascade, altering the food web and creating potentially destabilizing changes in the abundance of other species. Apex predators have been shown to control large-scale ecosystem processes, so eliminating vaquita would set off a domino effect for which the long-term biological fallout cannot be overstated.

"It is Mexico—and its unique marine environment—that will bear the most devastating consequences of the vaquita's extinction," wrote Omar Vidal for CNN. "Once the vaquita is gone, environmental protections would likely evaporate with it; the remaining marine life—including totoaba, shrimp, corvina, sharks, and sea turtles—will follow the same tragic path." He concluded, "In the end, local fishermen and their families will find themselves in an even more desperate situation. Today, essentially all fisheries in this isolated region are overexploited and sustainable economic alternatives have not yet been developed. If the ecosystem falls apart here, the cost will be much more than environmental."

No a ver peces, no a ver comer, no a ver dinero. No fish, no food, no money.

But there is another crucial reason to save vaquita. "The main risk factor for coastal marine mammals around the world are gillnets," Lorenzo told me. "I am a member of many international teams that deal with that. In Argentina, in New Zealand, in Taiwan, we are all facing the same challenge. If you let vaquita go extinct and nobody pays for that, then you open the door for other extinctions to follow."

Barb said the same thing. "Vaquita is such an important battle because the biggest threat to marine mammals worldwide is gillnets. They're amazingly good at killing things. And they're cheap. If we don't do something, we're going to lose a lot of life. Dolphins, porpoises, sharks, sea turtles—they're all going down the tubes."

This moment is a chance for change. If we learn from the vaquita crisis and push for sanctions on gillnet fishing around the world, we just might stop the ecological bleeding before another marine mammal is forced to assume the dubious title of "most endangered."

And who, if we fail, will that be?

It's difficult to say—several species are in peril.

A likely candidate is the Irrawaddy dolphin, *Orcaella brevirostris*, a bubble-faced cetacean found in the coastal waters of Southeast Asia. But low numbers for the giant North Atlantic right whale, *Eubalaena glacialis*, and some strange, pink-skinned Taiwanese humpback dolphin, *Sousa chinensis*, also have scientists justifiably worried. If we are not careful, all of these—and others too—will go the way of baiji.

As Paco pointed out, though, sending someone to jail for killing a particular species is not conservation. You may put three men in jail, but the species is no better off. Conservation requires understanding the history and all the species that are related. Biodiversity is like an intricate clock, designed to tick on and on in perpetuity. From the largest gear to the tiniest screw, every part has its function; no piece is extraneous or irrelevant. Only the creator can say why an itty-bitty bracket hidden from view is essential to the clockworks. But it is.

One adventuresome philosopher-author from the United Kingdom is pedaling a bamboo bicycle down the latitudes of South America. In 2017, Kate Rawles embarked on a yearlong, six-thousand-mile mission to engage people in conversations about the definition and significance of biodiversity. Most habitats are protected (if they are protected at all) because people are trying to save a certain animal. Kate's premise shifts our focus from genera to biomes. If we think of ecosystems as they really are—multispecies bionetworks that demand all parts to function—everyone and everything within those ecosystems should be cared for.

I think it's a brilliant strategy, especially given that humans are blatantly biased when it comes to picking and choosing which animals are worthy of care.

Here's a case in point. A friend from my animal rescue circles recently posted a photo of a giant slug on her Facebook page. Her caption read, "I'm going to vomit now." The comments that followed were equally pert. "Ewww," wrote one person. Another typed, "<barf>." Someone suggested to ". . . throw some salt on it!! It will melt just like the witch in oz!!!"

Slugs don't have a lot of fans.

But the irony was found a half-scroll above this exchange. My friend's cover photo, the banner she chose to represent her as a person and animal advocate, contained six words.

Hate Is Easy, Love Takes Courage.

Alas, certain animals seem to require more courage than we have.

~

If I have learned anything since my first trip into Mexico to investigate the plight of vaquita, it's that conservation is complicated. Shaking hands with Gustavo at the Hotel Los Angeles in the spring of 2016 and jumping into his red truck to go meet Paco and Javier, I could never have known—or even imagined—what awaited me in the twenty months that followed.

Drawn into this contentious drama, I have found myself stumbling around in the dark corners of human frailty. Yet I have also witnessed greatness. A shining beam of courage and optimism has driven humans through millennia. In its light, we rise up and forge onward.

Through the efforts of many people, vaquita is now a flagship species, a living symbol for conservation worldwide. As we watch this enchanting porpoise fight against the eternity of extinction—as sea pens are anchored in the waves and the capture team prepares its tackle—we are painfully trapped between the prospect of a heroic conclusion and the agony of a dreadful one.

The situation is bleak, but we cannot lose hope. Should apathy prevail, every step toward positive change will falter. In times of strain, I oft recall Jane Goodall's four sensible reasons for hope: "(1) the human brain; (2) the resilience of nature; (3) the energy and enthusiasm that is found or can be kindled among young people worldwide; and (4) the indomitable human spirit." These strengths must keep us going.

"I very often feel discouraged, but I can't give up because there's one thing that's for sure—that if you give up, there is no more hope," Oona told me. "So, I just want to keep going. That's how, maybe, we could save ourselves, and save the animals of this planet."

Will vaquita survive tomorrow and beyond? No one can say. But I can't help thinking that as we contemplate the outcome ahead, as we look to the future, perhaps feeling a little crushed by the weight of it, we just might discover what we're made of.

If we listen to our hearts, really listen, maybe at long last we'll know what to do, not do.

Epilogue

THERE ARE JUST NO WORDS." That was the shared sentiment of everyone who tried to describe their emotional state after the first vaquita capture—the tangled mix of fear and relief, hope and vexation that knotted stomachs and prevented peaceful sleep.

On October 18, the catch team had closed in on a mother and calf pair swimming in the Vaquita Refuge. A large net was dropped, and three small boats circled. As skilled observers watched for trouble, a flurry of radio calls, measured but for their anxious undertones, coordinated every movement. Quickly and cautiously, the vaquitas were herded into the net, but just as the procedure reached completion, the mother slipped the lattice, leaving her daughter, less skilled at evasion, alone in the mesh. The panicked youngster bucked and tossed as the closest boatmen moved in to assist.

VaquitaCPR had officially commenced five days earlier. Thanks to daily acoustic reports providing clues to the animals' whereabouts, the search team sighted vaquitas every trip out, without the aid of US Navy dolphins. But the porpoises proved difficult to catch. They were fast, intelligent, and agile. The first one detained was this six-month-old calf. A photo shows the little girl—light gray skin, facial markings faint but visible—poised on the edge of a Zodiac in the arms of several Danish men.

Placed in a padded transport cradle, the agitated calf underwent a one-hour boat ride to an aboveground pool at the Vaquita Care Center in San Felipe for observation and evaluation. When she failed to settle, the team tried her out in the sea pen, but the youngster continued to show signs of life-threatening respiratory distress. Heart racing, she swam erratically with her head held above the water. Although her teeth had already erupted, suggesting that she was of weaning age and capable of consuming solid foods, losing contact with her mother was clearly causing strain. The veterinarians made the call.

Within five hours of meeting human hands, the first vaquita ever captured was set free in the exact location where she had been found.

∼

Minister Rafael Pacchiano tweeted that sixty-nine experts from nine countries had converged in Mexico to contribute to the vaquita recovery program. During the scheduled capture period—October 12 to November 11, 2017—their work was intensive. Lorenzo and Cynthia led the massive VaquitaCPR team. Armando, Gustavo, and Mauricio managed an unwieldy amount of acoustic data, relying on the Islas del Golfo contractors to wrangle c-pods in whatever weather greeted them. Sara continued to coordinate with Sea Shepherd, the *Narval*, Pesca ABC, and the Mexican Navy to hunt and extract ghost nets. And documentary filmmakers Matt and Sean shot footage of the unfolding events—now in collaboration with Appian Way, Leonardo DiCaprio's production company.

Netting the calf proved that capture was possible, but unfavorable sea conditions frequently kept the specialists ashore, and missed attempts foiled them on the water. Vaquitas that were sighted seemed to vanish before the eye, prompting one observer to nickname them "ghost porpoises." As precious days ticked past, supporters fretted that the effort could end empty-handed.

Thus, relief was palpable on the afternoon of November 4, seventeen days after the calf was let go, when a full-sized female was safely secured. Unlike the juvenile, the adult remained calm during capture and transport, her respiration and heart rate steady. Her age and disposition gave reason for optimism—that is, until she was released into the sea pen. There, she raced forward, crashing into the soft siding, and then frantically darted back and forth, narrowly avoiding the mesh walls and eventually falling limp in the middle of the pool.

Despite an emergency release, the situation deteriorated. Back in open water, the female swam away at full speed only to make an abrupt one-eighty, charging back toward the humans, who caught her just before she hit the boat. She wasn't breathing. Diagnosing a cardiac arrest, the veterinarians began cardiopulmonary resuscitation, quickly supplying intubated oxygen and intravenous fluids. For three unwavering hours, they brought all their medical skill to bear, but when the animal was stricken by a second heart attack, nothing more could be done.

Under the glow of a full moon, she was pronounced dead.

With the capture plan aborted, heartbroken advocates are now forced back to plan A: in situ conservation. Unequivocally, *Phocoena sinus*, unsuited for captivity, requires enforced protection and net removal inside the Vaquita Refuge. No other options remain.

~

I went back one last time, like visiting a gravesite.

The morning air was quiet and moist, the tide slowly rising. A waddle of beachcombers—willets, plovers, and sandpipers—waded in the surf. Sitting where Ps2's body once rested on the sand, I tried to settle my mind. I was seized with an agonizing question: what will come of the remaining vaquitas?

Their fate is cast to the sea.

They will not endure life in captivity.

How long, though, until the nets of the *bucheros* find them?

Fraught with worry, I offered the one and only thing I could—a promise. It was the same promise I made to Ps2 the first time I wept for her, a promise I have repeated every day since.

"I will tell your story," I whispered seaward, my words borne by wind and wave. "I will tell the story of your tribe so the world remembers."

Just then, a flock of gulls passed overhead like a symbol of continued life. I laid my head back and watched them sail. With snow-white underbellies, they were living angels against the royal blue sky.

Author's Note

THE STORY OF VAQUITA IS COMPLEX and detailed. In an effort to keep it as comprehensible as possible for US readers, I have made a couple of style choices worth mentioning. First, although both Mexico and science describe the world in metric units, I have elected to use the more familiar United States customary units for dimensions, distances, and temperatures. If metric figures are held within quotes, a conversion is provided parenthetically. Second, most institutions with lengthy multiword names use acronyms as their common names—phonetically pronounced. To streamline the reading experience, I have opted to use those commonly recognized acronyms and thus exclude long Spanish names for governmental institutions and organizations throughout the text. Full names can be found in the Guide to Acronyms.

Guide to Acronyms

CEDO   Intercultural Center for the Study of Deserts and Oceans (*Centro Intercultural de Estudios de Desiertos y Océanos*)

CICESE   Mexico's Center for Scientific Research and Higher Education at Ensenada (*Centro de Investigación Científica y de Educación Superior de Ensenada*)

CIRVA   International Committee for the Recovery of Vaquita (*Comité Internacional para la Recuperación de la Vaquita*)

CITES   Convention on International Trade in Endangered Species

CONABIO   National Commission for the Knowledge and Use of Biodiversity (*Comisión Nacional para el Conocimiento y Uso de la Biodiversidad*)

CONANP   Mexico's National Commission of Natural Protected Areas (*Comisión Nacional de Areas Naturales Protegidas*)

CONAPESCA   Mexico's National Commission of Aquaculture and Fisheries (*Comisión Nacional de Acuacultura y Pesca*)

EDF   Environmental Defense Fund

EDGE   evolutionarily distinct, globally endangered; from Zoological Society of London's EDGE of Existence program

ENDESU   Natural Spaces and Sustainable Development (*Espacios Naturales y Desarrollo Sustentable*)

INAPESCA	Mexico's National Fisheries Institute (*Instituto Nacional de la Pesca*)
INECC	Mexico's National Institute of Ecology and Climate Change (*Instituto Nacional de Ecología y Cambio Climático*)
INTERPOL	International Police Organization
IUCN	International Union for Conservation of Nature
IWC	International Whaling Commission
MIA	environmental impact study (*Manifestación de Impacto Ambiental*)
MMPA	US Marine Mammal Protection Act
MOU	memorandum of understanding
NASA	US National Aeronautics and Space Administration
NOAA	US National Oceanic and Atmospheric Administration
NOM	Mexico's National Regulations (*Normas Oficiales Mexicanas*); official system of standards and regulations, including NOM-059 for protection of at-risk species
NRDC	Natural Resources Defense Council
PACE-Vaquita	Mexico's Species Conservation Action Plan for Vaquita (*Programa de Acción para la Protección de la Especie de la Vaquita*)
PAM	passive acoustic monitoring
Pesca	Short for CONAPESCA and INAPESCA combined (*pesca* is Spanish for fishing)
Pesca ABC	Alternative Fishing of Baja California (*Pesca Alternativa de Baja California*)
PRI	Institutional Revolutionary Party (*Partido Revolucionario Institucional*)
PROCETUS	Cetacean Observation Program (*Programa de Observación de Cetáceos*)
PROFEPA	Mexico's Federal Agency of Environmental Protection (*Procuraduria Federal de Protección al Ambiente*)

RMB	Renminbi; the currency of the People's Republic of China
SAGARPA	Mexico's Secretary of Agriculture, Livestock, Rural Development, Fisheries and Food (*Secretaría de Agricultura, Ganadería, Desarrollo Rural, Pesca y Alimentación*)
SEDENA	Mexico's Secretary of National Defense (*Secretaría de la Defensa Nacional*)
SEMARNAT	Mexico's Secretary of Environment and Natural Resources (*Secretaría del Medio Ambiente y Recursos Naturales*)
UNESCO	United Nations Educational, Scientific and Cultural Organization
WAP	World Animal Protection
WWF	World Wildlife Fund

Acknowledgments

This book could never have come into existence without the generous support and input of a great many people to whom I owe boundless credit. My deepest thanks go to three capable and dedicated scientists, Lorenzo Rojas Bracho, Barbara Taylor, and Armando Jaramillo Legorreta, who opened to me the world of *Phocoena sinus*, sharing a glimpse into their exceptional careers and arranging many critical connections. I am equally indebted to Gustavo Cárdenas Hinojosa, who not only presented essential introductions and opportunities but also helped me navigate every turn. To Mauricio Nájera Caballero and Sara Amozurrutia, who took me into the field and into their homes, I am ever grateful. *Abrazos de gracias* to Javier and Paco Valverde for teaching me about culture and history—and courage, too. And to Ramon Arozamena, Alán Valverde, Gilberto "Giby" Ruiz, Rafael "Gordis" Sánchez, Victor Orozco, Luis "Taladro" Martínez, Antonio "Tonicho" García, Armando "Muelas" Castro, Carlos Samudio, and all the other alternative-gear fishermen for welcoming me into their yards and pangas and working tirelessly for change.

Oona Layolle, I salute you for speaking up when others could not. I also extend my appreciation to Paul Watson and the entire Sea Shepherd crew as they undertake the day-to-day labor of protecting our oceans, especially Woody Henderson, Thomas Le Coz, Luisa Albera,

Patricia Gandolfo, Jean Paul "JP" Geoffroy, Paloma de Castilla, Roy Sasano, Corey Dahlquist, Adam Conniss, Rodrigo Gil Kuri, Jack Hutton, Mike Sine, CB Nolen, Mark Crowder, Fernando Schnitzer, and Sheila Hanney. To Ricardo Rebolledo, thank you for my visit aboard the *Narval*. To Elizabeth Hogan, Jared Berg, and Andy Walling for the lesson in side-scan sonar. To Steve Walker for my tour of the Vaquita Care Center. And to Chris Snyder for talking with me when it probably felt like stepping into a firestorm. Profound thanks are due to several more people who shared time, knowledge, or resources: Alán Alexis Valverde, Elizabeth Brassea Pérez, Claudia Cecilia Olimon, Sergio Perez, Emilia Marín, Ivan Jaramillo, Gladys Cossio, Jose Maria Cuevas, Daniel Gonzales, Mario López Paloma, Fernanda Urrutia, Alex López, Jaime Gonzáles Huerta, and Luis Tiznado. I also benefited from conversations with the late Dale Vinnedge, who will always be remembered for his love of whales.

For lending their expertise, I am ever grateful to Cynthia Smith, Peggy Turk Boyer, Sarah Mesnick, Conal David True, Frances Gulland, Tom Jefferson, Alex Olivera, Zak Smith, Rafael Ortiz, Juan Carlos Cantu, Sarah Uhlemann, and Antonella Wilby. I especially wish to acknowledge Guillermo Munro Collosio (Memuco), Leonardo Gonzales Rodriguez, and Pedro Camancho for bringing vaquita to life through the magic of paint; Matt Podolsky and Sean Bogle for crusading through film; and Guillermo Munro Palacio, Aidan Bodeo-Lomicky, and Jen and Sander Gabler for finding the words. Maria Johnson gave me insight into the atrocities of bycatch as well as hope that we may forge a more compassionate future. Yolanda Madueño Santiesteban was instrumental in helping me refresh my Spanish. And Gary Elbert was the perfect traveling companion to the eastern shores. My sincere thanks go to all.

More than two dozen of the aforementioned people reviewed some or all of the working manuscript to correct any mistakes or misconceptions, and every comment and suggestion progressed this work. Special thanks go to Barb Taylor for her thorough and thoughtful feedback. For photos, I owe credit to Sea Shepherd Conservation Society with help from Zorianna Kit, Mike Bales of Cortez Publications, Tom Gorman, Todd Pusser, and US Fish and Wildlife Service. I also wish to express gratitude to several people whom I did not interview, but whose professional strides contributed significantly to this book: Enrique Peña Nieto, Rafael Pacchiano Alamán, and all the CIRVA members not previously acknowledged, including Jay Barlow, Tim Gerrodette, and Robert Brownell; also Ken Norris, Gregory Silber, Omar Vidal, Nick Trigenza, Robert Pitman, Kerri Danil, Randy Wells, Leonardo DiCaprio, Carlos Slim, Todd Gloria, Chris Johnson, and William Whittenbury.

Heartfelt thanks go to my trusted editor, Erin Johnson, for believing in this book and providing such astute guidance. Thanks also to David Miller, Julie Marshall, Sharis Simonian, and the entire Island Press team for their extraordinary care. I am forever grateful to Carl Safina for taking time to write his eloquent foreword and to Sy Montgomery for her boundless encouragement and beautiful words. Several early readers helped me find my way. An ocean of thanks goes to Heather Baldwin, who offered brilliant notes on every chapter—she was my guiding light. To Bob Albano for his editorial expertise and sage council. To Peter Lourie for giving me the courage to dive into the deep end. And to Lisa Schnebly Heidinger, my very first reader, for saying all the right things.

Numerous colleagues, friends, and family members have, through my life, contributed to the knowledge, skill, and passion required to carry out this journey; I heartily regret that I cannot name them all here. But I do wish to acknowledge a few who listened and encouraged, following this adventure in real time: Gary Galbreath, Donna Gabriel, Becci Gurski, Dan and Mary Bessesen, Marie-Laure Bessesen, Kathryn Koenig, Sharon Hurd, Greg Brown, and my HSUS teammates. An enormous hug of thanks goes to my cherished mother, Barbara Bessesen, for talking through daily thoughts and ideas and always sharing a soft shoulder when the road was rough. And to my beloved husband and best friend, Kevin Steiner, for giving me a mini tape recorder all those years ago when I casually mentioned that someday I'd like to write a book—and for believing in me every minute since.

Notes

Chapter 1: The Dead Girl

p. 3   fewer than sixty: CIRVA, *Report of the Seventh Meeting of the Comité Internacional para la Recuperación de la Vaquita (CIRVA-7)*, 2016, http://www.iucn-csg.org/index.php/downloads/, p. 5.

p. 6   "aquatic cocaine": K. Lah and A. Moya, "Aquatic Cocaine: Fish Bladders Are Latest Mexican Smuggling Commodity," CNN, May 23, 2016, http://www.cnn.com.

p. 8   up to 40 percent: Oceana, *Wasted Catch: Unsolved Problems in U.S. Fisheries*, Oceana report, 2014, pp. 3, 5.

p. 9   A satellite image: Environmental Investigation Agency, *Duel Extinction: The Illegal Trade in the Endangered Totoaba and Its Impact on the Critically Endangered Vaquita*, Environmental Investigation Agency Briefing to the 66th Standing Committee of CITES, January 11–15, 2016, p. 4.

p. 10   the country's national marine mammal: V. Jaggard, "Ten Unusual National Animals That Rival the Unicorn," *Smithsonian*, September 22, 2014, http://www.smithsonianmag.com.

p. 10   "The [president's gillnet] ban": Center for Biological Diversity, *Trade Sanctions Sought Against Mexico in Fight to Save Vanishing Porpoise*, press release, June 28, 2016, http://www.biologicaldiversity.org.

p. 10   A single *buche* can put: US Department of Justice, *Fishy Business— Smuggler of Swim Bladders Is Sentenced in Federal Court*, US Attorney's Office Southern District of California, press release, August 11, 2014, https://www.justice.gov/.

p. 10   as high as $50,000: Environmental Investigation Agency, *Collateral Damage: How Illegal Trade in Totoaba Swim Bladders Is Driving the Vaquita to Extinction* (London: Environmental Investigation Agency, 2016), pp. 2, 4, 5.

p. 11   a shocking 80 percent: A. M. Jaramillo-Legorreta et al., "Passive Acoustic Monitoring of the Decline of Mexico's Critically Endangered Porpoise," *Conservation Biology* 31, no. 1 (2016): 183.

p. 11   "Science explains": P. Fleishmann, *Eyes Wide Open: Going Behind the Environmental Headlines* (Somerville, MA: Candlewick Press, 2014), p. 7.

p. 11   "nobody noticed—": S. Haro Cordero, "Pesca illegal de totoaba: Corrupción y Simulación," *ZETA*, April 11, 2016, http://zetatijuana.com.

p. 11   More than two dozen seizures: Environmental Investigation Agency, *Collateral Damage*, pp. 12, 13.

p. 12   valued at $3.6 million: US Department of Justice, *Fishy Business*.

p. 12   "no apparent evidence": E. Mendéz, "Encuentran segunda vaquita marina muerta en menos de 10 días," *Excelsior*, March 16, 2016, http://www.excelsior.com.mx.

p. 13   "trauma, entanglement": IUCN, "Vaquita Update: Three Documented Deaths in One Month, Not Good," *IUCN Cetacean Specialist Group*, April 13, 2016, http://www.iucn-csg.org/index.php/2016/04/13/.

p. 14   Ps2 turned out to be: F. Gulland, "Necropsy Form for Vaquita Ps2, Completed March 24," *IUCN Cetacean Specialist Group*, accessed April 18, 2016, http://www.iucn-csg.org/index.php/downloads/.

Chapter 2: Resource Extraction

p. 23   a new species of porpoise: K. S. Norris and W. N. McFarland, "A New Harbor Porpoise of the Genus Phocoena from the Gulf of California," *Journal of Mammalogy* 39 (1958): 22–39.

p. 23   in scientific literature: K. S. Norris and J. S. Prescott, "Observations on Pacific Cetaceans of Californian and Mexican Waters," *University of California Publications in Zoology* 63 (1961): 291–402.

p. 25   "Pink gold": R. Cudney Bueno and P. J. Turk Boyer, *Pescando Entre Mareas del Alto Golfo de California: Una Guía sobre la Pesca Artesanal,*

su Gente y sus Propuestas de Manejo (Puerto Peñasco, Sonora: Centro
Intercultural de Estudios de Desiertos y Océanos [CEDO], 1998), p. 6.

p. 25   less than sixty tons: C. A. Flanagan and R. Hendrickson, "Observa-
tions on the Commercial Fishery and Reproductive Biology of the
Totoaba *Cynoscion macdonaldi* in the Northern Gulf of California,"
Fish Bulletin 74 (1976): 531–44.

p. 26   "to ensure that international": Convention on International Trade
in Endangered Species, "What Is CITES?," Convention on International Trade in Endangered Species of Wild Fauna and Flora website,
accessed September 8, 2016, https://cites.org/eng/disc/what.php.

p. 26   Scientists who later scrutinized: Flanagan and Hendrickson, "Observations," p. 542; M. A. Cisneros-Mata, G. Montemayor-López, and
M. J. Román-Rodríguez, "Life History and Conservation of *Totoaba
macdonaldi*," *Conservation Biology* 9, no. 4 (1995): 806–14.

p. 26   each year in the decade: Cisneros-Mata, Montemayor-López, and
Román-Rodríguez, "Life History," p. 806.

p. 27   "The Mexican Government has": R. L. Brownell, "Vaquita or Cochito," in *Red Data Book*, vol. 1, *Mammalia*, eds. H.A. Goodwin and
C.W. Holloway (Gland, Switzerland: IUCN, 1978), pp. unknown.

p. 27   "during totoaba gillnet fishing": R. L. Brownell, "Status of the Cochito, *Phocoena sinus*, in the Gulf of California," in *Mammals in the
Seas*, vol. 4, *Small Cetaceans, Seals, Sirenians, and Otters*, FAO Fisheries Series (Rome: Food and Agriculture Organization of the United
Nations, 1982), p. 88.

p. 27   vaquita's unique markings: R. L. Brownell, L. T. Findley, O. Vidal, A.
Robles, and N. S. Manzanilla, "External Morphology and Pigmenta-
tion of the Vaquita, *Phocoena sinus* (Cetacea: Mammalia)," *Marine
Mammal Science* 3 (1987): 22–30.

p. 29   catches had dropped: Cudney Bueno and Turk Boyer, *Pescando Entre
Mareas*, p. 7.

p. 30   mortality studies: C. D'Agrosa, C. E. Lennert-Cody, and O. Vidal,
"Vaquita Bycatch in Mexico's Artisanal Gillnet Fisheries: Driving
a Small Population to Extinction," *Conservation Biology* 14 (2000):
1115; photo of dead calves: L. Rojas-Bracho, R. R. Reeves, and
A. Jaramillo-Legorreta, "Conservation of the Vaquita *Phocoena sinus*,"

Mammal Review 36 (2006): 188, Fig. 4; O. Vidal, "Population Biology and Incidental Mortality of the Vaquita, *Phocoena sinus*," *Reports of the International Whaling Commission*, Special Issue 16 (1995): 247.

p. 31   "to preserve and protect": Cudney Bueno and Turk Boyer, *Pescando Entre Mareas*, p. 10.

p. 31   the men reported: Cudney Bueno and Turk Boyer, *Pescando Entre Mareas*, p. 103.

p. 31   Only 567 individuals: A. M. Jaramillo-Legorreta, L. Rojas-Bracho, and T. Gerrodette, "A New Abundance Estimate for Vaquitas: First Step for Recovery," *Marine Mammal Science* 15 (1999): 957.

p. 31   potential causes of: L. Rojas-Bracho and B. L. Taylor, "Risk Factors Affecting the Vaquita (*Phocoena sinus*)," *Marine Mammal Science* 15, no. 4 (1999): 974–89; J. Calambokidis, *Chlorinated Hydrocarbon Concentrations in the Gulf of California Harbor Porpoise* (Phocoena sinus), Cascadia Research Collective, unpublished contract report, 1988.

p. 32   "gillnets are the greatest risk": CIRVA, *Comité Internacional para la Recuperación de la Vaquita (CIRVA), Scientific Reports of First, Second and Third Meetings*, 2004, http://www.vivavaquita.org, p. 1-16.

p. 33   "We need to act fast": EDGE, "Mammals: Overview," EDGE website, accessed September 8, 2016, http://www.edgeofexistence.org /mammals/.

p. 33   just 245 survivors: T. Gerrodette et al., "A Combined Visual and Acoustic Estimate of 2008 Abundance, and Change in Abundance since 1997, for the Vaquita, *Phocoena sinus*," *Marine Mammal Science* 27 (2011): E79.

p. 33   PACE-Vaquita: L. Rojas-Bracho and R. R. Reeves, "Vaquita and Gillnets: Mexico's Ultimate Cetacean Conservation Challenge," *Endangered Species Research* 21 (2013): 80–81.

p. 35   "Within days following": B. Taylor, "Vaquita Gillnet Ban Begins April 29, 2015," Society for Marine Mammalogy website, April 30, 2015, https://www.marinemammalscience.org/.

p. 36   "Culture does not change": F. Hesselbein, "The Key to Cultural Transformation," *Leader to Leader* 12 (1999): 1–7.

p. 36   an interesting psychological: Cudney Bueno and Turk Boyer, *Pescando Entre Mareas*, pp. 106, 109.

Chapter 3: Chasing a Myth

p. 41   another 57 percent: T. Gerrodette et al., "A Combined Visual and Acoustic Estimate of 2008 Abundance, and Change in Abundance since 1997, for the Vaquita, *Phocoena sinus*," *Marine Mammal Science* 27 (2011): E79.

p. 49   Barb had written: B. L. Taylor and T. Gerrodette, "The Uses of Statistical Power in Conservation Biology: The Vaquita and Northern Spotted Owl," *Conservation Biology* 7 (1993): 489–500.

p. 50   "cessation of fishing": J. Afflerbach et al., *An Analysis of Bioeconomic Tradeoffs in Vaquita Conservation Policies*, Group Project Report, Bren School of Environmental Science and Management, University of California, Santa Barbara, 2013, pp. 5, 10.

Chapter 4: Tangled Agendas

p. 55   90 percent of the shrimp: G. Rodríguez-Quiroz, E. A. Aragon-Noriega, and A. Ortega-Rubio, "Artisanal Shrimp Fishing in the Biosphere Reserve of the Upper Gulf of California," *Crustaceana* 82, no. 12 (2009): 1481–93.

p. 55   435 miles of gillnets: Marine Mammal Center, "Vaquita, the World's Most Endangered Marine Mammal," Marine Mammal Center website, accessed September 13, 2017, http://www.marinemammalcenter .org.

p. 57   There are about 2,770 people: A. Olivera, "Compensación por no pescar," *BCS Noticias*, August 22, 2016, http://www.bcsnoticias.mx.

p. 59   "the average biomass": J. H. Ruelas-Peña, C. Valdez-Muñoz, and E. A. Aragón-Noriega, "Analysis of the Corvina Gulf Fishery as a Function of Management Actions in the Upper Gulf of California, Mexico," *Latin American Journal of Aquatic Research* 41, no. 3 (2013): 498.

p. 60   "the main modus operandi": "Fish Bladders Fetch More than Cocaine," *Mexico Daily News*, August 23, 2016, http://mexiconewsdaily .com.

p. 62   he had been receiving: E. Méndez, "Abaten a pescador furtivo de totoaba, que recibía recursos federales," *Excelsior*, March 28, 2016, http://www.excelsior.com.mx.

p. 62   "That size implies corruption": S. Haro Cordero, "Pesca illegal de totoaba: Corrupción y Simulación," *ZETA*, April 11, 2016, http://zetatijuana.com.

p. 64   "This crime is more than": L. Fendt, "4 Convicted, 3 Acquitted in Jairo Mora Murder Trial," *Tico Times*, March 29, 2014, http://www.ticotimes.net.

p. 64   On Tuesday, June 11: C. Mejia Giraldo and J. Bargent, "Are Mexican Narcos Moving into Lucrative Fish Bladder Market?," *InSight Crime*, August 6, 2014, http://www.insightcrime.org.

Chapter 5: Death, Drugs, and Accountability

p. 69   "the permittee knocked him out": S. Haro Cordero, "Crisis en San Felipe," *ZETA*, March 28, 2016, http://zetatijuana.com.

p. 70   "drowned by ambition": Haro Cordero, "Crisis en San Felipe."

p. 73   "used electoral fraud, corruption": T. L. Merrill and R. Miro, eds., "Institutional Revolutionary Party (PRI)," in *Mexico: A Country Study* (Washington, DC: GPO for the Library of Congress, 1996), http://countrystudies.us/mexico/84.htm.

p. 73   "29% of the thesis": Associated Press, Mexico City, "Mexico President Enrique Peña Nieto Plagiarized Thesis for Law Degree: Report," *The Guardian*, August 22, 2016, https://www.theguardian.com.

p. 74   "unevenness of Peña Nieto's": Biography.com Editors, "Enrique Peña Nieto," Biography.com, accessed September 25, 2016, https://www.biography.com.

p. 76   "Curbing vicious cycles": O. Aburto-Oropeza et al., "Endangered Species, Ecosystem Integrity, and Human Livelihoods," *Conservation Letters*, March 24, 2017, p. 6. doi:10.1111/conl.12358.

p. 77   "promotion of fishing": Gob.mx, "Mario Gilberto Aguilar Sanchez," CONAPESCA Directory, accessed June 10, 2016, https://www.gob.mx.

p. 77   "contributed to the population": Oscar CaboExpeditions, "Conoce BCS. Expositores: Dr. Luis Fleisher [sic]," *Facebook* posting, June 11, 2011.

p. 77   "espoused allowing gray whaling": D. Russell, *Eye of the Whale: Epic Passage from Baja to Siberia* (Washington, DC: Island Press, 2004), pp. 77, 81.

p. 78   "In the absence of constant": E. Dinerstein, *The Kingdom of Rarities* (Washington, DC: Island Press, 2013), p. 268.

p. 78   zero vaquita mortalities: L. Fleischer et al., "Mortalidad incidental de la vaquita, *Phocoena sinus*. Historia y actualidad (abril de 1996)," *Ciencia Pesquera* 13 (1996): 78–82.

p. 78   "They should just declare": Agence France-Presse, "Ban Fishing to Save World's Smallest Porpoise—WWF," *GMA News*, May 17, 2016, http://www.gmanetwork.com.

p. 78   "It is difficult to get a man": U. Sinclair, *I, Candidate for Governor: And How I got Licked* (Berkeley: University of California Press, 1994), p. 109.

p. 79   "'quick-fix' . . . in which": Aburto-Oropeza et al., "Endangered Species," p. 1.

p. 80   "fishing industry advocates": R. Dalton, "Endangered Porpoise Worse Off than Thought," *Nature* website, November 16, 2007, http://www .nature.com.

p. 80   "some of the fishermen blamed": J. Johnson, "Mexico Gets Serious about Saving Its Tiny Endangered Porpoise," *McClatchy DC Bureau*, March 18, 2015, http://www.mcclatchydc.com.

p. 81   "in defense of": Sea Shepherd, "Operation Milagro II," Sea Shepherd website, accessed March 30, 2016, http://www.seashepherd.org.

Chapter 6: Pirates on Patrol

p. 85   the meat is primarily marketed: Kyodo, "Whale Meat Back on School Lunch Menus," *Japan Times*, September 5, 2010, https://www.japan times.co.jp.

p. 85   "In the case concerning": International Court of Justice, 2014. "Whaling in the Antarctic," *ICJ Reports of Judgments, Advisory Opinions and Orders, Judgment of 31 March 2014*, pp. 8, 76.

p. 85   When Japanese whalers returned: K. Beesley, "Japanese Fleet Kills 333 Whales in the Antarctic," *The Two-Way*, NPR, March 25, 2016, http://www.npr.org.

p. 91   "It is an honor to be able": Sea Shepherd, "Captain Oona Layolle Calls for Increased Patrols to Protect the Vaquita," Sea Shepherd website, March 26, 2016, http://www.seashepherd.org.

p. 91   "We found a third dead": Sea Shepherd, "Sea Shepherd Finds Third

Dead Vaquita in Three Weeks," Sea Shepherd website, March 28, 2016, http://www.seashepherd.org.

Chapter 7: Searching for Vaquita

p. 96   "I am happy to be": Sea Shepherd, "The M/V Farley Mowat Crew: Rodrigo Gil," Sea Shepherd website, accessed March 30, 2016, http://www.seashepherd.org.

p. 98   "a unique oceanographic area": Marine Conservation Biology Institute, *Marine Priority Conservation Areas: Baja California to the Bering Sea (B2B)*, Report of the Commission for Environmental Cooperation of North America, 2005, pp. 100, 101.

p. 101   "This latest death shows": Sea Shepherd, "Gillnets Claim Another Humpback," Sea Shepherd website, April 6, 2016, http://www.sea shepherd.org.

p. 102   "an era dominated by industry": R. Carson, *Silent Spring* (1962; repr. Boston: Houghton Mifflin, 2002), p. 23.

p. 103   up to 90 percent: E. Gavenus, M. Johnson, and E. Magrane, "Bycatch—the Complexities for Shrimp Trawling in the Gulf of California," *MAHB Arts Community*, May 25, 2017, https://mahb.stanford .edu/creative-expressions/bycatch-complexities/.

p. 104   "to help this shy": Sea Shepherd, "Operation Milagro II—Vaquita Porpoise Defense Campaign," Sea Shepherd website, accessed November 12, 2016, http://www.seashepherd.org.

Chapter 8: Hearing Is Believing

p. 113   "self-contained ultrasound": Chelonia Limited, *The Software User Guide for CPOD.EXE*, accessed December 10, 2014, http://www .chelonia.co.uk/downloads/CPOD.pdf.

p. 116   decode a visual scene: M. C. Potter, C. E. Hagmann, and E. S. McCourt, "Attention, Detecting Meaning in RSVP at 13 ms per Picture," *Attention, Perception, and Psychophysics* 76, no. 2 (2014): 270–79.

p. 117   "*Phocoena sinus* acoustic signals": G. K. Silber, "Acoustic Signals of the Vaquita (*Phocoena sinus*)," *Aquatic Mammals* 17 (1991): 130.

p. 118   From 1997 to 2007: T. Gerrodette et al., "A Combined Visual and Acoustic Estimate of 2008 Abundance, and Change in Abundance since 1997, for the Vaquita, *Phocoena sinus*," *Marine Mammal Science* 27 (2011): E79.

p. 123   "phocoenid porpoises are able": Silber, "Acoustic Signals," p. 132.

p. 124   "a passionate roboticist": National Geographic Society, "National Geographic Young Explorer: Antonella Wilby," National Geographic (blog), accessed August 18, 2016, https://voices.nationalgeographic .org/author/awilby/.

Chapter 9: Science in the Sea

p. 130   bronze-striped grunts: J. E. Fitch and R. L. Brownell, "Fish Otoliths in Cetacean Stomachs and Their Importance in Interpreting Feeding Habits," *Journal of the Fisheries Research Board of Canada* 25 (1968): 2561–74; H. Pérez-Cortés, G. K. Silber, and B. Villa Ramírez, "Contribución al conocimiento de la biología de la vaquita, *Phocoena sinus*," *Ciencia Pesquera* 13 (1996): 66–72.

p. 130   rate of 34 percent: A. M. Jaramillo-Legorreta et al., "Passive Acoustic Monitoring of the Decline of Mexico's Critically Endangered Porpoise," *Conservation Biology* 31, no. 1 (2016): 183.

p. 132   "The difficulty of obtaining": B. Taylor et al., "Extinction Is Imminent for Mexico's Endemic Porpoise Unless Fishery Bycatch Is Eliminated," *Conservation Letters* 10, no. 5 (2017): 589.

p. 134   "If the vaquita population could": Taylor et al. "Extinction Is Imminent," p. 4.

p. 138   "certify Mexico for failing": Center for Biological Diversity, *Trade Sanctions Sought Against Mexico in Fight to Save Vanishing Porpoise*, Center for Biological Diversity press release, June 28, 2016, http:// www.biologicaldiversity.org.

p. 138   "the Integral Strategy": UNESCO World Heritage Committee, "Report on the Reactive Monitoring Mission to Islands and Protected Areas of the Gulf of California (Mexico)," Convention Concerning the Protection of the World Cultural and Natural Heritage, 41st Session, Krakow, Poland, 2017, p. 5.

p. 138   "Mexico will make permanent": White House of President Barack Obama, "FACT SHEET: United States–Mexico Relations," White House, July 22, 2016, https://obamawhitehouse.archives.gov.

p. 139   "hasten the implementation": IUCN, "Motion 013—Actions to Avert the Extinction of the Vaquita Porpoise (*Phocoena sinus*)," IUCN World Conservation Congress, Hawaii, September 1–10, 2016, https://portals.iucn.org/congress/motion/013.

p. 139   tasked with opening up: CITES, "Decisions of the Conference of the Parties to CITES in Effect after Its 17th Meeting, 17.145–151," CoP17, Johannesburg, South Africa, September 24–October 5, 2016, pp. 33–34.

p. 139   "Noting that the Commission": Multiple Nations, "Draft Resolution on the Critically Endangered Vaquita," International Whaling Commission, Portorož, Slovenia, IWC/66/20 Rev, 2017, pp. 1–2.

p. 140   ghost net removal project: CIRVA, *Report of the Eighth Meeting of the Comité Internacional para la Recuperación de la Vaquita (CIRVA-8)*, 2016, http://www.iucn-csg.org/index.php/downloads, pp. 30–35.

p. 141   finally poised to reform: Notimex, "Avalan endurecer penas contra pesca furtive; entre ellas, de totoaba," *El Universal*, December 13, 2016, http://www.eluniversal.com.mx/.

p. 141   "About 100 enforcement officers": CITES, "China, U.S. and Mexico Collaborate to Protect Endangered Totoaba and Vaquita," *Endangered Species Scientific Commission, P. R. C.*, December 13, 2016, http://www.cites.org.cn.

Chapter 10: Witnessing Extinction

p. 143   "Mexico's minister": K. Kumar, "Vaquita Porpoise Facing Survival Risk: Activists Call for Boycott of Mexican Shrimp in the US," *Tech Times*, March 18, 2017, http://www.techtimes.com.

p. 144   a premature fetus: O. Vidal, "Population Biology and Incidental Mortality of the Vaquita, *Phocoena sinus*," *Reports of the International Whaling Commission*, Special Issue 16 (1995): 247.

p. 145   "with net marks": Sea Shepherd, "Operation Milagro III Update: Day of the Dead Dolphins," Sea Shepherd website, February 18, 2017, http://www.seashepherd.org.

p. 146   "*Hay otro amigo*": Sea Shepherd, "Sea Shepherd Rescues Drowning Fisherman in Gulf of California," Sea Shepherd video, January 27, 2017, http://www.seashepherd.org.

p. 147   "Last night virtually all": F. Mejia, "Violencia en el Golfo De Santa Clara," *La Voz de la Frontera*, March 8, 2016, https://www.lavozdela frontera.com.mx.

p. 148   thirty porpoises left: CIRVA, *Report of the Eighth Meeting of the Comité Internacional para la Recuperación de la Vaquita (CIRVA-8)*, 2016, http://www.iucn-csg.org/index.php/downloads, p. 3; L. Thomas et al., "Last Call: Passive Acoustic Monitoring Shows Continued Rapid Decline of Critically Endangered Vaquita," *Journal of the Acoustical Society of America* 142, no. 5 (2017): EL512.

p. 149   "This shocking new report": Center for Biological Diversity, "Report: Only 30 Vaquita Porpoises Remain on Earth," press release, February 2, 2017, http://www.biologicaldiversity.org.

p. 149   "wherever they are found": World Wildlife Fund, *Vanishing Vaquita*, WWF Analysis, 2017, p. 6.

p. 152   "They knew my name": Sea Shepherd, "Sea Shepherd Crew's Life Threatened by Mexican 'Cartels' in the Gulf of California," Sea Shepherd website, September 9, 2016, http://www.seashepherd.org.

p. 153   alleged crime leader: Televisa, "Crimen y corrupción, las otras redes que afectan a la vaquita marina," *Noticieros Televisa*, November 9, 2017.

p. 154   "Sea Shepherd is not": MarEx, "Mexican Fishermen Threaten Sea Shepherd," *Maritime Executive*, April 4, 2017, http://maritime-exec utive.com.

p. 155   two types of rarity: E. Dinerstein, *The Kingdom of Rarities* (Washington, DC: Island Press, 2013), pp. 42–43.

p. 155   the limited genetic variability: B. L. Taylor and L. Rojas-Bracho, "Examining the Risk of Inbreeding Depression in a Naturally Rare Cetacean, the Vaquita (*Phocoena sinus*)," *Marine Mammal Science*, 15, no. 4 (1999): 1004–28.

p. 157   "The marine ecosystem": R. C. Brusca et al., "Colorado River Flow and Biological Productivity in the Northern Gulf of California, Mexico," *Earth-Science Reviews*, 164 (2017): 1.

p. 159   the tiny fetus would be labeled: CIRVA, *Report of the Ninth Meeting of the Comité Internacional para la Recuperación de la Vaquita (CIRVA-9)*, 2017, http://www.iucn-csg.org/index.php/downloads/, pp. 26–30.

p. 159   "If good enforcement": R. L. Brownell, "Status of the Cochito, *Pho-coena sinus*, in the Gulf of California," in *Mammals in the Seas*, vol. 4, *Small Cetaceans, Seals, Sirenians, and Otters*, FAO Fisheries Series (Rome: Food and Agriculture Organization of the United Nations, 1982), p. 88.

Chapter 11: Saving Bigfoot

p. 167   "This one specimen bleached": E. Magrane, "Bycatch: Poems by Eric Magrane, Artwork by Maria Johnson," *Terrain*, July 7, 2016, http://www.terrain.org/2016/poetry/bycatch-eric-magrane-maria-johnson/.

p. 172   identified four individuals: T. A. Jefferson, P. A. Olson, T. R. Kieck-hefer, and L. Rojas-Bracho, "Photo-Identification of the Vaquita (*Phocoena sinus*): The World's Most Endangered Cetacean," *Latin American Journal of Aquatic Mammals* 7 (2009): 53–56.

p. 175   "how illegal trade in totoaba": Environmental Investigation Agency, *Collateral Damage: How Illegal Trade in Totoaba Swim Bladders Is Driving the Vaquita to Extinction*, Environmental Investigation Agency video, uploaded September 20, 2016, https://www.youtube.com/embed/CTFNGR1tukc.

Chapter 12: Sending Out an SOS

p. 186   "with the mission of protecting": Leonardo DiCaprio Foundation, "About Us," Leonardo DiCaprio Foundation website, accessed June 20, 2017, https://www.leonardodicaprio.org/about/.

p. 186   "benefited millions": Fundación Carlos Slim, "Who We Are: About Us," Fundación Carlos Slim website, accessed June 21, 2017, http://fundacioncarlosslim.org/english/quienes-somos/.

p. 187   "fishing gear may not": Ustados Unidos Mexicanos Secretaría de Go-biernación, "DOF: 30/06/2017," *Diario Oficial de la Federación*, June 30, 2017, http://www.dof.gob.mx/nota_detalle.php?codigo=5488674&fecha=30/06/2017.

p. 191   "pointed out that lactating": *Comité Internacional para la Recuperación de la Vaquita (CIRVA), Scientific Reports of First, Second and Third Meetings*, 2004, http://www.vivavaquita.org, p. 1-5.

p. 193   "ecologically very good": J. A. Trigueros Almeron, "Selectividad del arte de pesca suripera en la pesquería artesanal del camarón en norte de Sinaloa," Universidad De Occidente Departamento De Ciencias Biológic, Los Mochis, Sonaloa, 2012, pp. 2, 12, 13.

p. 193 "the only shrimp fishery": Del Pacifico, "Sustainable Shrimp," Del Pacifico website, accessed April 18, 2017, http://www.delpacificosea foods.com.

p. 194 "Fisheries policies should": A. Olivera, "Compensación por no pescar," *BCS Noticias*, August 22, 2016, http://www.bcsnoticias.mx.

p. 196 "requires that all imported": Z. Smith et al., "Net Loss: The Killing of Marine Mammals in Foreign Fisheries," Natural Resources Defense Council report, 2014, p. 4, https://www.nrdc.org.

p. 196 640,000 tons of ghost nets: G. Macfadyen, T. Huntington, and R. Cappell, *Abandoned, Lost or Otherwise Discarded Fishing Gear*. Food and Agriculture Organization of the United Nations and United Nations Environment Programme report, 2009, pp. xv, 11, www.fao.org.

p. 197 "unlawful for any person": T. Gloria, "Assembly Bill AB-1151 Vaquita-Friendly Fish and Fish Products," California Legislative Information website, accessed April 18, 2017, https://leginfo.legislature .ca.gov.

p. 198 more than $274 million: Animal Welfare Institute, "Why Are You Asking People to Boycott Shrimp?," *Boycott Mexican Shrimp* website, accessed June 10, 2017, http://www.boycottmexicanshrimp.com/.

Chapter 13: Meet the Totoaba

p. 201 capture-induced barotrauma: C. David True, A. Silva Loera, and N. Castro Castro, "Technical Notes: Acquisition of Broodstock of *Totoaba macdonaldi*: Field Handling, Decompression, and Prophylaxis of an Endangered Species," *Progressive Fish-Culturist* 59, no. 3 (1997): 246–48.

p. 212 predict the size: C. D. True, L. Enríque, and M. Burnham-Curtis, "Genetic Traceability of Wild and Captive-Reared Totoaba Stocks: A Tool for Population Recovery Assessment and Law Enforcement," Presentation, Trilaterial Committee for Wildlife and Ecosystem Conservation and Management, 20th annual meeting, April 13–17, 2015, San Diego, pp. 10–14.

Chapter 14: Last-Ditch Effort

p. 216 "over 90% of the total": SOS Dolfijn, "Rescue and Rehabilitation," SOS Dolfijn website, accessed April 2, 2017, https://www.sosdolfijn .nl/english.

p. 216 "it would be irresponsible": CIRVA, *Report of the Seventh Meeting of the Comité Internacional para la Recuperación de la Vaquita (CIRVA-7)*, 2016, http://www.iucn-csg.org/index.php/downloads/, p. 28.

p. 223 rarely seen Burmeister's: R. L. Brownell Jr. and P. J. Clapman, "Burmeister's Porpoise," in *Handbook of Marine Mammals: The Second Book of Dolphins and Porpoises*, ed. S. H. Ridgway and R. J. Harrison (Amsterdam: Elsevier, 1998), p. 407.

p. 224 "I think it's going to be": R. Melsky, "Dolphins Will Be Shipped to the Arizona Desert So People Can Swim with Them," *The Dodo*, June 27, 2016, https://www.thedodo.com.

p. 227 "shore-based sea pen": CIRVA, *Report of the Eighth Meeting of the Comité Internacional para la Recuperación de la Vaquita (CIRVA-8)*, 2016, http://www.iucn-csg.org/index.php/downloads, p. 56.

p. 227 online petition begging Americans: L. Dee, "A Big 'NO' to Captive Dolphins in Arizona!," *Care2 Petitions*, accessed December 3, 2016, http://www.thepetitionsite.com.

p. 231 "This drastic measure": D. Mosbergen, "World's Smallest Porpoise Inches Closer to Extinction," *Huffpost*, February 3, 2017, http:// www.huffingtonpost.com.

p. 231 "amidst dire prognostications": S. A. H. Osborn, *Condors in Canyon Country* (Grand Canyon, AZ: Grand Canyon Association, 2007), p. 32.

p. 233 "The challenge ahead": E. Dinerstein, *The Kingdom of Rarities* (Washington, DC: Island Press, 2013), pp. 268–69.

Chapter 15: Hope Is a Life Raft (with a Persistent Leak)

p. 235 "Some of the scientists": R. Nordland, "Only Captivity Will Save the Vaquita, Experts Say," *New York Times*, April 27, 2017, https://www .nytimes.com.

p. 236 Biologist Stuart Pimm: E. Dinerstein, *The Kingdom of Rarities* (Washington, DC: Island Press, 2013), p. 5.

p. 236 Living Planet Index: World Wildlife Fund, *Living Planet Report 2016: Summary* (Gland, Switzerland: World Wildlife Fund, 2016), p. 6.

p. 236 "Saving only one population": Dinerstein, *Kingdom of Rarities*, p. 6.

p. 237 "gives the ecological systems": H. Whitehead and L. Rendell, *The Cultural Lives of Whales and Dolphins* (Chicago: University of Chicago Press, 2015), Kindle ed. location 6535.

p. 237 "We cannot recover a lost world": G. Schaller, *The Last Panda* (Chicago: University of Chicago Press, 1994), p. 252.

p. 241 "Despite all the legislation": S. Turvey, *Witness to Extinction: How We Failed to Save the Yangtze River Dolphin* (Oxford, UK: Oxford University Press, 2008), p. 66.

p. 241 no baijis left: S. T. Turvey et al., "First Human-Caused Extinction of a Cetacean Species?," *Biology Letters* 3 (2007): 537–40.

p. 241 "This is a tragedy": Turvey, *Witness to Extinction*, p. 197.

p. 245 "Many Chinese gangs": C4ADS, "Hooked: How Demand for a Protected Fish Lined the Pockets of Mexican Cartels and Sunk the Future of an Endangered Porpoise Species," August 2017, https://c4ads .org/s/Hooked.pdf.

p. 245 "undercover investigations": C4ADS, "Hooked," pp. 56, 64.

p. 245 "organized criminal groups": C4ADS, "Hooked," p. 6.

p. 247 "It is Mexico": O. Vidal, "Mr. President, Save Mexico's 'Panda of the Sea,'" CNN, May 16, 2016, http://www.cnn.com.

p. 250 "(1) the human brain": J. Goodall, *Reason for Hope: A Spiritual Journey* (New York: Grand Central Publishing, 1999), p. 233.

Epilogue

p. 252 Placed in a padded: CIRVA, *Report of the Tenth Meeting of the Comité Internacional para la Recuperación de la Vaquita (CIRVA-10)*, 2018, http://www.iucn-csg.org/index.php/downloads/, pp. 24–26.

Selected Bibliography

Brownell, R. L. 1982. "Status of the Cochito, *Phocoena sinus*, in the Gulf of California." Pp. 85–90 in *Mammals in the Seas*, vol. 4, *Small Cetaceans, Seals, Sirenians, and Otters*, FAO Fisheries Series. Rome: Food and Agriculture Organization of the United Nations. 531 pp.

C4ADS. 2017. "Hooked: How Demand for a Protected Fish Lined the Pockets of Mexican Cartels and Sunk the Future of an Endangered Porpoise Species." C4ADS report, 106 pp. https://c4ads.org/s/Hooked.pdf.

Cantú-Guzmán, J. C., A. Olivera-Bonilla, and M. E. Sánchez-Saldaña. 2015. "A History (1990–2015) of Mismanaging the Vaquita into Extinction—A Mexican NGO's Perspective." *Journal of Marine Animals and Their Ecology* 8, no. 1: 15–25.

CIRVA. 2004. *Comité Internacional para la Recuperación de la Vaquita (CIRVA), Scientific Reports of the First, Second, and Third Meetings.* 67 pp. http://www.vivavaquita.org.

———. 2012. *Report of the Fourth Meeting of the Comité Internacional para la Recuperación de la Vaquita.* 47 pp. http://www.iucn-csg.org/index.php /downloads/.

———. 2014. *Report of the Fifth Meeting of the Comité Internacional para la Recuperación de la Vaquita (CIRVA-5).* 43 pp. http://www.iucn-csg.org /index.php/downloads/.

———. 2015. *Report of the Sixth Meeting of the Comité Internacional para la Recuperación de la Vaquita (CIRVA-6).* 57 pp. http://www.iucn-csg.org /index.php/downloads/.

————. 2016. *Report of the Seventh Meeting of the Comité Internacional para la Recuperación de la Vaquita (CIRVA-7)*. 76 pp. http://www.iucn-csg.org/index.php/downloads/.

————. 2016. *Report of the Eighth Meeting of the Comité Internacional para la Recuperación de la Vaquita (CIRVA-8)*. 69 pp. http://www.iucn-csg.org/index.php/downloads.

————. 2017. *Report of the Ninth Meeting of the Comité Internacional para la Recuperación de la Vaquita (CIRVA-9)*. 32 pp. http://www.iucn-csg.org/index.php/downloads/.

————. 2018. *Report of the Tenth Meeting of the Comité Internacional para la Recuperación de la Vaquita (CIRVA-10)*. 66 pp. http://www.iucn-csg.org/index.php/downloads/.

Cudney Bueno, R., and P. J. Turk Boyer. 1998. *Pescando Entre Mareas del Alto Golfo de California: Una Guía sobre la Pesca Artesanal, su Gente y sus Propuestas de Manejo*. Puerto Peñasco, Sonora: Centro Intercultural de Estudios de Desiertos y Océanos (CEDO), 164 pp.

Dinerstein, E. 2013. *The Kingdom of Rarities*. Washington, DC: Island Press. 312 pp.

EIA. 2016. *Collateral Damage: How Illegal Trade in Totoaba Swim Bladders Is Driving the Vaquita to Extinction*. Environmental Investigation Agency Organization Report, London, 19 pp.

Gerrodette, T., B. L. Taylor, R. Swift, S. Rankin, A. M. Jaramillo-Legorreta, and L. Rojas-Bracho. 2011. "A Combined Visual and Acoustic Estimate of 2008 Abundance, and Change in Abundance since 1997, for the Vaquita, *Phocoena sinus*." *Marine Mammal Science* 27: E79–100.

Jaramillo-Legorreta, A. M., G. Cardenas-Hinojosa, E. Nieto-Garcia, L. Rojos-Bracho, J. Ver Hoef, J. Moore, N. Tegenza, et al. 2016. "Passive Acoustic Monitoring of the Decline of Mexico's Critically Endangered Porpoise." *Conservation Biology* 31, no. 1: 183–91.

Jaramillo-Legorreta, A. M., L. Rojas-Bracho, and T. Gerrodette. 1999. "A New Abundance Estimate for Vaquitas: First Step for Recovery." *Marine Mammal Science* 15: 957–73.

Rojas-Bracho, L., and R. R. Reeves. 2013. "Vaquita and Gillnets: Mexico's Ultimate Cetacean Conservation Challenge." *Endangered Species Research* 21: 77–87.

Rojas-Bracho, L., R. R. Reeves, and A. Jaramillo-Legorreta. 2006. "Conservation of the Vaquita *Phocoena sinus*." *Mammal Review* 36: 179–216.

Taylor, B. L., L. Rojas-Bracho, J. Moore, A. Jaramillo-Legorreta, J. M. Ver Hoef, G. Cardenas-Hinojosa, E. Nieto-Garcia, et al. 2017. "Extinction Is Imminent for Mexico's Endemic Porpoise Unless Fishery Bycatch Is Eliminated." *Conservation Letters* 10, no. 5: 588–95.

Thomas, L., A. Jaramillo-Legorreta, G. Cardenas-Hinojosa, E. Nieto-Garcia, L. Rojas-Bracho, J. M. Ver Hoef, J. Moore, B. Taylor, J. Barlow, and N. Tregenza. 2017. "Last Call: Passive Acoustic Monitoring Shows Continued Rapid Decline of Critically Endangered Vaquita." *Journal of the Acoustical Society of America* 142, no. 5: EL512–17.

Turvey, S. 2008. *Witness to Extinction: How We Failed to Save the Yangtze River Dolphin.* Oxford, UK: Oxford University Press. 233 pp.

Vidal, O. 1995. "Population Biology and Incidental Mortality of the Vaquita, *Phocoena sinus*." *Reports of the International Whaling Commission*, Special Issue, 16: 247–72.

Index

Note: page numbers in *italics* refer to photographs.